About the Illustrator

Hi, I'm Cassandre Bolan. I was so excited about this project when Natalie told me it was a story about women setting themselves free; who doesn't love that!

See my work at

www.cassandrebolan.com

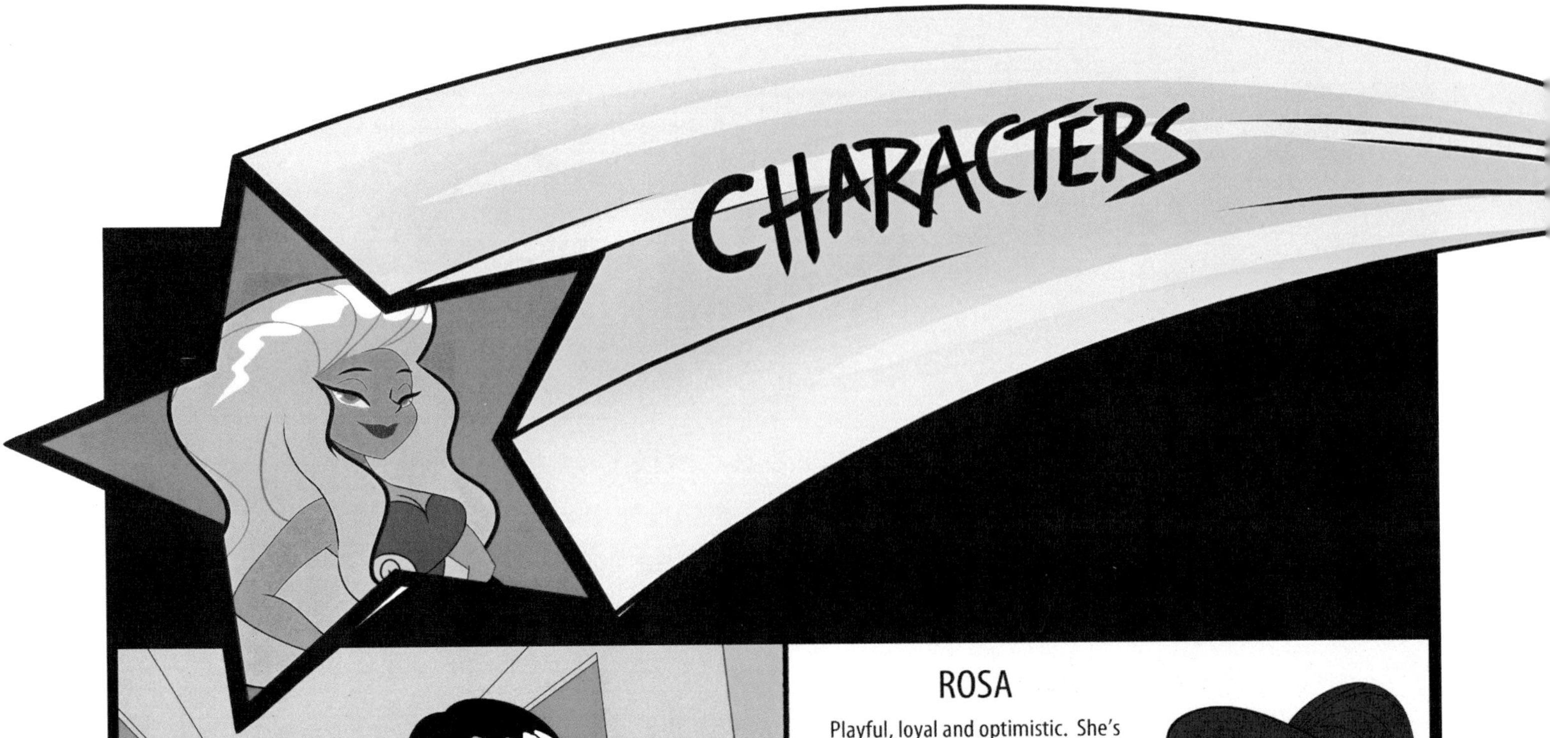

CHARACTERS

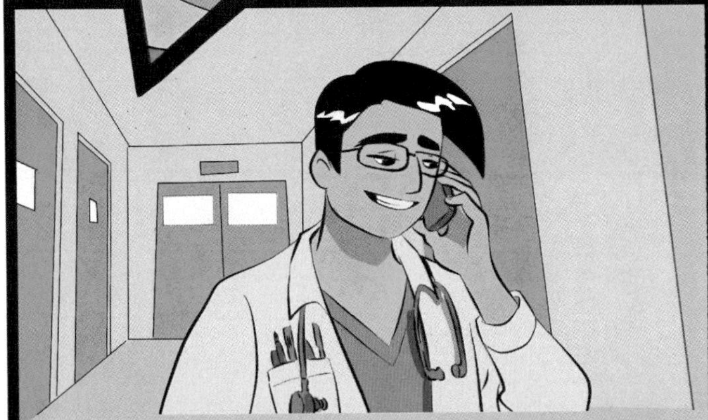

ALAN

A metropolitan, regal, educated well-traveled immigrant from pre-revolutionary Iran with a strong cultural family. He fell into a romantic, emotionally supportive relationship with Talia.

ROSA

Playful, loyal and optimistic. She's an Earth and animal loving best friend to Talia. Rosa is also on her own journey of surviving a failed marriage of deceit. Her ex-husband was a Jehovah's Witness Elder who committed credit fraud with her accounts, and didn't come out of the closet until well after getting married. Rosa still has flashbacks of being raised in an intense Hispanic Jehovah's Witness household. Talia and Rosa have a beautiful, therapeutic relationship of exploring life outside of the Jehovah's Witnesses.

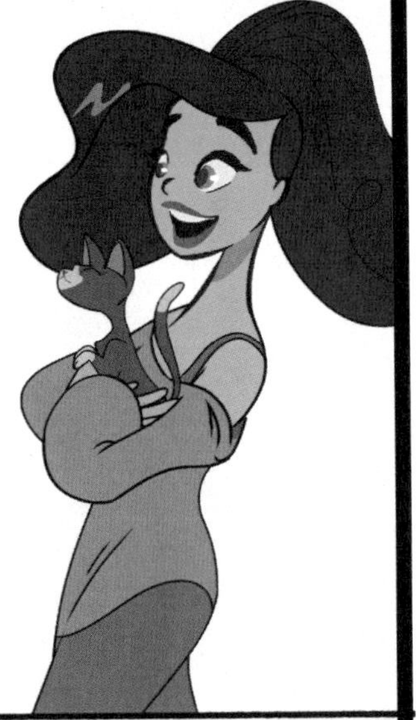

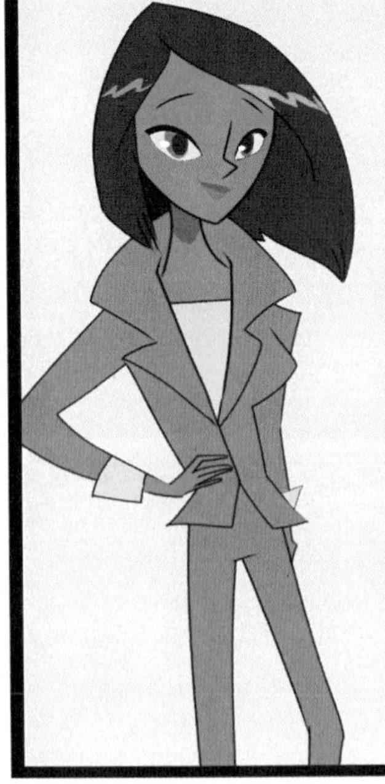

SANDY

Sandy is cheerful, professional, logical and mildly naive from marrying young out of a strict Jehovah's Witness household. Sandy is in a functional, healthy relationship with a husband who stands by her side as she slowly slips away from the Jehovah's Witness religion. She replaces her religious needs with professional life as she climbs the corporate ladder, raising scholastically successful children who engage in extracurricular activities that are normally banned in the cult. Her supportive husband allows her to make religious decisions for herself and her children, which is rare in a Jehovah's Witness household.

ROCHELLE

A classic nurturing sweetheart that's fun loving and the perfect mother and wife as well as a lifelong friend with Talia. Rochelle's husband defends his wife's honor to the Jehovah's Witness Elders and has a deep love for her. Rochelle's deepest desire is to provide a warm and loving childhood for her children wanting them to have culture in their life and make their own decisions.

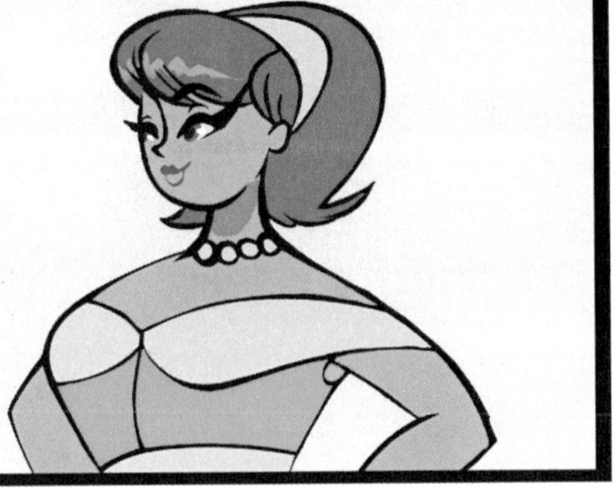

happy Hanukkah
2022

Created & Written: Natalie Grand

Illustrated: Cassandre Bolan

Colors: Kunna Aulia

Letters: Nikki Powers

Cover: Cassandre Bolan

Editor: N. Scott Robinson, Ph.D.

PUBLISHER: ALEX GRAND
ISBN: 978-1-7367647-9-4
PUBLISHED BY COMIC BOOK HISTORIANS, LLC.

About the Author

Talia in Cult Girls is an inspired story of my life as a young divorced Californian woman who left . . .

The story also covers the inspiring and supportive friends I had along the way telling how they were able to find new purposes in their lives. Specifically, how they, like myself, dealt with the reality of being raised, married, and eventually having rejected this particular suppressive religion.

It's a beautiful story filled with hope, romance, female empowerment, and self-exploration with therapeutic humor throughout the journey. Once you've left a cult, take it from me, flashbacks remain while the routines and doctrines take some more time to break. Cult Girls can be appreciated by those who've left a similarly suppressive religion and/or had experience with oppressive relationships and misguided parental control.

Learn more about me at

www.NatalieGrandAuthor.com

TALIA'S FATHER

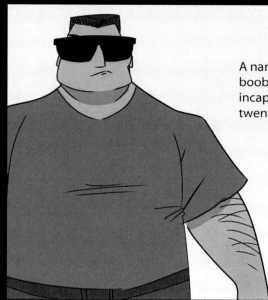

A narcissistic, volatile, hypocritical, boob-obsessed Jehovah's Witness who is incapable of loving his daughter and thinks he is twenty years younger than he really is.

TALIA'S MOTHER

An emotionally damaged woman, who was abused by Talia's father and has a weak, introverted personality. She finds it easier to be in a religion that thinks for her and provides her with a false hope for her future.

RUTHIE
Talia's sister

She is a devoted Jehovah's Witness that basks in her father's approval of being in submission to the religion and borders on extremism in the way she raises her kids.

TIMMY

Ruthie's husband is a kind and passive guy raised as a Jehovah's Witness. He actually grew up as childhood friends with Ruthie and Talia. He loves Ruthie very much, and it's better for his marriage to appease and try to please Ruthie's father.

MARIA AND CALEB

Rosa's older sister is young and parades her husband in front of her younger sister to push the concept of early marriage from the religion. Maria is in a constant state of elation as a Jehovah's Witness and cannot come to terms with her husband's unbiblical hobby as a Peeping Tom.

THE EX

Talia's ex-husband was her rushed teen marriage that was founded on religious convenience instead of mutual passion.

THE ELDERS

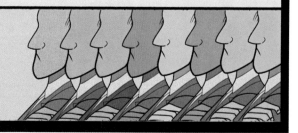

This is an organized body of men in the local congregation who conduct themselves as makeshift intermediaries of God in a pseudo-judicial system.

ROSA'S STORY

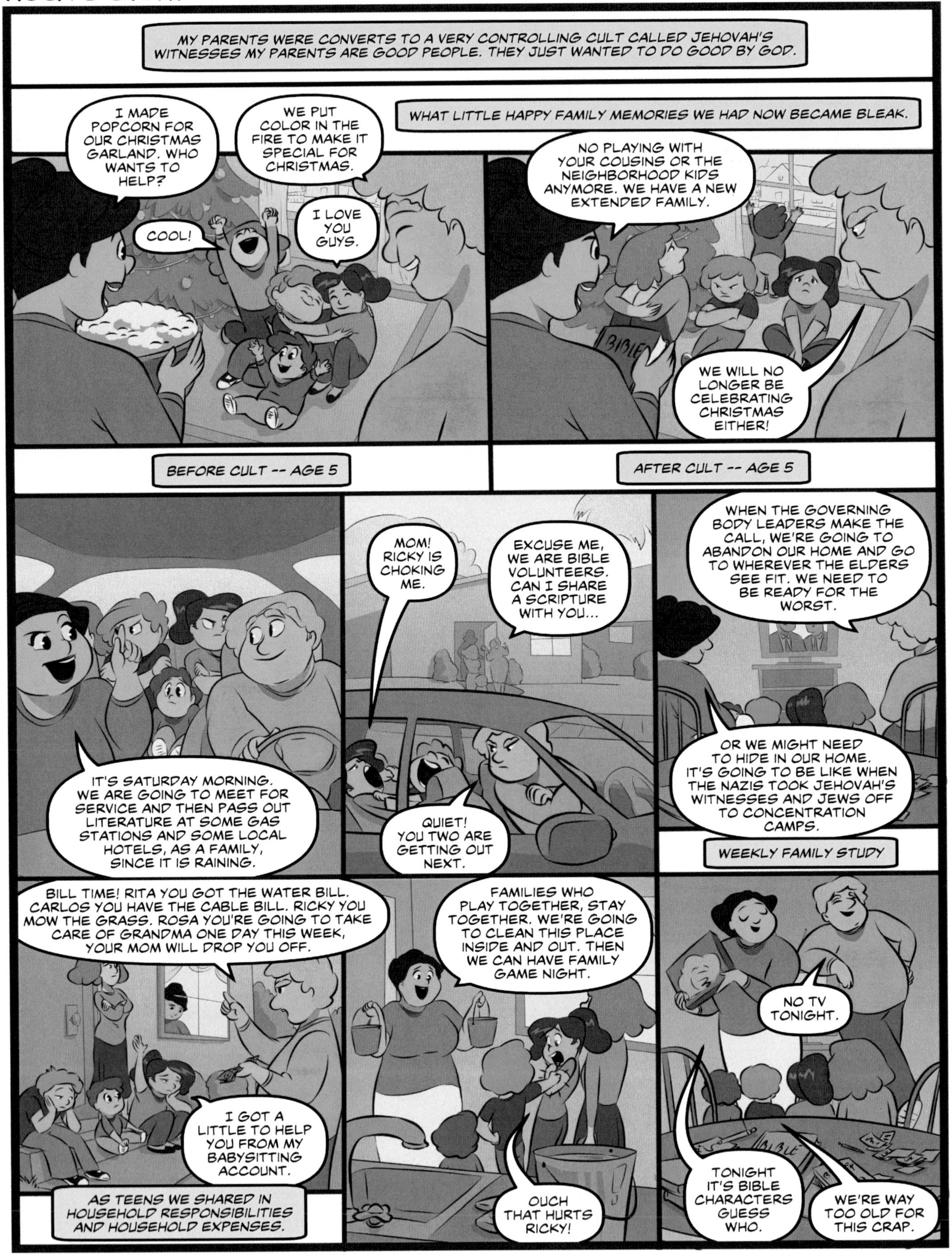

MY PARENTS WERE CONVERTS TO A VERY CONTROLLING CULT CALLED JEHOVAH'S WITNESSES MY PARENTS ARE GOOD PEOPLE. THEY JUST WANTED TO DO GOOD BY GOD.
I MADE POPCORN FOR OUR CHRISTMAS GARLAND. WHO WANTS TO HELP?
WE PUT COLOR IN THE FIRE TO MAKE IT SPECIAL FOR CHRISTMAS.
COOL!
I LOVE YOU GUYS.
BEFORE CULT -- AGE 5
WHAT LITTLE HAPPY FAMILY MEMORIES WE HAD NOW BECAME BLEAK.
NO PLAYING WITH YOUR COUSINS OR THE NEIGHBORHOOD KIDS ANYMORE. WE HAVE A NEW EXTENDED FAMILY.
BIBLE
WE WILL NO LONGER BE CELEBRATING CHRISTMAS EITHER!
AFTER CULT -- AGE 5
IT'S SATURDAY MORNING. WE ARE GOING TO MEET FOR SERVICE AND THEN PASS OUT LITERATURE AT SOME GAS STATIONS AND SOME LOCAL HOTELS, AS A FAMILY, SINCE IT IS RAINING.
MOM! RICKY IS CHOKING ME.
EXCUSE ME, WE ARE BIBLE VOLUNTEERS. CAN I SHARE A SCRIPTURE WITH YOU...
QUIET! YOU TWO ARE GETTING OUT NEXT.
WHEN THE GOVERNING BODY LEADERS MAKE THE CALL, WE'RE GOING TO ABANDON OUR HOME AND GO TO WHEREVER THE ELDERS SEE FIT. WE NEED TO BE READY FOR THE WORST.
OR WE MIGHT NEED TO HIDE IN OUR HOME. IT'S GOING TO BE LIKE WHEN THE NAZIS TOOK JEHOVAH'S WITNESSES AND JEWS OFF TO CONCENTRATION CAMPS.
WEEKLY FAMILY STUDY
BILL TIME! RITA YOU GOT THE WATER BILL. CARLOS YOU HAVE THE CABLE BILL. RICKY YOU MOW THE GRASS. ROSA YOU'RE GOING TO TAKE CARE OF GRANDMA ONE DAY THIS WEEK, YOUR MOM WILL DROP YOU OFF.
I GOT A LITTLE TO HELP YOU FROM MY BABYSITTING ACCOUNT.
AS TEENS WE SHARED IN HOUSEHOLD RESPONSIBILITIES AND HOUSEHOLD EXPENSES.
FAMILIES WHO PLAY TOGETHER, STAY TOGETHER. WE'RE GOING TO CLEAN THIS PLACE INSIDE AND OUT. THEN WE CAN HAVE FAMILY GAME NIGHT.
OUCH THAT HURTS RICKY!
NO TV TONIGHT.
TONIGHT IT'S BIBLE CHARACTERS GUESS WHO.
WE'RE WAY TOO OLD FOR THIS CRAP.

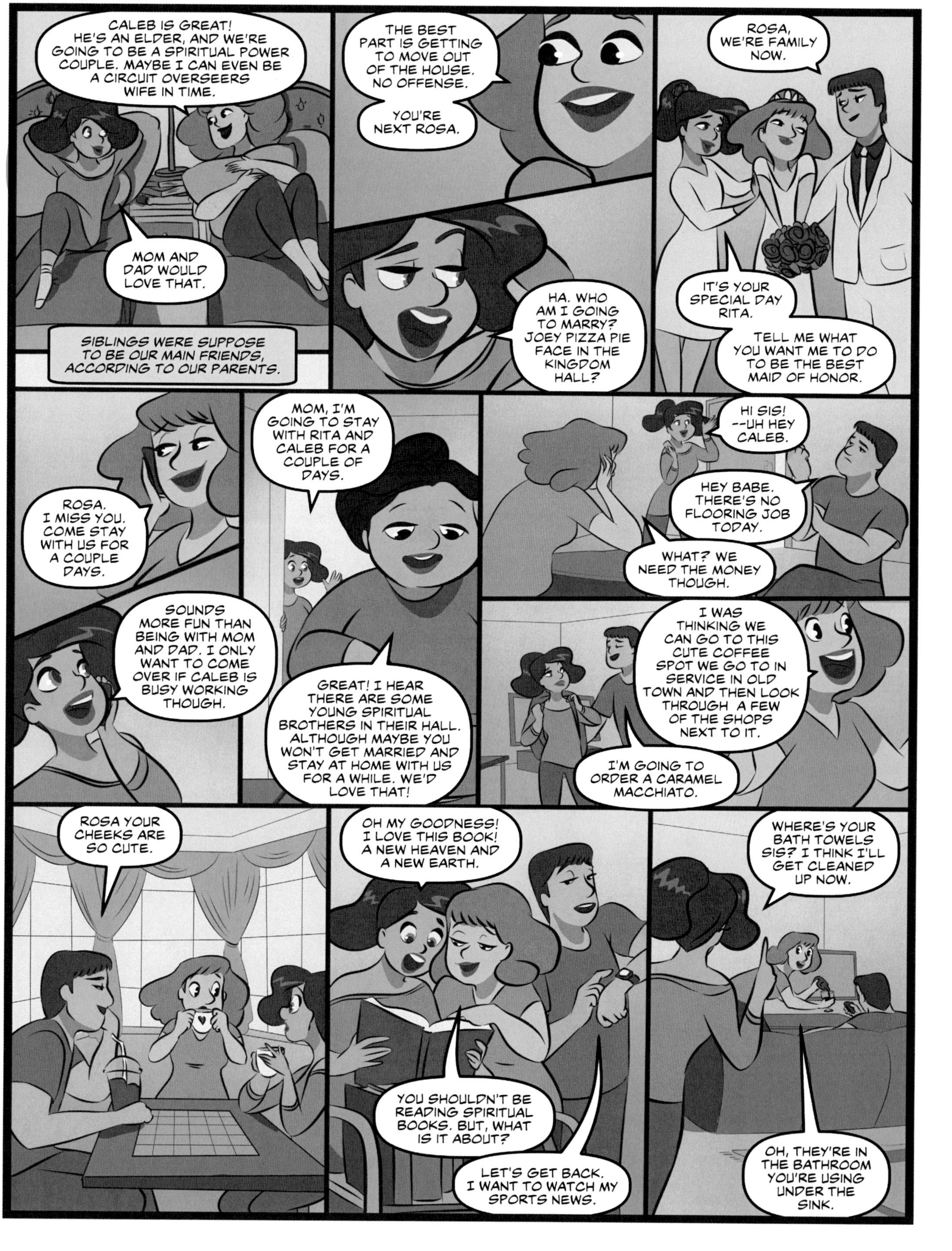
CALEB IS GREAT! HE'S AN ELDER, AND WE'RE GOING TO BE A SPIRITUAL POWER COUPLE. MAYBE I CAN EVEN BE A CIRCUIT OVERSEERS WIFE IN TIME.
MOM AND DAD WOULD LOVE THAT.
SIBLINGS WERE SUPPOSE TO BE OUR MAIN FRIENDS, ACCORDING TO OUR PARENTS.
THE BEST PART IS GETTING TO MOVE OUT OF THE HOUSE. NO OFFENSE.
YOU'RE NEXT ROSA.
HA. WHO AM I GOING TO MARRY? JOEY PIZZA PIE FACE IN THE KINGDOM HALL?
ROSA, WE'RE FAMILY NOW.
IT'S YOUR SPECIAL DAY RITA.
TELL ME WHAT YOU WANT ME TO DO TO BE THE BEST MAID OF HONOR.
ROSA. I MISS YOU. COME STAY WITH US FOR A COUPLE DAYS.
SOUNDS MORE FUN THAN BEING WITH MOM AND DAD. I ONLY WANT TO COME OVER IF CALEB IS BUSY WORKING THOUGH.
MOM, I'M GOING TO STAY WITH RITA AND CALEB FOR A COUPLE OF DAYS.
GREAT! I HEAR THERE ARE SOME YOUNG SPIRITUAL BROTHERS IN THEIR HALL. ALTHOUGH MAYBE YOU WON'T GET MARRIED AND STAY AT HOME WITH US FOR A WHILE. WE'D LOVE THAT!
HI SIS! --UH HEY CALEB.
HEY BABE. THERE'S NO FLOORING JOB TODAY.
WHAT? WE NEED THE MONEY THOUGH.
I WAS THINKING WE CAN GO TO THIS CUTE COFFEE SPOT WE GO TO IN SERVICE IN OLD TOWN AND THEN LOOK THROUGH A FEW OF THE SHOPS NEXT TO IT.
I'M GOING TO ORDER A CARAMEL MACCHIATO.
ROSA YOUR CHEEKS ARE SO CUTE.
OH MY GOODNESS! I LOVE THIS BOOK! A NEW HEAVEN AND A NEW EARTH.
YOU SHOULDN'T BE READING SPIRITUAL BOOKS. BUT, WHAT IS IT ABOUT?
LET'S GET BACK. I WANT TO WATCH MY SPORTS NEWS.
WHERE'S YOUR BATH TOWELS SIS? I THINK I'LL GET CLEANED UP NOW.
OH, THEY'RE IN THE BATHROOM YOU'RE USING UNDER THE SINK.

PEEPER

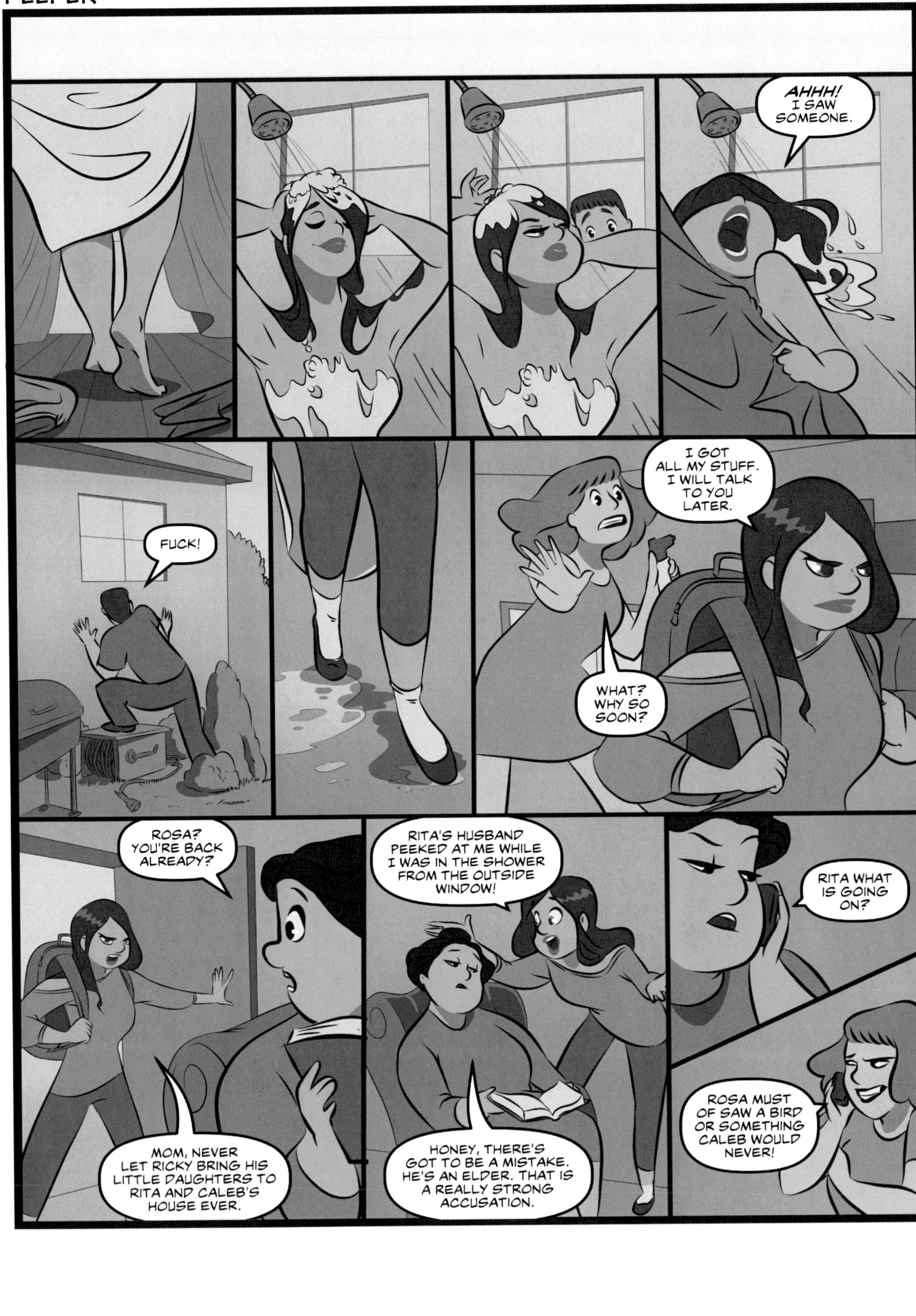
AHHH! I SAW SOMEONE.
FUCK!
I GOT ALL MY STUFF. I WILL TALK TO YOU LATER.
WHAT? WHY SO SOON?
ROSA? YOU'RE BACK ALREADY?
MOM, NEVER LET RICKY BRING HIS LITTLE DAUGHTERS TO RITA AND CALEB'S HOUSE EVER.
RITA'S HUSBAND PEEKED AT ME WHILE I WAS IN THE SHOWER FROM THE OUTSIDE WINDOW!
HONEY, THERE'S GOT TO BE A MISTAKE. HE'S AN ELDER. THAT IS A REALLY STRONG ACCUSATION.
RITA WHAT IS GOING ON?
ROSA MUST OF SAW A BIRD OR SOMETHING CALEB WOULD NEVER!

ABORTION

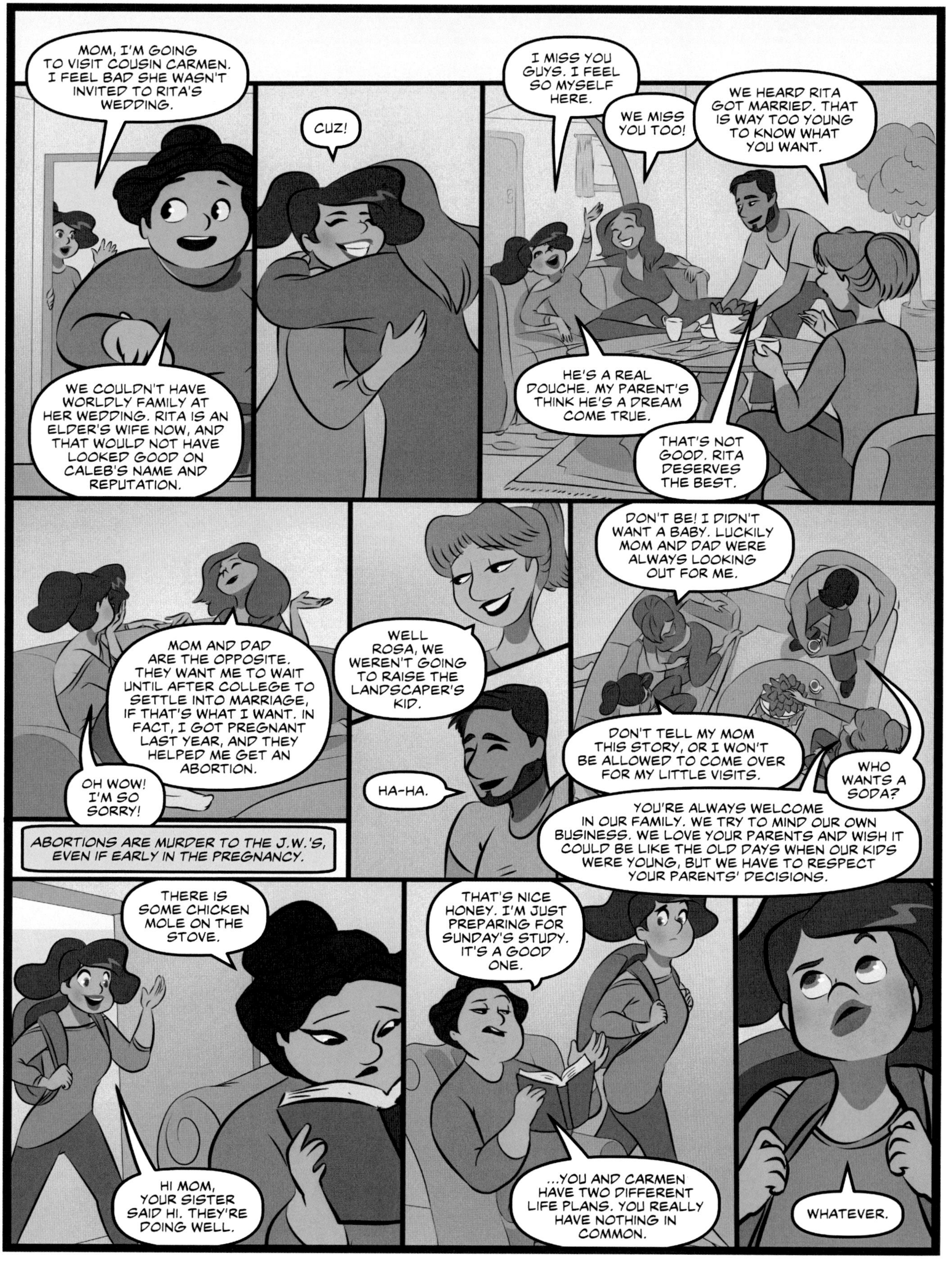

MOM, I'M GOING TO VISIT COUSIN CARMEN. I FEEL BAD SHE WASN'T INVITED TO RITA'S WEDDING.
WE COULDN'T HAVE WORLDLY FAMILY AT HER WEDDING. RITA IS AN ELDER'S WIFE NOW, AND THAT WOULD NOT HAVE LOOKED GOOD ON CALEB'S NAME AND REPUTATION.
CUZ!
I MISS YOU GUYS. I FEEL SO MYSELF HERE.
WE MISS YOU TOO!
WE HEARD RITA GOT MARRIED. THAT IS WAY TOO YOUNG TO KNOW WHAT YOU WANT.
HE'S A REAL DOUCHE. MY PARENT'S THINK HE'S A DREAM COME TRUE.
THAT'S NOT GOOD. RITA DESERVES THE BEST.
MOM AND DAD ARE THE OPPOSITE. THEY WANT ME TO WAIT UNTIL AFTER COLLEGE TO SETTLE INTO MARRIAGE, IF THAT'S WHAT I WANT. IN FACT, I GOT PREGNANT LAST YEAR, AND THEY HELPED ME GET AN ABORTION.
OH WOW! I'M SO SORRY!
ABORTIONS ARE MURDER TO THE J.W.'S, EVEN IF EARLY IN THE PREGNANCY.
WELL ROSA, WE WEREN'T GOING TO RAISE THE LANDSCAPER'S KID.
HA-HA.
DON'T BE! I DIDN'T WANT A BABY. LUCKILY MOM AND DAD WERE ALWAYS LOOKING OUT FOR ME.
DON'T TELL MY MOM THIS STORY, OR I WON'T BE ALLOWED TO COME OVER FOR MY LITTLE VISITS.
WHO WANTS A SODA?
YOU'RE ALWAYS WELCOME IN OUR FAMILY. WE TRY TO MIND OUR OWN BUSINESS. WE LOVE YOUR PARENTS AND WISH IT COULD BE LIKE THE OLD DAYS WHEN OUR KIDS WERE YOUNG, BUT WE HAVE TO RESPECT YOUR PARENTS' DECISIONS.
HI MOM, YOUR SISTER SAID HI. THEY'RE DOING WELL.
THERE IS SOME CHICKEN MOLE ON THE STOVE.
THAT'S NICE HONEY. I'M JUST PREPARING FOR SUNDAY'S STUDY. IT'S A GOOD ONE.
...YOU AND CARMEN HAVE TWO DIFFERENT LIFE PLANS. YOU REALLY HAVE NOTHING IN COMMON.
WHATEVER.

ROSA'S STORY OF HER DIVORCE FROM IAN

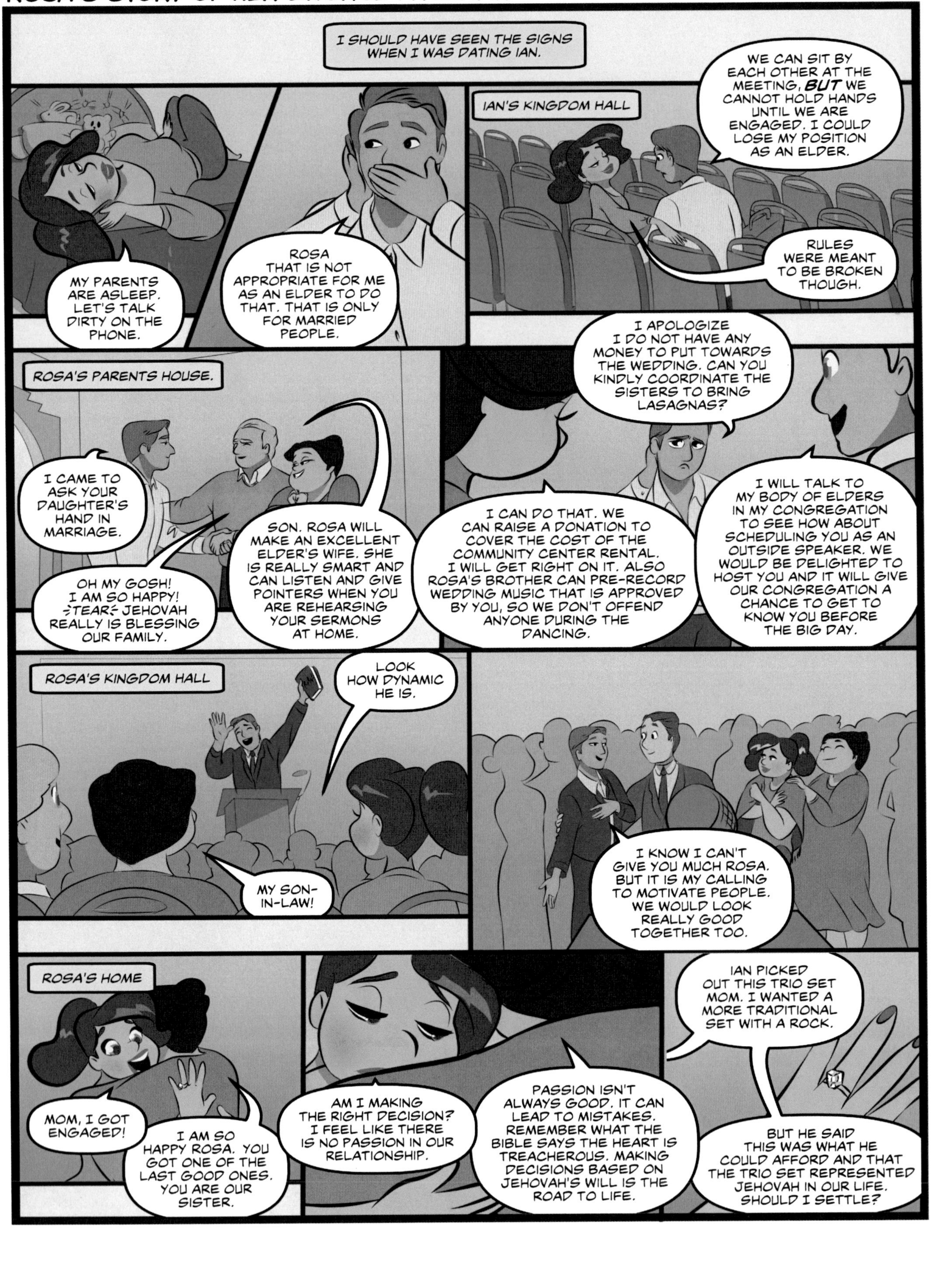
I SHOULD HAVE SEEN THE SIGNS WHEN I WAS DATING IAN.
MY PARENTS ARE ASLEEP. LET'S TALK DIRTY ON THE PHONE.
ROSA THAT IS NOT APPROPRIATE FOR ME AS AN ELDER TO DO THAT. THAT IS ONLY FOR MARRIED PEOPLE.
IAN'S KINGDOM HALL
WE CAN SIT BY EACH OTHER AT THE MEETING, BUT WE CANNOT HOLD HANDS UNTIL WE ARE ENGAGED. I COULD LOSE MY POSITION AS AN ELDER.
RULES WERE MEANT TO BE BROKEN THOUGH.
ROSA'S PARENTS HOUSE.
I CAME TO ASK YOUR DAUGHTER'S HAND IN MARRIAGE.
OH MY GOSH! I AM SO HAPPY! -TEAR- JEHOVAH REALLY IS BLESSING OUR FAMILY.
SON. ROSA WILL MAKE AN EXCELLENT ELDER'S WIFE. SHE IS REALLY SMART AND CAN LISTEN AND GIVE POINTERS WHEN YOU ARE REHEARSING YOUR SERMONS AT HOME.
I APOLOGIZE I DO NOT HAVE ANY MONEY TO PUT TOWARDS THE WEDDING. CAN YOU KINDLY COORDINATE THE SISTERS TO BRING LASAGNAS?
I CAN DO THAT. WE CAN RAISE A DONATION TO COVER THE COST OF THE COMMUNITY CENTER RENTAL. I WILL GET RIGHT ON IT. ALSO ROSA'S BROTHER CAN PRE-RECORD WEDDING MUSIC THAT IS APPROVED BY YOU, SO WE DON'T OFFEND ANYONE DURING THE DANCING.
I WILL TALK TO MY BODY OF ELDERS IN MY CONGREGATION TO SEE HOW ABOUT SCHEDULING YOU AS AN OUTSIDE SPEAKER. WE WOULD BE DELIGHTED TO HOST YOU AND IT WILL GIVE OUR CONGREGATION A CHANCE TO GET TO KNOW YOU BEFORE THE BIG DAY.
ROSA'S KINGDOM HALL
LOOK HOW DYNAMIC HE IS.
MY SON-IN-LAW!
I KNOW I CAN'T GIVE YOU MUCH ROSA. BUT IT IS MY CALLING TO MOTIVATE PEOPLE. WE WOULD LOOK REALLY GOOD TOGETHER TOO.
ROSA'S HOME
MOM, I GOT ENGAGED!
I AM SO HAPPY ROSA. YOU GOT ONE OF THE LAST GOOD ONES. YOU ARE OUR SISTER.
AM I MAKING THE RIGHT DECISION? I FEEL LIKE THERE IS NO PASSION IN OUR RELATIONSHIP.
PASSION ISN'T ALWAYS GOOD. IT CAN LEAD TO MISTAKES. REMEMBER WHAT THE BIBLE SAYS THE HEART IS TREACHEROUS. MAKING DECISIONS BASED ON JEHOVAH'S WILL IS THE ROAD TO LIFE.
IAN PICKED OUT THIS TRIO SET MOM. I WANTED A MORE TRADITIONAL SET WITH A ROCK.
BUT HE SAID THIS WAS WHAT HE COULD AFFORD AND THAT THE TRIO SET REPRESENTED JEHOVAH IN OUR LIFE. SHOULD I SETTLE?

THEATER

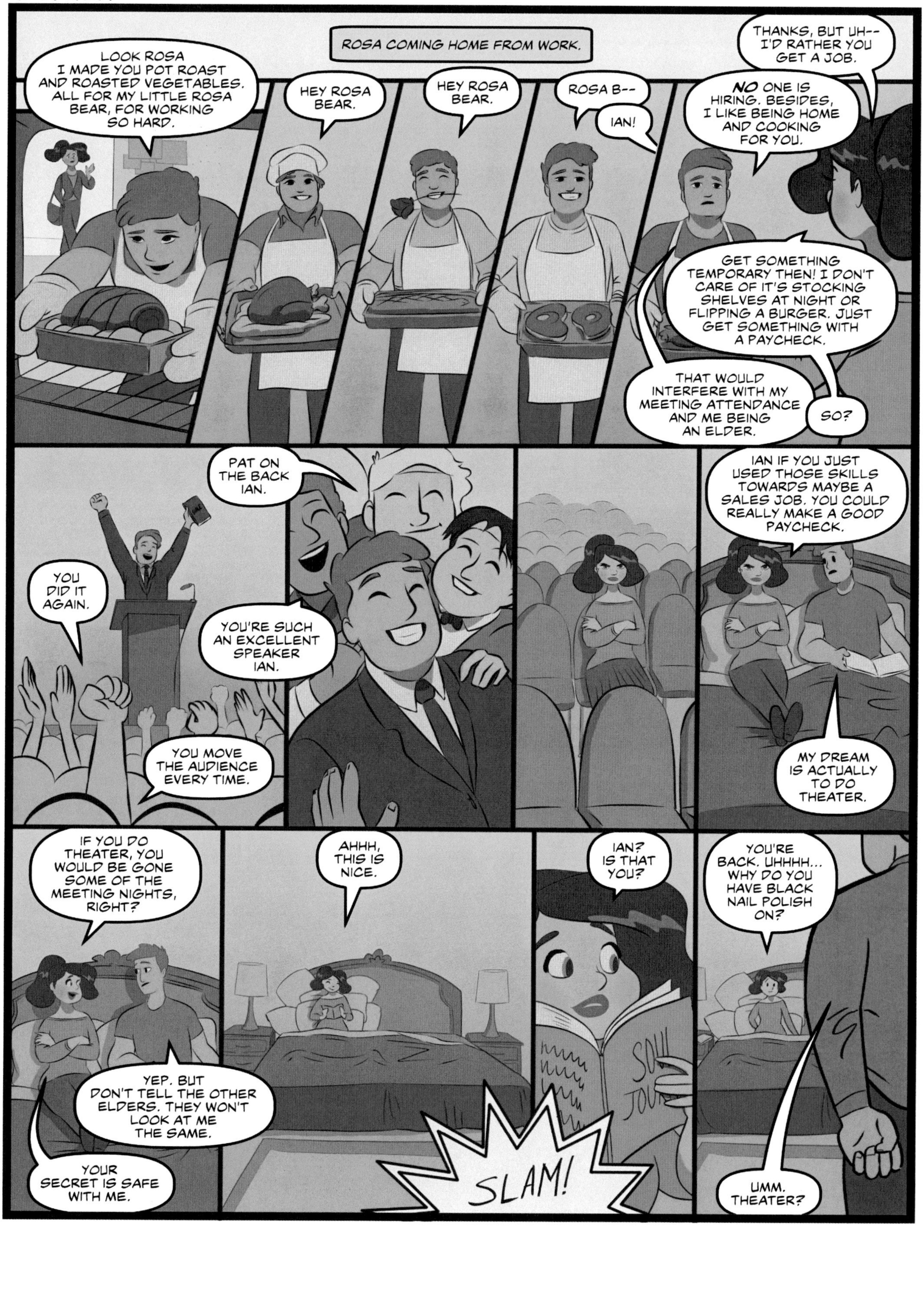
ROSA COMING HOME FROM WORK.
LOOK ROSA I MADE YOU POT ROAST AND ROASTED VEGETABLES. ALL FOR MY LITTLE ROSA BEAR, FOR WORKING SO HARD.
HEY ROSA BEAR.
HEY ROSA BEAR.
ROSA B--
IAN!
THANKS, BUT UH-- I'D RATHER YOU GET A JOB.
NO ONE IS HIRING. BESIDES, I LIKE BEING HOME AND COOKING FOR YOU.
GET SOMETHING TEMPORARY THEN! I DON'T CARE OF IT'S STOCKING SHELVES AT NIGHT OR FLIPPING A BURGER. JUST GET SOMETHING WITH A PAYCHECK.
THAT WOULD INTERFERE WITH MY MEETING ATTENDANCE AND ME BEING AN ELDER.
SO?
YOU DID IT AGAIN.
YOU MOVE THE AUDIENCE EVERY TIME.
PAT ON THE BACK IAN.
YOU'RE SUCH AN EXCELLENT SPEAKER IAN.
IAN IF YOU JUST USED THOSE SKILLS TOWARDS MAYBE A SALES JOB, YOU COULD REALLY MAKE A GOOD PAYCHECK.
MY DREAM IS ACTUALLY TO DO THEATER.
IF YOU DO THEATER, YOU WOULD BE GONE SOME OF THE MEETING NIGHTS, RIGHT?
YEP. BUT DON'T TELL THE OTHER ELDERS. THEY WON'T LOOK AT ME THE SAME.
YOUR SECRET IS SAFE WITH ME.
AHHH, THIS IS NICE.
SLAM!
IAN? IS THAT YOU?
YOU'RE BACK. UHHHH... WHY DO YOU HAVE BLACK NAIL POLISH ON?
UMM. THEATER?

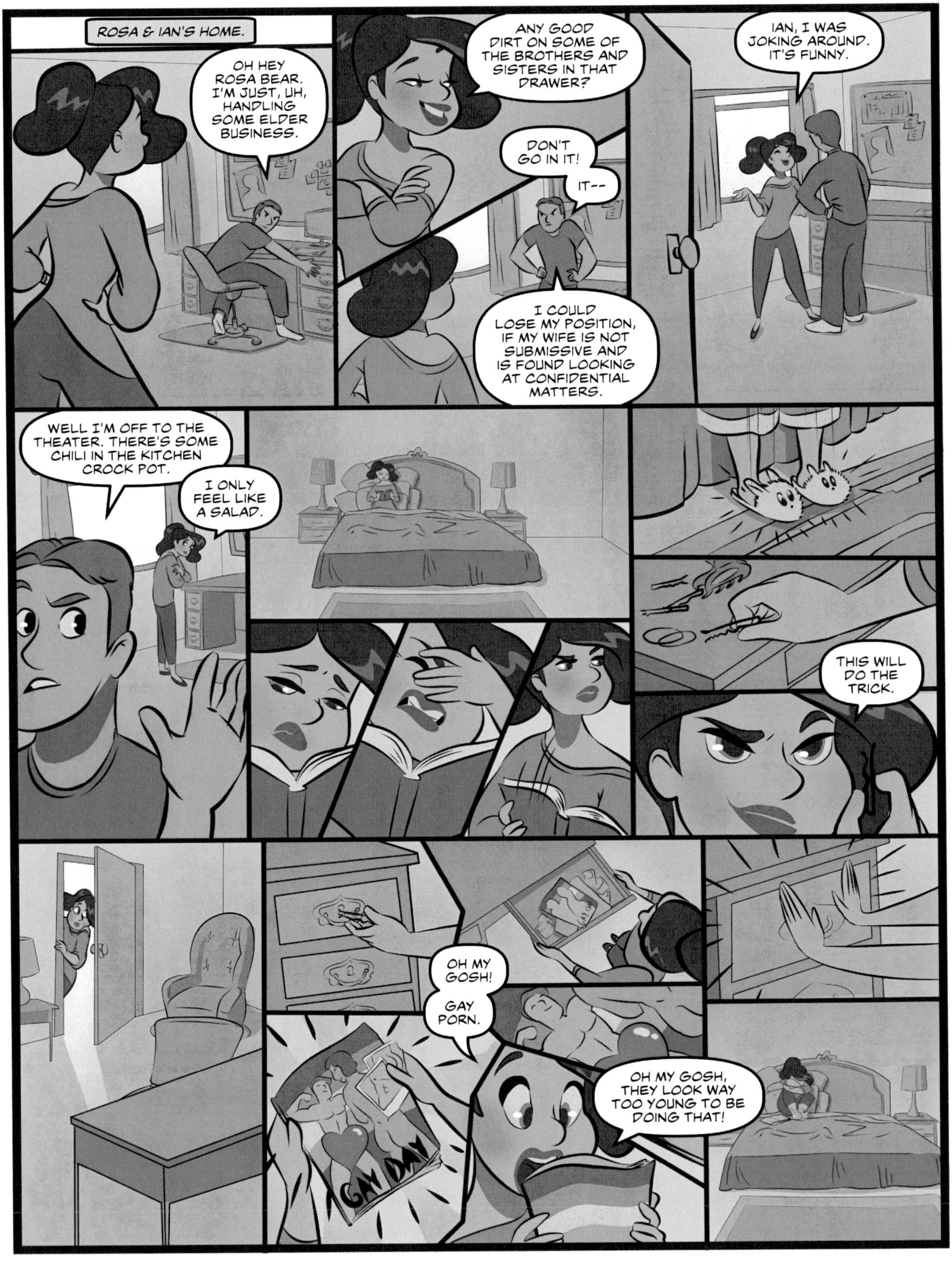
ROSA & IAN'S HOME.
OH HEY ROSA BEAR. I'M JUST, UH, HANDLING SOME ELDER BUSINESS.
ANY GOOD DIRT ON SOME OF THE BROTHERS AND SISTERS IN THAT DRAWER?
DON'T GO IN IT!
IT--
I COULD LOSE MY POSITION, IF MY WIFE IS NOT SUBMISSIVE AND IS FOUND LOOKING AT CONFIDENTIAL MATTERS.
IAN, I WAS JOKING AROUND. IT'S FUNNY.
WELL I'M OFF TO THE THEATER. THERE'S SOME CHILI IN THE KITCHEN CROCK POT.
I ONLY FEEL LIKE A SALAD.
THIS WILL DO THE TRICK.
OH MY GOSH!
GAY PORN.
GAY DAY
OH MY GOSH, THEY LOOK WAY TOO YOUNG TO BE DOING THAT!

DIVORCE PAPERS

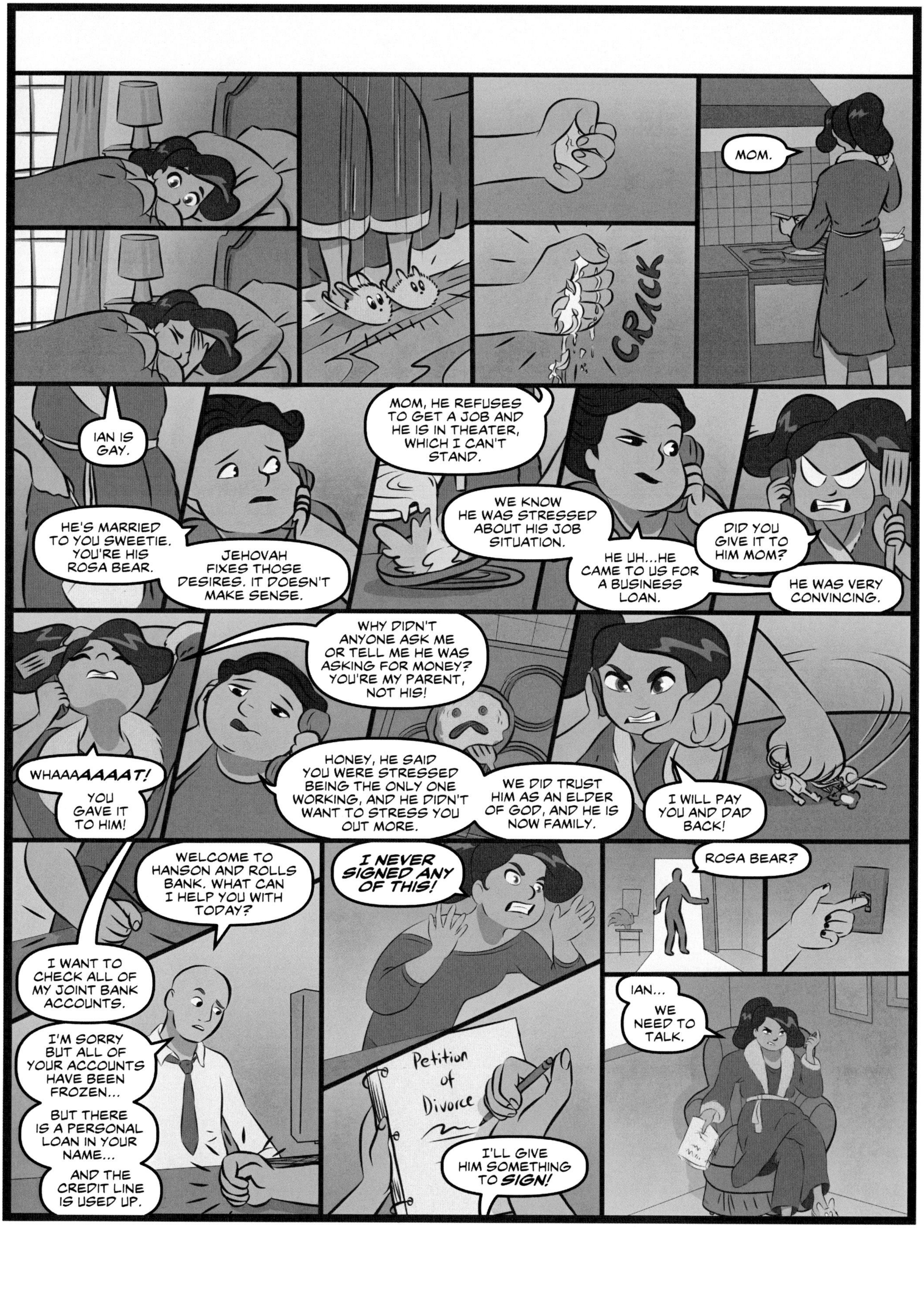

MOM.
IAN IS GAY.
HE'S MARRIED TO YOU SWEETIE. YOU'RE HIS ROSA BEAR.
JEHOVAH FIXES THOSE DESIRES. IT DOESN'T MAKE SENSE.
MOM, HE REFUSES TO GET A JOB AND HE IS IN THEATER, WHICH I CAN'T STAND.
WE KNOW HE WAS STRESSED ABOUT HIS JOB SITUATION.
HE UH...HE CAME TO US FOR A BUSINESS LOAN.
DID YOU GIVE IT TO HIM MOM?
HE WAS VERY CONVINCING.
WHAAAAAAAT!
YOU GAVE IT TO HIM!
WHY DIDN'T ANYONE ASK ME OR TELL ME HE WAS ASKING FOR MONEY? YOU'RE MY PARENT, NOT HIS!
HONEY, HE SAID YOU WERE STRESSED BEING THE ONLY ONE WORKING, AND HE DIDN'T WANT TO STRESS YOU OUT MORE.
WE DID TRUST HIM AS AN ELDER OF GOD, AND HE IS NOW FAMILY.
I WILL PAY YOU AND DAD BACK!
WELCOME TO HANSON AND ROLLS BANK. WHAT CAN I HELP YOU WITH TODAY?
I WANT TO CHECK ALL OF MY JOINT BANK ACCOUNTS.
I'M SORRY BUT ALL OF YOUR ACCOUNTS HAVE BEEN FROZEN...
BUT THERE IS A PERSONAL LOAN IN YOUR NAME...
AND THE CREDIT LINE IS USED UP.
I NEVER SIGNED ANY OF THIS!
Petition of Divorce
I'LL GIVE HIM SOMETHING TO SIGN!
ROSA BEAR?
IAN...
WE NEED TO TALK.

Talia's Story

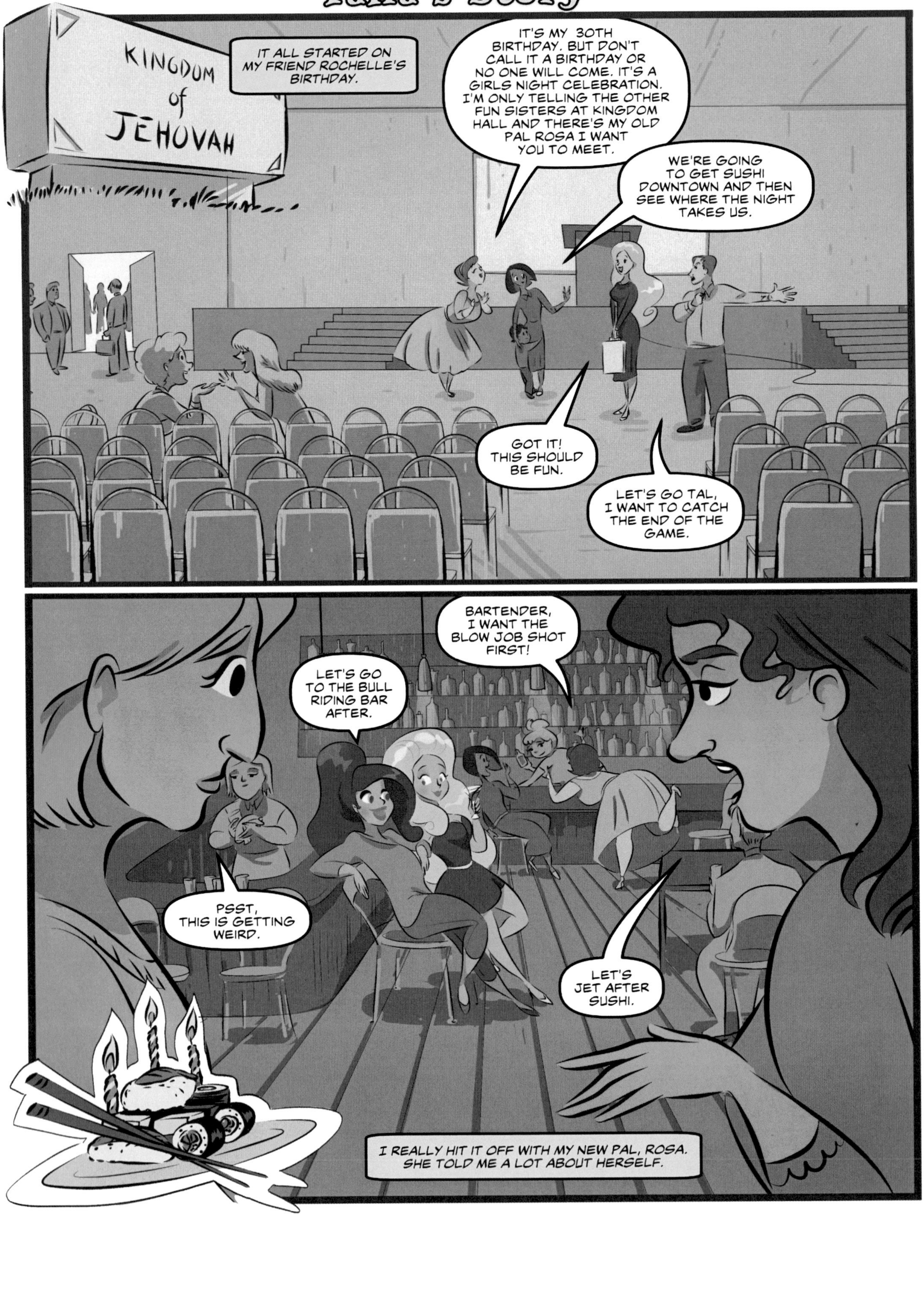

KINGDOM of JEHOVAH
IT ALL STARTED ON MY FRIEND ROCHELLE'S BIRTHDAY.
IT'S MY 30TH BIRTHDAY. BUT DON'T CALL IT A BIRTHDAY OR NO ONE WILL COME. IT'S A GIRLS NIGHT CELEBRATION. I'M ONLY TELLING THE OTHER FUN SISTERS AT KINGDOM HALL AND THERE'S MY OLD PAL ROSA I WANT YOU TO MEET.
WE'RE GOING TO GET SUSHI DOWNTOWN AND THEN SEE WHERE THE NIGHT TAKES US.
GOT IT! THIS SHOULD BE FUN.
LET'S GO TAL, I WANT TO CATCH THE END OF THE GAME.
BARTENDER, I WANT THE BLOW JOB SHOT FIRST!
LET'S GO TO THE BULL RIDING BAR AFTER.
PSST, THIS IS GETTING WEIRD.
LET'S JET AFTER SUSHI.
I REALLY HIT IT OFF WITH MY NEW PAL, ROSA. SHE TOLD ME A LOT ABOUT HERSELF.

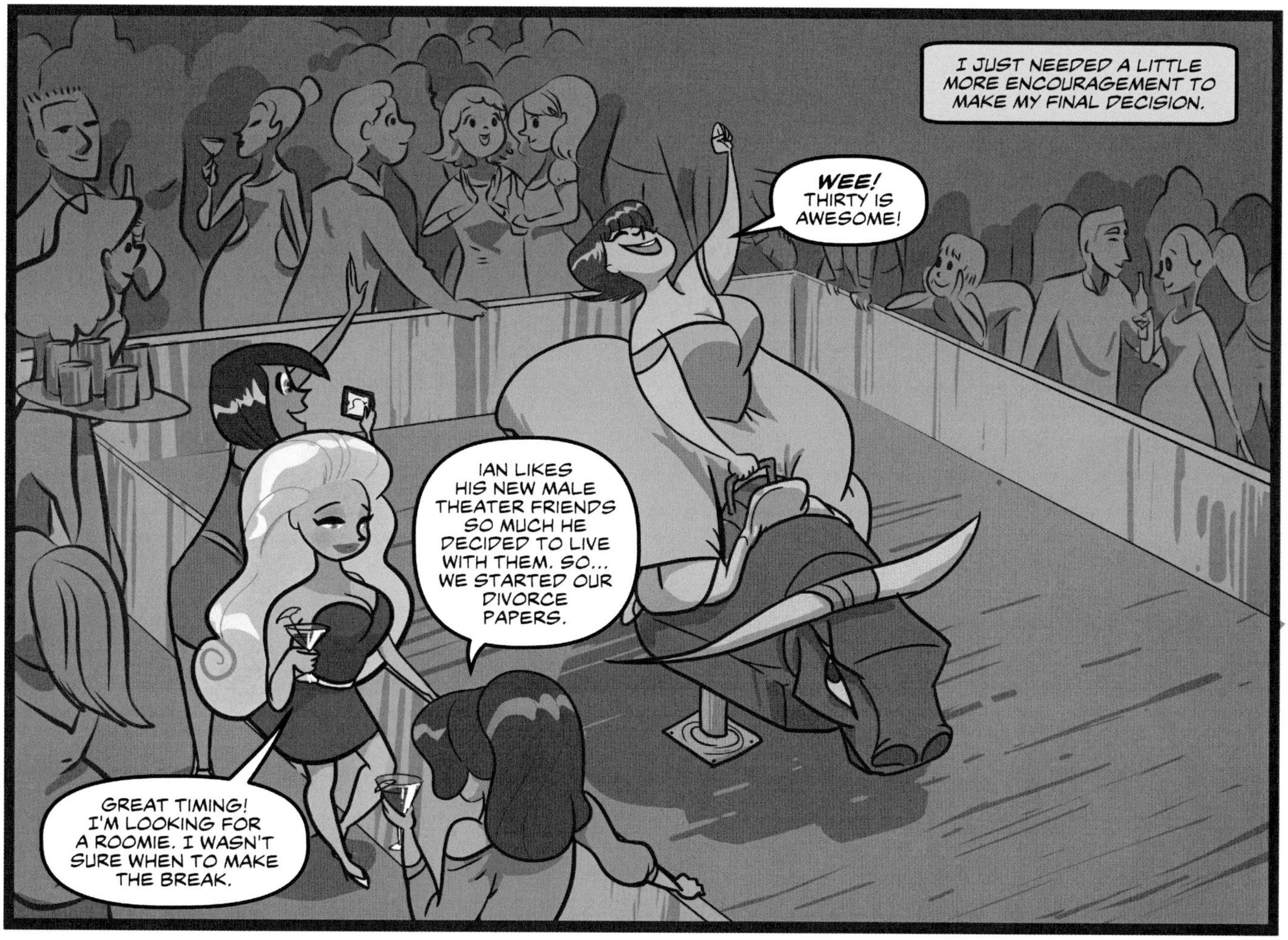
I JUST NEEDED A LITTLE MORE ENCOURAGEMENT TO MAKE MY FINAL DECISION.
WEE! THIRTY IS AWESOME!
IAN LIKES HIS NEW MALE THEATER FRIENDS SO MUCH HE DECIDED TO LIVE WITH THEM. SO... WE STARTED OUR DIVORCE PAPERS.
GREAT TIMING! I'M LOOKING FOR A ROOMIE. I WASN'T SURE WHEN TO MAKE THE BREAK.

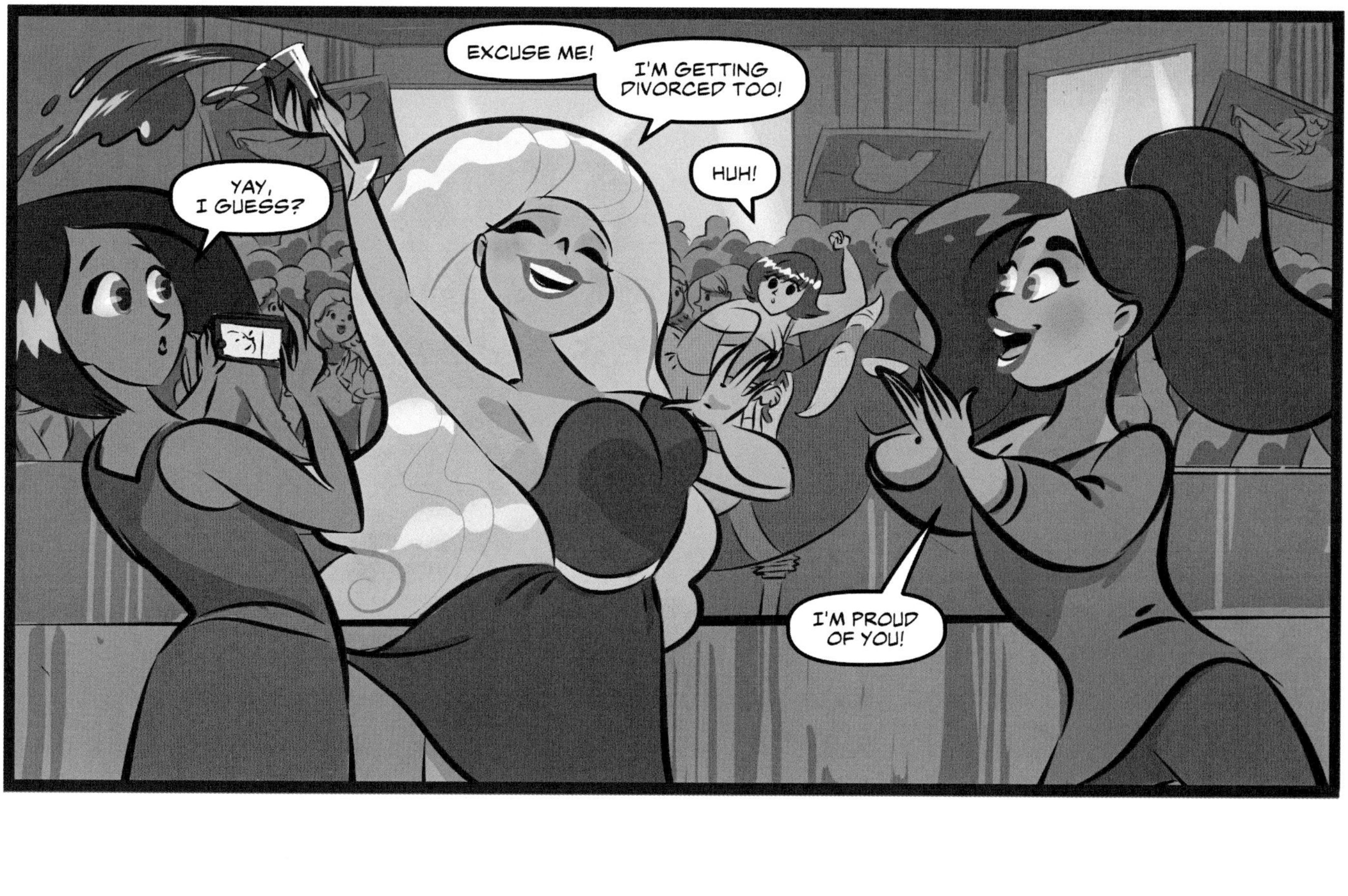
EXCUSE ME!
I'M GETTING DIVORCED TOO!
YAY, I GUESS?
HUH!
I'M PROUD OF YOU!

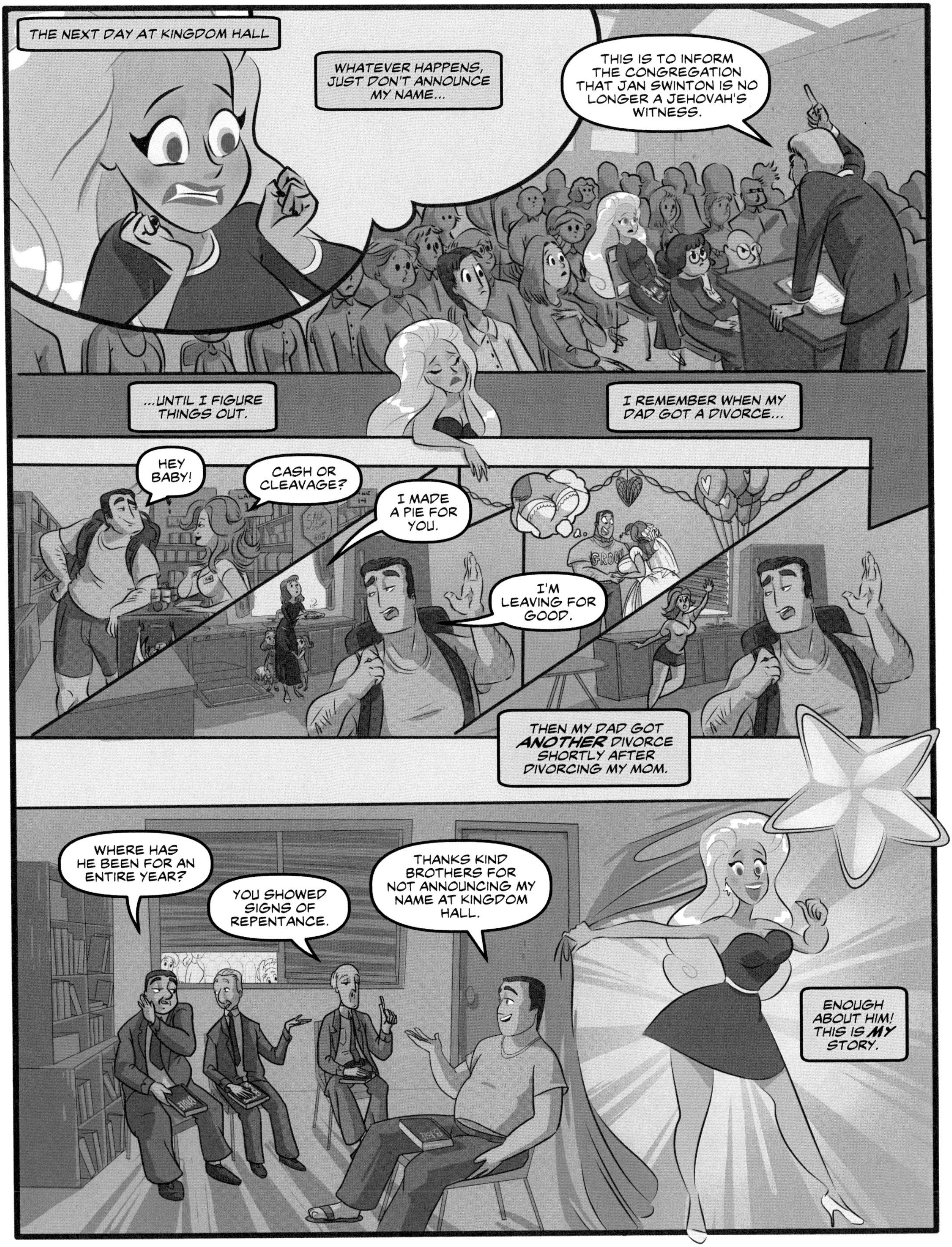
THE NEXT DAY AT KINGDOM HALL
WHATEVER HAPPENS, JUST DON'T ANNOUNCE MY NAME...
THIS IS TO INFORM THE CONGREGATION THAT JAN SWINTON IS NO LONGER A JEHOVAH'S WITNESS.
...UNTIL I FIGURE THINGS OUT.
I REMEMBER WHEN MY DAD GOT A DIVORCE...
HEY BABY!
CASH OR CLEAVAGE?
I MADE A PIE FOR YOU.
I'M LEAVING FOR GOOD.
THEN MY DAD GOT ANOTHER DIVORCE SHORTLY AFTER DIVORCING MY MOM.
WHERE HAS HE BEEN FOR AN ENTIRE YEAR?
YOU SHOWED SIGNS OF REPENTANCE.
THANKS KIND BROTHERS FOR NOT ANNOUNCING MY NAME AT KINGDOM HALL.
ENOUGH ABOUT HIM! THIS IS MY STORY.

REASONS JEHOVAH'S WITNESSES GET MARRIED YOUNG

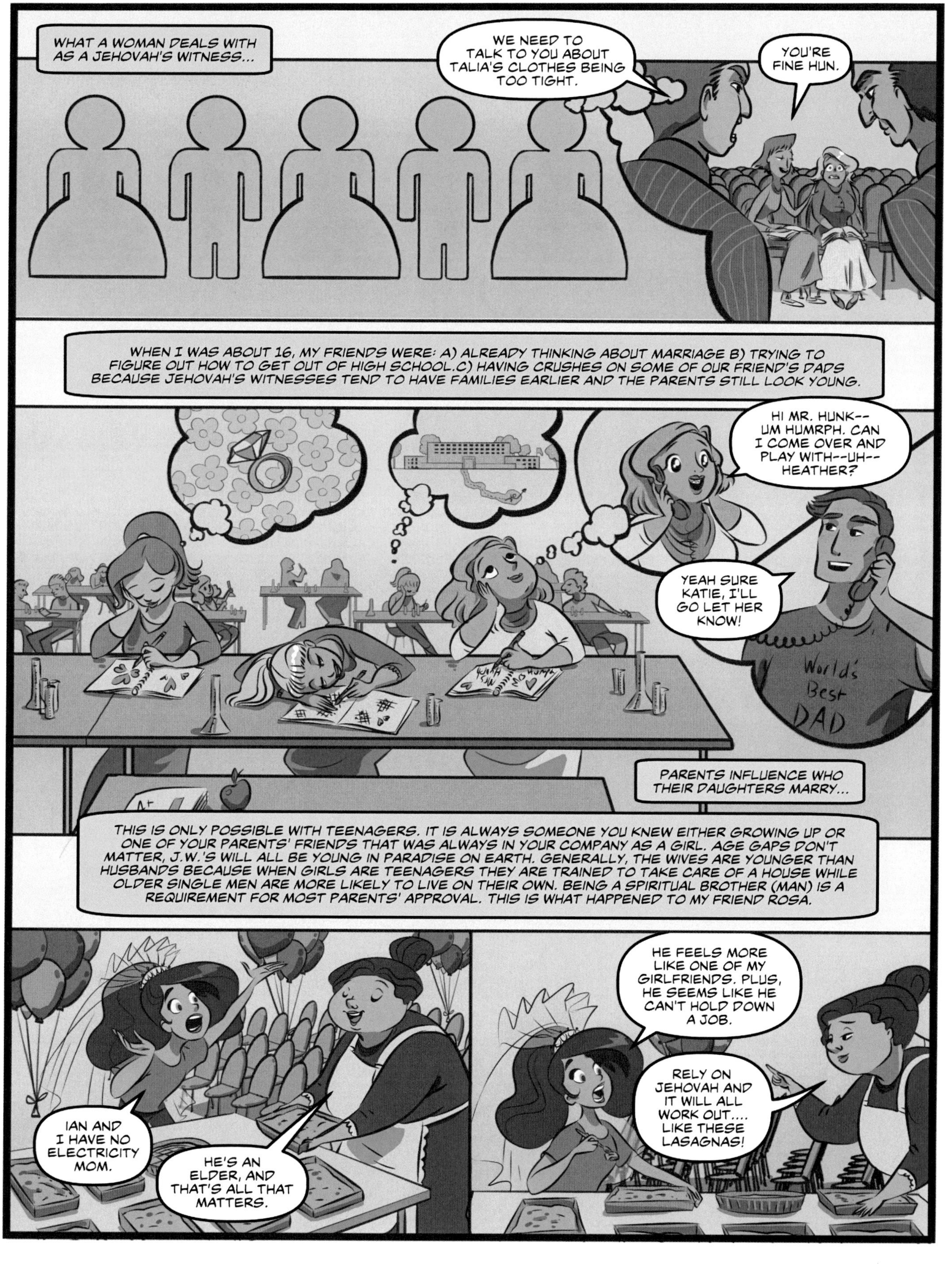
WHAT A WOMAN DEALS WITH AS A JEHOVAH'S WITNESS...
WE NEED TO TALK TO YOU ABOUT TALIA'S CLOTHES BEING TOO TIGHT.
YOU'RE FINE HUN.
WHEN I WAS ABOUT 16, MY FRIENDS WERE: A) ALREADY THINKING ABOUT MARRIAGE B) TRYING TO FIGURE OUT HOW TO GET OUT OF HIGH SCHOOL.C) HAVING CRUSHES ON SOME OF OUR FRIEND'S DADS BECAUSE JEHOVAH'S WITNESSES TEND TO HAVE FAMILIES EARLIER AND THE PARENTS STILL LOOK YOUNG.
HI MR. HUNK-- UM HUMRPH. CAN I COME OVER AND PLAY WITH--UH-- HEATHER?
YEAH SURE KATIE, I'LL GO LET HER KNOW!
World's Best DAD
PARENTS INFLUENCE WHO THEIR DAUGHTERS MARRY...
THIS IS ONLY POSSIBLE WITH TEENAGERS. IT IS ALWAYS SOMEONE YOU KNEW EITHER GROWING UP OR ONE OF YOUR PARENTS' FRIENDS THAT WAS ALWAYS IN YOUR COMPANY AS A GIRL. AGE GAPS DON'T MATTER, J.W.'S WILL ALL BE YOUNG IN PARADISE ON EARTH. GENERALLY, THE WIVES ARE YOUNGER THAN HUSBANDS BECAUSE WHEN GIRLS ARE TEENAGERS THEY ARE TRAINED TO TAKE CARE OF A HOUSE WHILE OLDER SINGLE MEN ARE MORE LIKELY TO LIVE ON THEIR OWN. BEING A SPIRITUAL BROTHER (MAN) IS A REQUIREMENT FOR MOST PARENTS' APPROVAL. THIS IS WHAT HAPPENED TO MY FRIEND ROSA.
IAN AND I HAVE NO ELECTRICITY MOM.
HE'S AN ELDER, AND THAT'S ALL THAT MATTERS.
HE FEELS MORE LIKE ONE OF MY GIRLFRIENDS. PLUS, HE SEEMS LIKE HE CAN'T HOLD DOWN A JOB.
RELY ON JEHOVAH AND IT WILL ALL WORK OUT.... LIKE THESE LASAGNAS!

VIEWS OF SEX IN A CULT

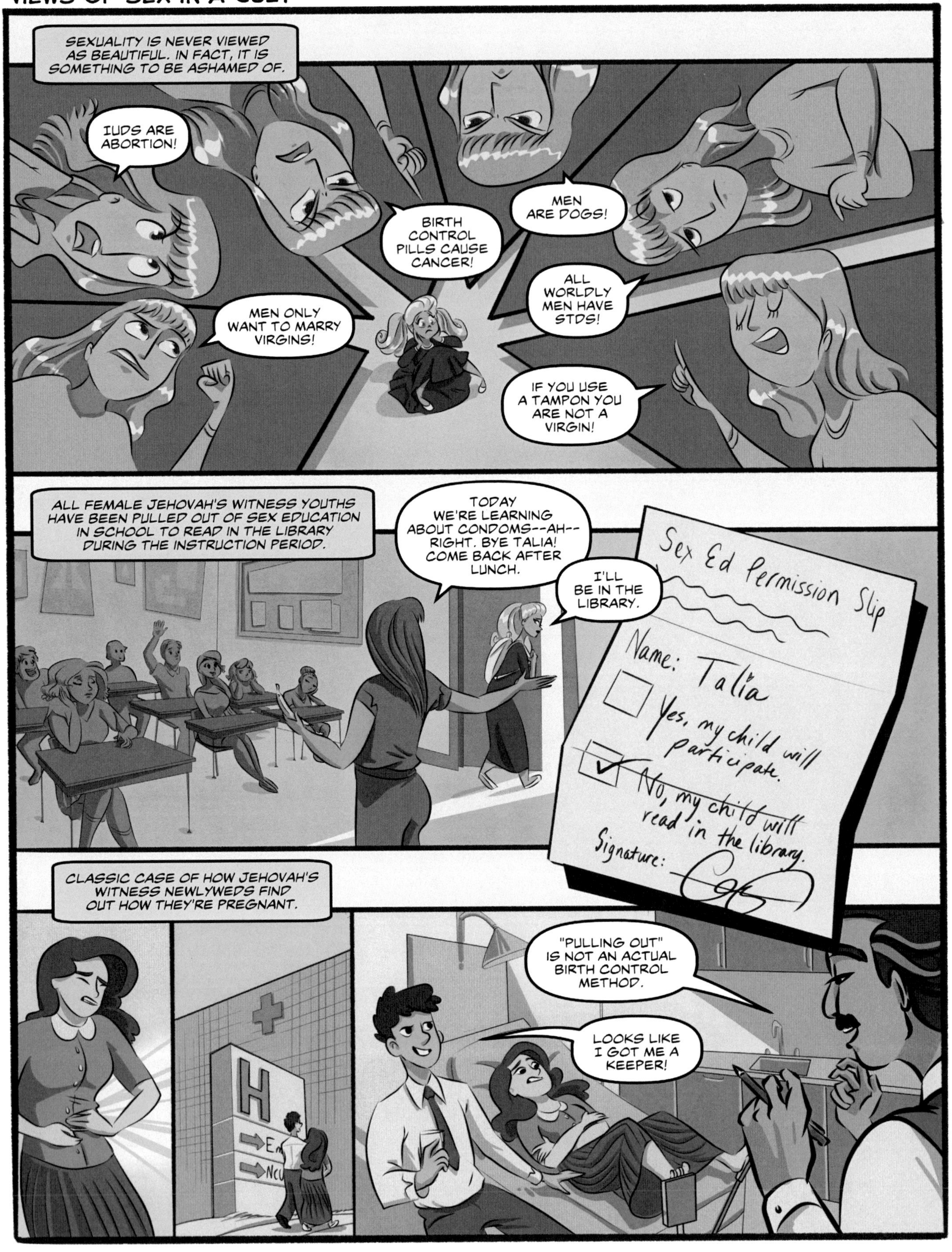
SEXUALITY IS NEVER VIEWED AS BEAUTIFUL. IN FACT, IT IS SOMETHING TO BE ASHAMED OF.
IUDS ARE ABORTION!
BIRTH CONTROL PILLS CAUSE CANCER!
MEN ARE DOGS!
ALL WORLDLY MEN HAVE STDS!
MEN ONLY WANT TO MARRY VIRGINS!
IF YOU USE A TAMPON YOU ARE NOT A VIRGIN!
ALL FEMALE JEHOVAH'S WITNESS YOUTHS HAVE BEEN PULLED OUT OF SEX EDUCATION IN SCHOOL TO READ IN THE LIBRARY DURING THE INSTRUCTION PERIOD.
TODAY WE'RE LEARNING ABOUT CONDOMS--AH--RIGHT. BYE TALIA! COME BACK AFTER LUNCH.
I'LL BE IN THE LIBRARY.
Sex Ed Permission Slip
Name: Talia
Yes, my child will participate.
No, my child will read in the library.
Signature:
CLASSIC CASE OF HOW JEHOVAH'S WITNESS NEWLYWEDS FIND OUT HOW THEY'RE PREGNANT.
"PULLING OUT" IS NOT AN ACTUAL BIRTH CONTROL METHOD.
LOOKS LIKE I GOT ME A KEEPER!

MARRIAGE FANTASY

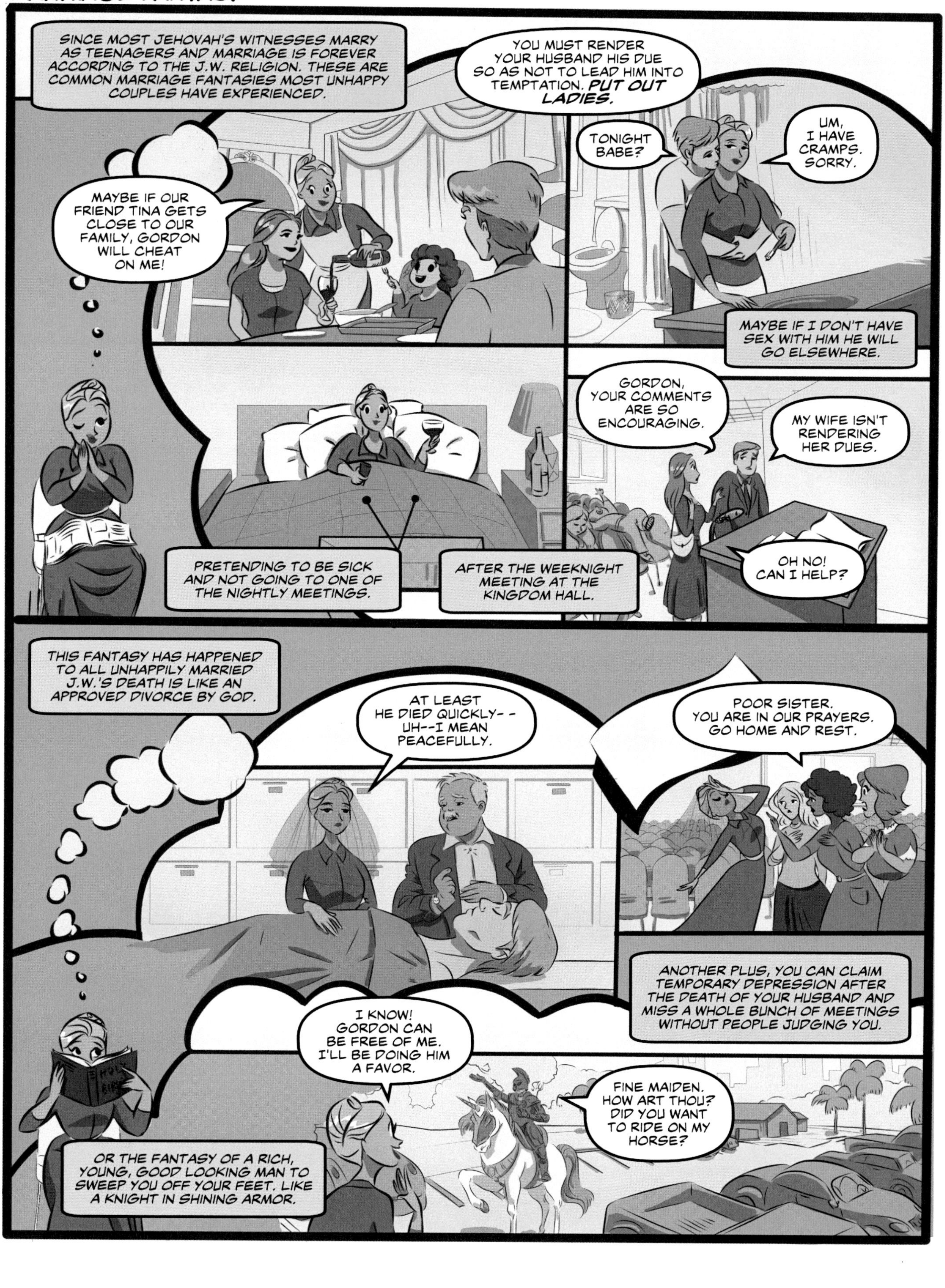

SINCE MOST JEHOVAH'S WITNESSES MARRY AS TEENAGERS AND MARRIAGE IS FOREVER ACCORDING TO THE J.W. RELIGION. THESE ARE COMMON MARRIAGE FANTASIES MOST UNHAPPY COUPLES HAVE EXPERIENCED.
YOU MUST RENDER YOUR HUSBAND HIS DUE SO AS NOT TO LEAD HIM INTO TEMPTATION. PUT OUT LADIES.
MAYBE IF OUR FRIEND TINA GETS CLOSE TO OUR FAMILY, GORDON WILL CHEAT ON ME!
TONIGHT BABE?
UM, I HAVE CRAMPS. SORRY.
MAYBE IF I DON'T HAVE SEX WITH HIM HE WILL GO ELSEWHERE.
PRETENDING TO BE SICK AND NOT GOING TO ONE OF THE NIGHTLY MEETINGS.
AFTER THE WEEKNIGHT MEETING AT THE KINGDOM HALL.
GORDON, YOUR COMMENTS ARE SO ENCOURAGING.
MY WIFE ISN'T RENDERING HER DUES.
OH NO! CAN I HELP?
THIS FANTASY HAS HAPPENED TO ALL UNHAPPILY MARRIED J.W.'S DEATH IS LIKE AN APPROVED DIVORCE BY GOD.
AT LEAST HE DIED QUICKLY- - UH--I MEAN PEACEFULLY.
POOR SISTER. YOU ARE IN OUR PRAYERS. GO HOME AND REST.
ANOTHER PLUS, YOU CAN CLAIM TEMPORARY DEPRESSION AFTER THE DEATH OF YOUR HUSBAND AND MISS A WHOLE BUNCH OF MEETINGS WITHOUT PEOPLE JUDGING YOU.
I KNOW! GORDON CAN BE FREE OF ME. I'LL BE DOING HIM A FAVOR.
FINE MAIDEN. HOW ART THOU? DID YOU WANT TO RIDE ON MY HORSE?
OR THE FANTASY OF A RICH, YOUNG, GOOD LOOKING MAN TO SWEEP YOU OFF YOUR FEET. LIKE A KNIGHT IN SHINING ARMOR.

THE ELDERS

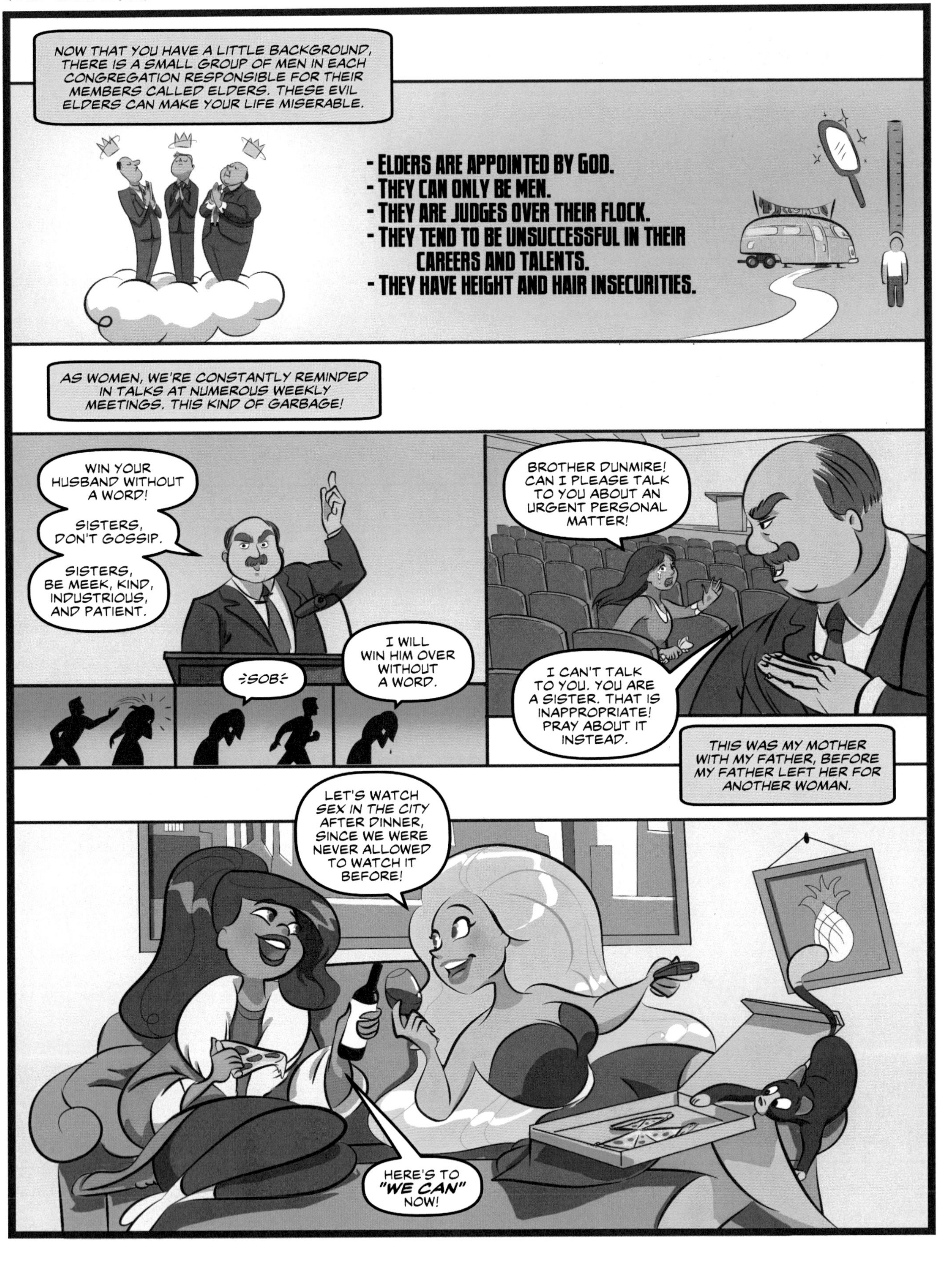
NOW THAT YOU HAVE A LITTLE BACKGROUND, THERE IS A SMALL GROUP OF MEN IN EACH CONGREGATION RESPONSIBLE FOR THEIR MEMBERS CALLED ELDERS. THESE EVIL ELDERS CAN MAKE YOUR LIFE MISERABLE.
- ELDERS ARE APPOINTED BY GOD.
- THEY CAN ONLY BE MEN.
- THEY ARE JUDGES OVER THEIR FLOCK.
- THEY TEND TO BE UNSUCCESSFUL IN THEIR CAREERS AND TALENTS.
- THEY HAVE HEIGHT AND HAIR INSECURITIES.
AS WOMEN, WE'RE CONSTANTLY REMINDED IN TALKS AT NUMEROUS WEEKLY MEETINGS. THIS KIND OF GARBAGE!
WIN YOUR HUSBAND WITHOUT A WORD!
SISTERS, DON'T GOSSIP.
SISTERS, BE MEEK, KIND, INDUSTRIOUS, AND PATIENT.
SOB
I WILL WIN HIM OVER WITHOUT A WORD.
BROTHER DUNMIRE! CAN I PLEASE TALK TO YOU ABOUT AN URGENT PERSONAL MATTER!
I CAN'T TALK TO YOU. YOU ARE A SISTER. THAT IS INAPPROPRIATE! PRAY ABOUT IT INSTEAD.
THIS WAS MY MOTHER WITH MY FATHER, BEFORE MY FATHER LEFT HER FOR ANOTHER WOMAN.
LET'S WATCH SEX IN THE CITY AFTER DINNER, SINCE WE WERE NEVER ALLOWED TO WATCH IT BEFORE!
HERE'S TO "WE CAN" NOW!

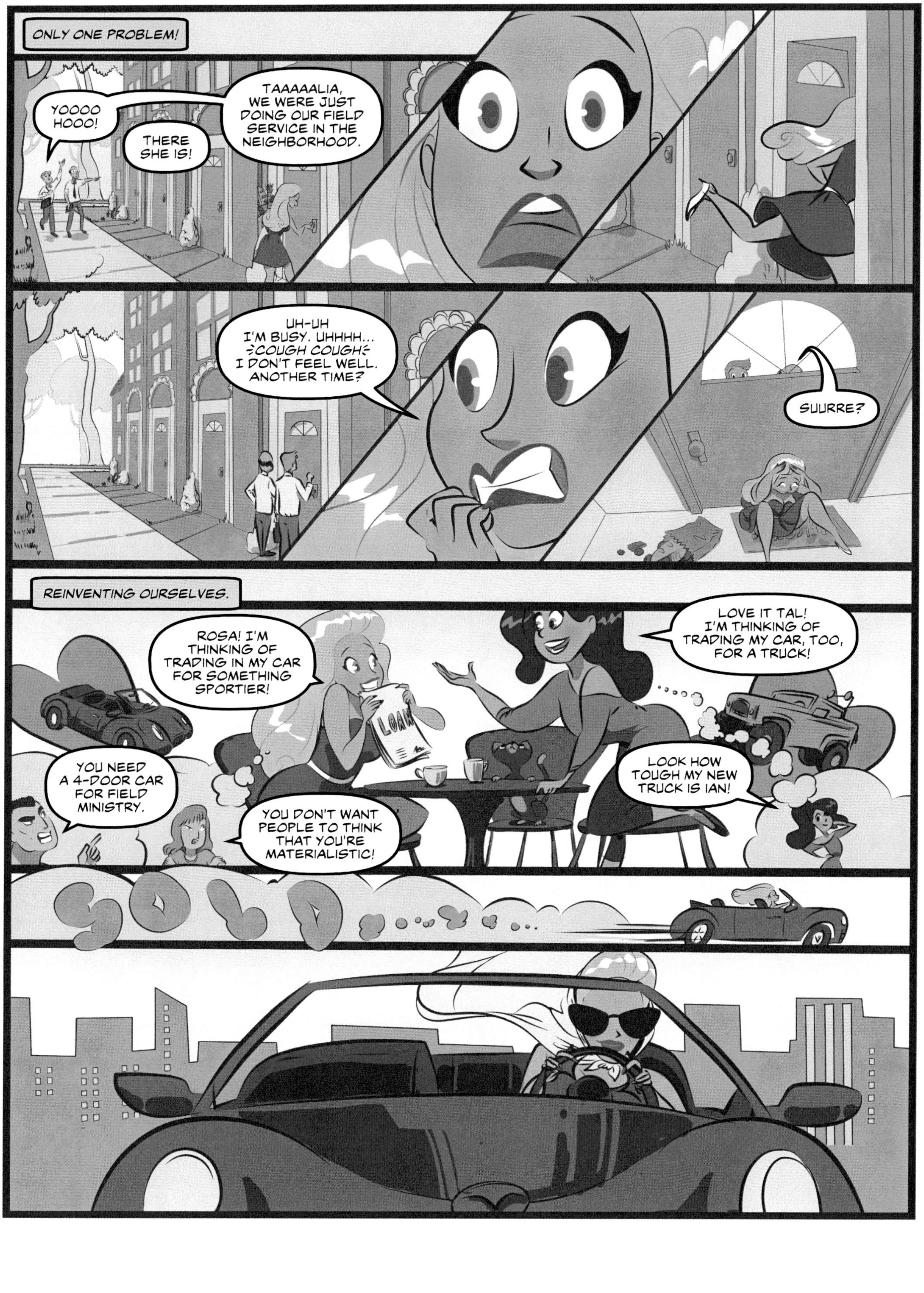
ONLY ONE PROBLEM!
YOOOO HOOO!
THERE SHE IS!
TAAAAALIA, WE WERE JUST DOING OUR FIELD SERVICE IN THE NEIGHBORHOOD.
UH-UH I'M BUSY. UHHHH... ≥COUGH COUGH≤ I DON'T FEEL WELL. ANOTHER TIME?
SUURRE?
REINVENTING OURSELVES.
ROSA! I'M THINKING OF TRADING IN MY CAR FOR SOMETHING SPORTIER!
LOAN
LOVE IT TAL! I'M THINKING OF TRADING MY CAR, TOO, FOR A TRUCK!
YOU NEED A 4-DOOR CAR FOR FIELD MINISTRY.
YOU DON'T WANT PEOPLE TO THINK THAT YOU'RE MATERIALISTIC!
LOOK HOW TOUGH MY NEW TRUCK IS IAN!
SOLD

ANNOUNCING & FADERS

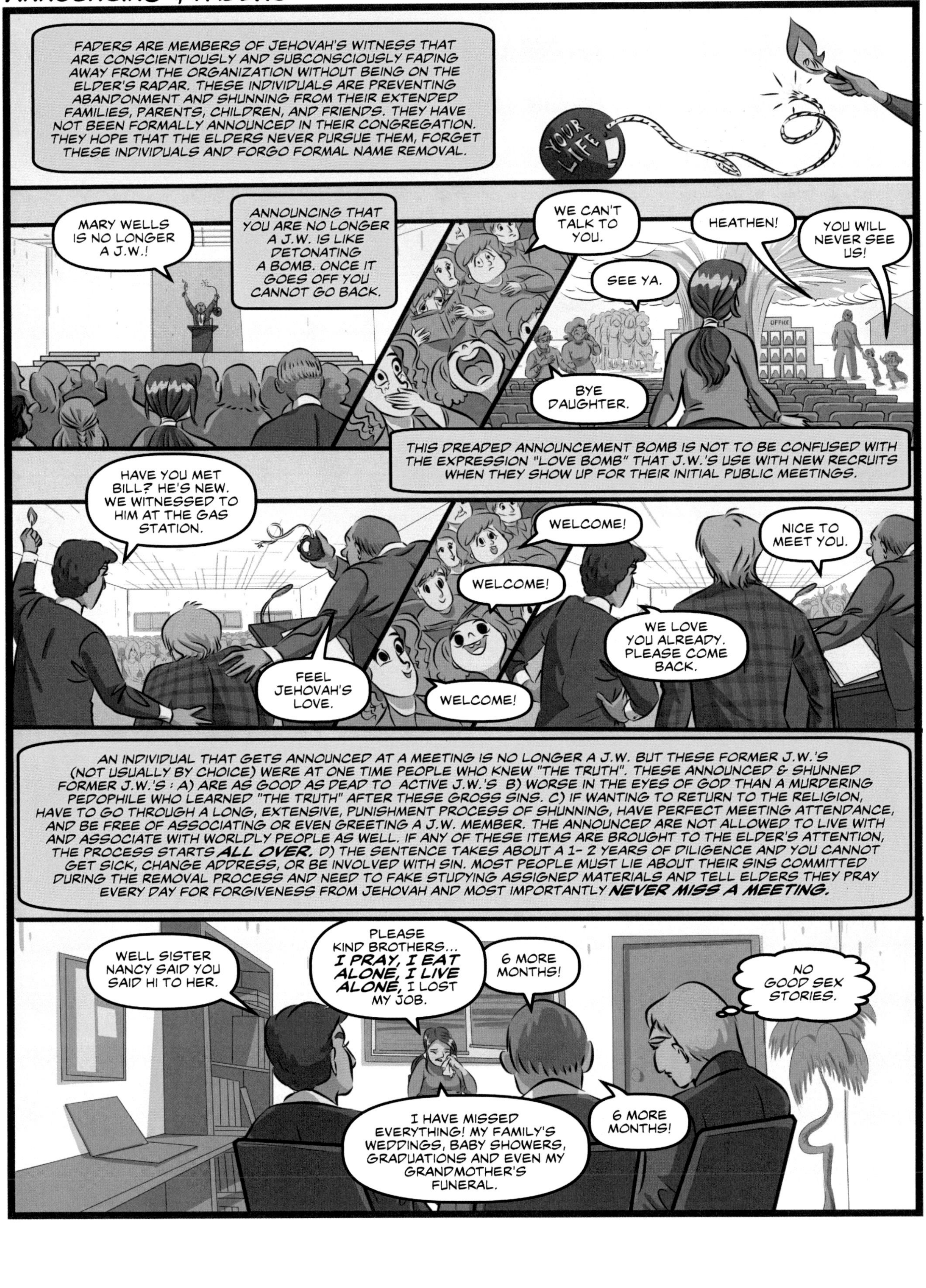
FADERS ARE MEMBERS OF JEHOVAH'S WITNESS THAT ARE CONSCIENTIOUSLY AND SUBCONSCIOUSLY FADING AWAY FROM THE ORGANIZATION WITHOUT BEING ON THE ELDER'S RADAR. THESE INDIVIDUALS ARE PREVENTING ABANDONMENT AND SHUNNING FROM THEIR EXTENDED FAMILIES, PARENTS, CHILDREN, AND FRIENDS. THEY HAVE NOT BEEN FORMALLY ANNOUNCED IN THEIR CONGREGATION. THEY HOPE THAT THE ELDERS NEVER PURSUE THEM, FORGET THESE INDIVIDUALS AND FORGO FORMAL NAME REMOVAL.
YOUR LIFE
MARY WELLS IS NO LONGER A J.W.!
ANNOUNCING THAT YOU ARE NO LONGER A J.W. IS LIKE DETONATING A BOMB. ONCE IT GOES OFF YOU CANNOT GO BACK.
WE CAN'T TALK TO YOU.
SEE YA.
HEATHEN!
YOU WILL NEVER SEE US!
OFFICE
BYE DAUGHTER.
THIS DREADED ANNOUNCEMENT BOMB IS NOT TO BE CONFUSED WITH THE EXPRESSION "LOVE BOMB" THAT J.W.'S USE WITH NEW RECRUITS WHEN THEY SHOW UP FOR THEIR INITIAL PUBLIC MEETINGS.
HAVE YOU MET BILL? HE'S NEW. WE WITNESSED TO HIM AT THE GAS STATION.
FEEL JEHOVAH'S LOVE.
WELCOME!
WELCOME!
WELCOME!
NICE TO MEET YOU.
WE LOVE YOU ALREADY. PLEASE COME BACK.
AN INDIVIDUAL THAT GETS ANNOUNCED AT A MEETING IS NO LONGER A J.W. BUT THESE FORMER J.W.'S (NOT USUALLY BY CHOICE) WERE AT ONE TIME PEOPLE WHO KNEW "THE TRUTH". THESE ANNOUNCED & SHUNNED FORMER J.W.'S : A) ARE AS GOOD AS DEAD TO ACTIVE J.W.'S B) WORSE IN THE EYES OF GOD THAN A MURDERING PEDOPHILE WHO LEARNED "THE TRUTH" AFTER THESE GROSS SINS. C) IF WANTING TO RETURN TO THE RELIGION, HAVE TO GO THROUGH A LONG, EXTENSIVE, PUNISHMENT PROCESS OF SHUNNING, HAVE PERFECT MEETING ATTENDANCE, AND BE FREE OF ASSOCIATING OR EVEN GREETING A J.W. MEMBER. THE ANNOUNCED ARE NOT ALLOWED TO LIVE WITH AND ASSOCIATE WITH WORLDLY PEOPLE AS WELL. IF ANY OF THESE ITEMS ARE BROUGHT TO THE ELDER'S ATTENTION, THE PROCESS STARTS ***ALL OVER.*** D) THE SENTENCE TAKES ABOUT A 1- 2 YEARS OF DILIGENCE AND YOU CANNOT GET SICK, CHANGE ADDRESS, OR BE INVOLVED WITH SIN. MOST PEOPLE MUST LIE ABOUT THEIR SINS COMMITTED DURING THE REMOVAL PROCESS AND NEED TO FAKE STUDYING ASSIGNED MATERIALS AND TELL ELDERS THEY PRAY EVERY DAY FOR FORGIVENESS FROM JEHOVAH AND MOST IMPORTANTLY ***NEVER MISS A MEETING.***
WELL SISTER NANCY SAID YOU SAID HI TO HER.
PLEASE KIND BROTHERS... ***I PRAY, I EAT ALONE, I LIVE ALONE,*** I LOST MY JOB.
6 MORE MONTHS!
NO GOOD SEX STORIES.
I HAVE MISSED EVERYTHING! MY FAMILY'S WEDDINGS, BABY SHOWERS, GRADUATIONS AND EVEN MY GRANDMOTHER'S FUNERAL.
6 MORE MONTHS!

THE DAY AFTER YOUR NAME IS ANNOUNCED

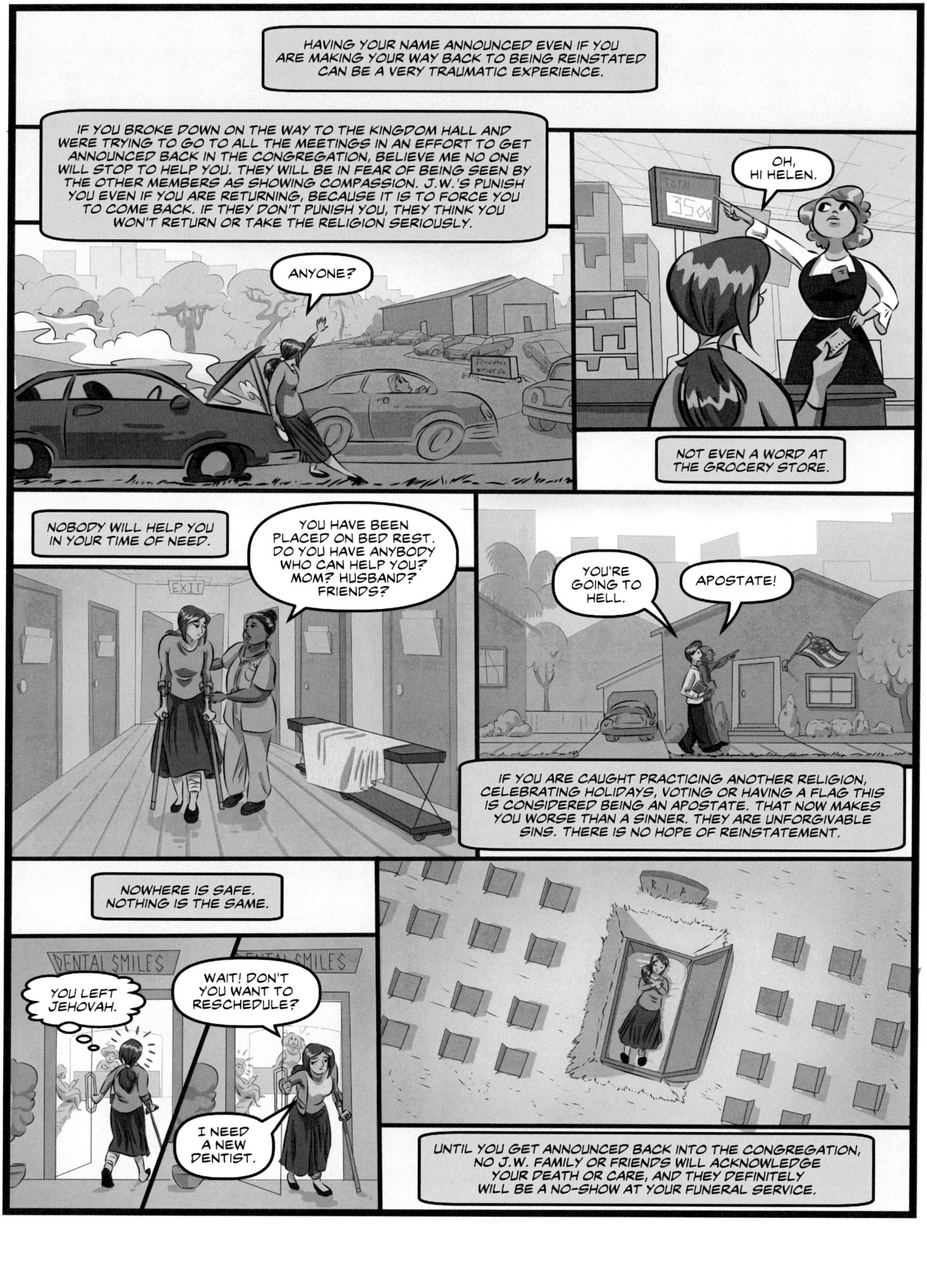
HAVING YOUR NAME ANNOUNCED EVEN IF YOU ARE MAKING YOUR WAY BACK TO BEING REINSTATED CAN BE A VERY TRAUMATIC EXPERIENCE.
IF YOU BROKE DOWN ON THE WAY TO THE KINGDOM HALL AND WERE TRYING TO GO TO ALL THE MEETINGS IN AN EFFORT TO GET ANNOUNCED BACK IN THE CONGREGATION, BELIEVE ME NO ONE WILL STOP TO HELP YOU. THEY WILL BE IN FEAR OF BEING SEEN BY THE OTHER MEMBERS AS SHOWING COMPASSION. J.W.'S PUNISH YOU EVEN IF YOU ARE RETURNING, BECAUSE IT IS TO FORCE YOU TO COME BACK. IF THEY DON'T PUNISH YOU, THEY THINK YOU WON'T RETURN OR TAKE THE RELIGION SERIOUSLY.
ANYONE?
OH, HI HELEN.
TOTAL
35.00
NOT EVEN A WORD AT THE GROCERY STORE.
NOBODY WILL HELP YOU IN YOUR TIME OF NEED.
YOU HAVE BEEN PLACED ON BED REST. DO YOU HAVE ANYBODY WHO CAN HELP YOU? MOM? HUSBAND? FRIENDS?
EXIT
YOU'RE GOING TO HELL.
APOSTATE!
IF YOU ARE CAUGHT PRACTICING ANOTHER RELIGION, CELEBRATING HOLIDAYS, VOTING OR HAVING A FLAG THIS IS CONSIDERED BEING AN APOSTATE. THAT NOW MAKES YOU WORSE THAN A SINNER. THEY ARE UNFORGIVABLE SINS. THERE IS NO HOPE OF REINSTATEMENT.
NOWHERE IS SAFE. NOTHING IS THE SAME.
DENTAL SMILES
YOU LEFT JEHOVAH.
WAIT! DON'T YOU WANT TO RESCHEDULE?
I NEED A NEW DENTIST.
R.I.P.
UNTIL YOU GET ANNOUNCED BACK INTO THE CONGREGATION, NO J.W. FAMILY OR FRIENDS WILL ACKNOWLEDGE YOUR DEATH OR CARE, AND THEY DEFINITELY WILL BE A NO-SHOW AT YOUR FUNERAL SERVICE.

COLLEGE

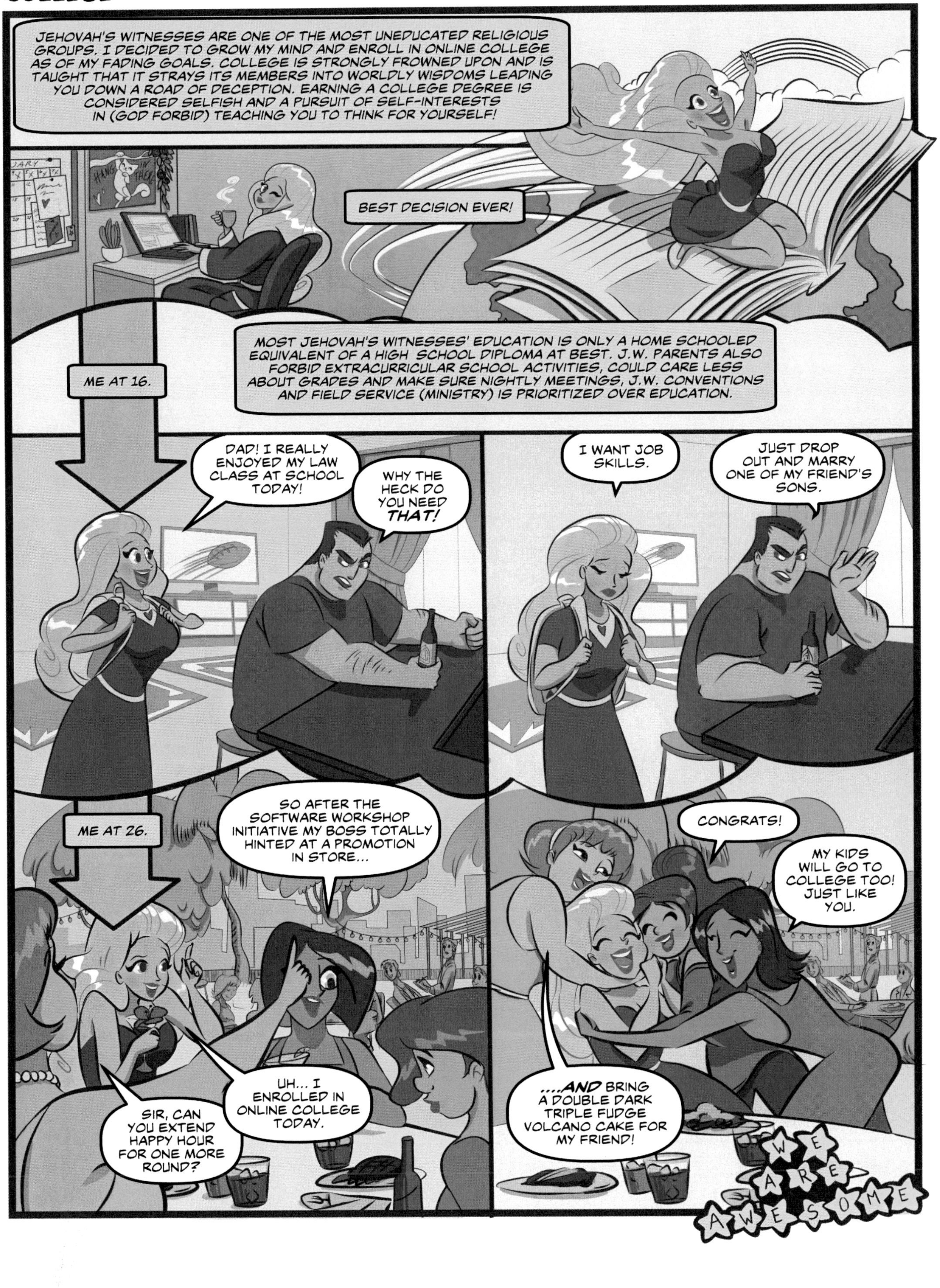
JEHOVAH'S WITNESSES ARE ONE OF THE MOST UNEDUCATED RELIGIOUS GROUPS. I DECIDED TO GROW MY MIND AND ENROLL IN ONLINE COLLEGE AS OF MY FADING GOALS. COLLEGE IS STRONGLY FROWNED UPON AND IS TAUGHT THAT IT STRAYS ITS MEMBERS INTO WORLDLY WISDOMS LEADING YOU DOWN A ROAD OF DECEPTION. EARNING A COLLEGE DEGREE IS CONSIDERED SELFISH AND A PURSUIT OF SELF-INTERESTS IN (GOD FORBID) TEACHING YOU TO THINK FOR YOURSELF!
HANG IN THERE
BEST DECISION EVER!
MOST JEHOVAH'S WITNESSES' EDUCATION IS ONLY A HOME SCHOOLED EQUIVALENT OF A HIGH SCHOOL DIPLOMA AT BEST. J.W. PARENTS ALSO FORBID EXTRACURRICULAR SCHOOL ACTIVITIES, COULD CARE LESS ABOUT GRADES AND MAKE SURE NIGHTLY MEETINGS, J.W. CONVENTIONS AND FIELD SERVICE (MINISTRY) IS PRIORITIZED OVER EDUCATION.
ME AT 16.
DAD! I REALLY ENJOYED MY LAW CLASS AT SCHOOL TODAY!
WHY THE HECK DO YOU NEED ***THAT!***
I WANT JOB SKILLS.
JUST DROP OUT AND MARRY ONE OF MY FRIEND'S SONS.
ME AT 26.
SO AFTER THE SOFTWARE WORKSHOP INITIATIVE MY BOSS TOTALLY HINTED AT A PROMOTION IN STORE...
UH... I ENROLLED IN ONLINE COLLEGE TODAY.
SIR, CAN YOU EXTEND HAPPY HOUR FOR ONE MORE ROUND?
CONGRATS!
MY KIDS WILL GO TO COLLEGE TOO! JUST LIKE YOU.
....AND BRING A DOUBLE DARK TRIPLE FUDGE VOLCANO CAKE FOR MY FRIEND!
WE ARE AWESOME

THE REASON FOR THE LACK OF EDUCATION

AS PUBLISHED STATISTICS SHOW, ONE REASON FOR THE LACK OF EDUCATION OF J.W.'S IS BECAUSE ALL OF THEIR TIME AND ENERGY HAS BEEN SUCKED AWAY THROUGH CONSTANT BRAINWASHING WEEKLY MEETINGS, REPRIMANDS IN THEIR LITERATURE, AND PUBLIC DISCOURSES THAT WARN J.W. MEMBERS THAT SELF IMPROVEMENT IS SATANIC AND SELFISH.
WHAT J.W. ADVANCEMENT LOOKS LIKE...
CONSTANT MEETINGS
FIELD SERVICE TIME AGAIN
ADVANCE AS JW YOU CAN ALWAYS DO MORE
DAILY BIBLE STUDY
...WHAT IT FEELS LIKE
JW MATH
1x2=1
EDUCATION +self = SELFISH!
FULLTIME WORK +self = EVIL!
3+self=sin
ANYTHING NEW +self = SHOWING OFF!
Retirement savings +self = BAD!
2+2=4
BECAUSE OF THE LACK OF JOB SKILLS YOU HAVE THESE 3 PROBLEMS...
DISABILITY
WELFARE
LACK of HEALTHCARE
YOU GET THE POINT.
THIS IS ANOTHER REASON J.W.'S HAVE ONE OF THE HIGHEST RATIOS OF UNEDUCATED PEOPLE.
MID-WEEK FIELD SERVICE 9:00 A.M.
NOT HOME
ON DISABILITY
NOT HOME
NOT HOME
HOUSE ARREST
BESIDES NOT HAVING TIME OR BEING ALLOWED TO PURSUE PASSIONS OR HOBBIES, YOU ARE RAISED AS A J.W. TO NEVER FEEL SPECIAL. J.W. MEMBERS CAN BE COLD, ROBOTIC, AND NICE ONLY IF THEY ARE INTERESTED IN MAKING A GOOD IMPRESSION. THIS IS SO YOU CAN BE RECRUITED AND SPEND ALL OF YOUR TIME AND RESOURCES IN GIVING YOUR LIFE TO THEIR RELIGION. THEN YOU ARE WORTHY OF THEIR EMOTIONAL SUPPORT AND KIND WORDS.
HERE ARE THE 3 BIG HOLIDAYS YOU CAN CELEBRATE THAT ARE THE SHINING RARE EXCEPTIONS TO J.W. MATH. ONCE THEY ARE OVER, THAT'S THE END OF CELEBRATIONS FOR YOU.
HOMESCHOOL GRADUATION
WEDDING DAY
BAPTISM
FUN'S OVER! BACK TO ENDLESS SELF SACRIFICE! FUN+SELF=NO! 2+2=NOT YOU! 1+4=3 2+
TYPICAL PRESSURES PUT ON PARENTS IN FIELD SERVICE ARE MONTHLY HOUR LONG FIELD MINISTRY TIME REQUIREMENTS IN ORDER TO REMAIN AN ACTIVE J.W. NOBODY LIKES FIELD SERVICE.
THE J.W. ORGANIZATION DOES NOT VALUE THE YEARS OF TIME THEIR MEMBERS HAVE SPENT RECRUITING AND EVEN CLEANING THE BUILDING OF KINGDOM HALL. IN FACT, NON-J.W. EMPLOYERS CARE MORE ABOUT THE WELFARE OF THEIR J.W. EMPLOYEES THAN THE RELIGION DOES!
JACK'S WORLDLY DAD PUT JR. IN SOCCER.
GASP! BUT WHAT IF HE'S GOOD?
WE ARE ALL VOLUNTEERS. ANY MONEY YOU GIVE GOES ONLY TO THE ORGANIZATION, NOT FOR OUR GAS, FOOD, OR HEALTH CARE.

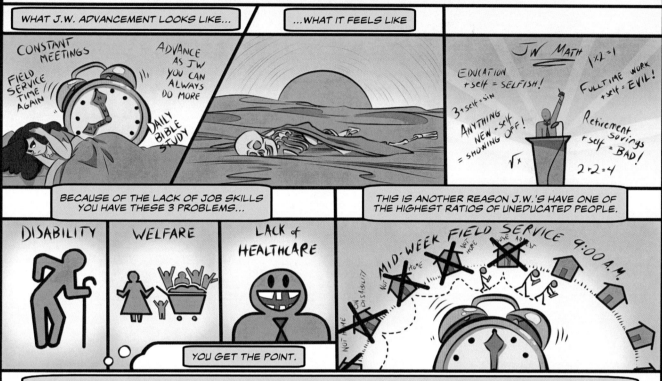

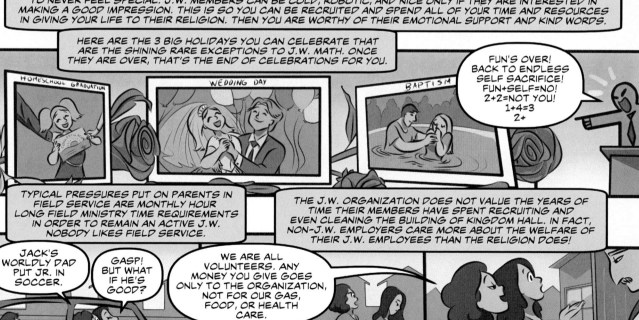

ARE THERE A LOT OF PEDOPHILE J.W.'S?

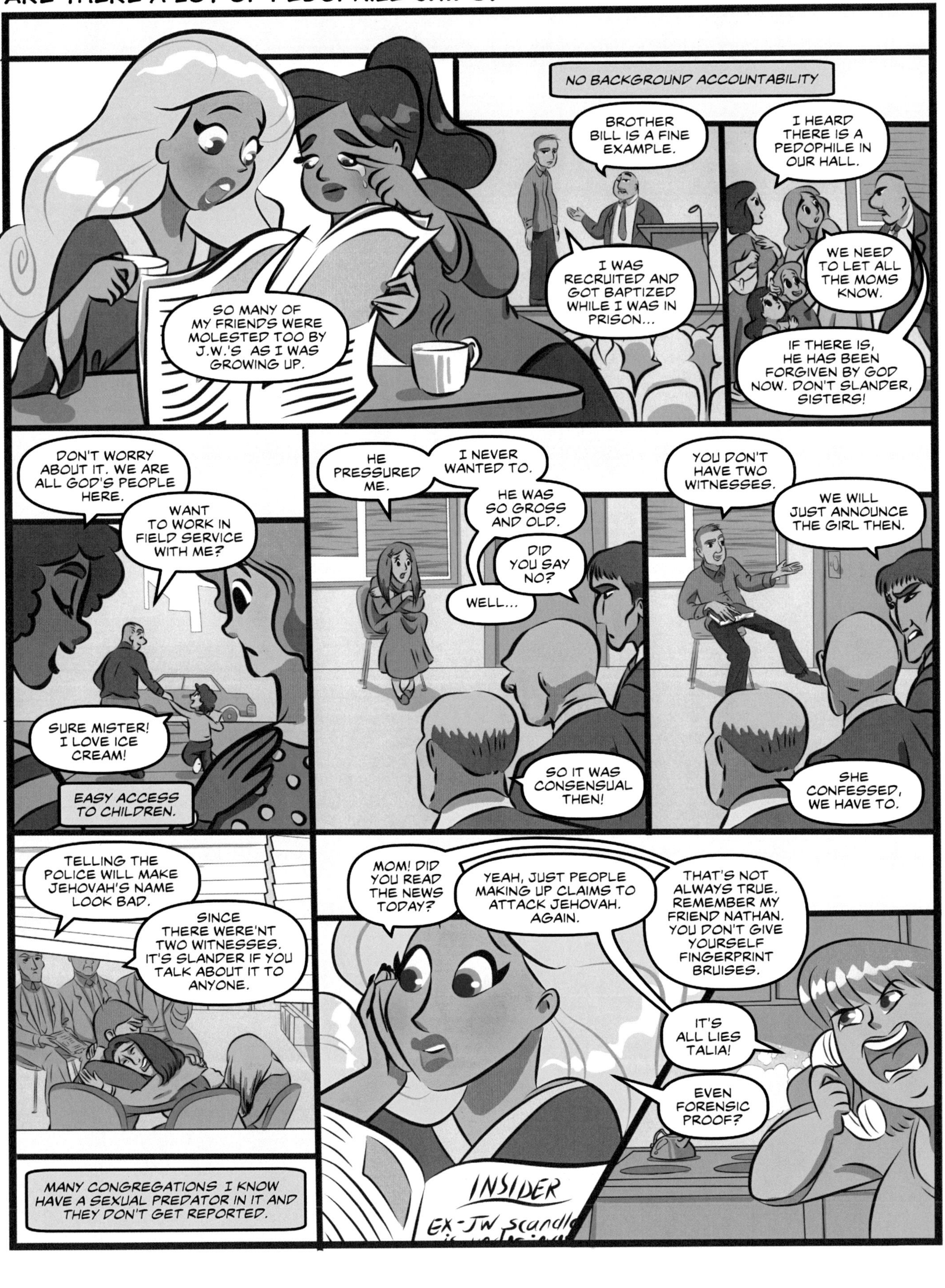

SO MANY OF MY FRIENDS WERE MOLESTED TOO BY J.W.'S AS I WAS GROWING UP.
NO BACKGROUND ACCOUNTABILITY
BROTHER BILL IS A FINE EXAMPLE.
I WAS RECRUITED AND GOT BAPTIZED WHILE I WAS IN PRISON...
I HEARD THERE IS A PEDOPHILE IN OUR HALL.
WE NEED TO LET ALL THE MOMS KNOW.
IF THERE IS, HE HAS BEEN FORGIVEN BY GOD NOW. DON'T SLANDER, SISTERS!
DON'T WORRY ABOUT IT. WE ARE ALL GOD'S PEOPLE HERE.
WANT TO WORK IN FIELD SERVICE WITH ME?
SURE MISTER! I LOVE ICE CREAM!
EASY ACCESS TO CHILDREN.
HE PRESSURED ME.
I NEVER WANTED TO.
HE WAS SO GROSS AND OLD.
DID YOU SAY NO?
WELL...
SO IT WAS CONSENSUAL THEN!
YOU DON'T HAVE TWO WITNESSES.
WE WILL JUST ANNOUNCE THE GIRL THEN.
SHE CONFESSED, WE HAVE TO.
TELLING THE POLICE WILL MAKE JEHOVAH'S NAME LOOK BAD.
SINCE THERE WERE'NT TWO WITNESSES. IT'S SLANDER IF YOU TALK ABOUT IT TO ANYONE.
MANY CONGREGATIONS I KNOW HAVE A SEXUAL PREDATOR IN IT AND THEY DON'T GET REPORTED.
MOM! DID YOU READ THE NEWS TODAY?
YEAH, JUST PEOPLE MAKING UP CLAIMS TO ATTACK JEHOVAH. AGAIN.
THAT'S NOT ALWAYS TRUE. REMEMBER MY FRIEND NATHAN. YOU DON'T GIVE YOURSELF FINGERPRINT BRUISES.
IT'S ALL LIES TALIA!
EVEN FORENSIC PROOF?
INSIDER

HOLIDAY TIME

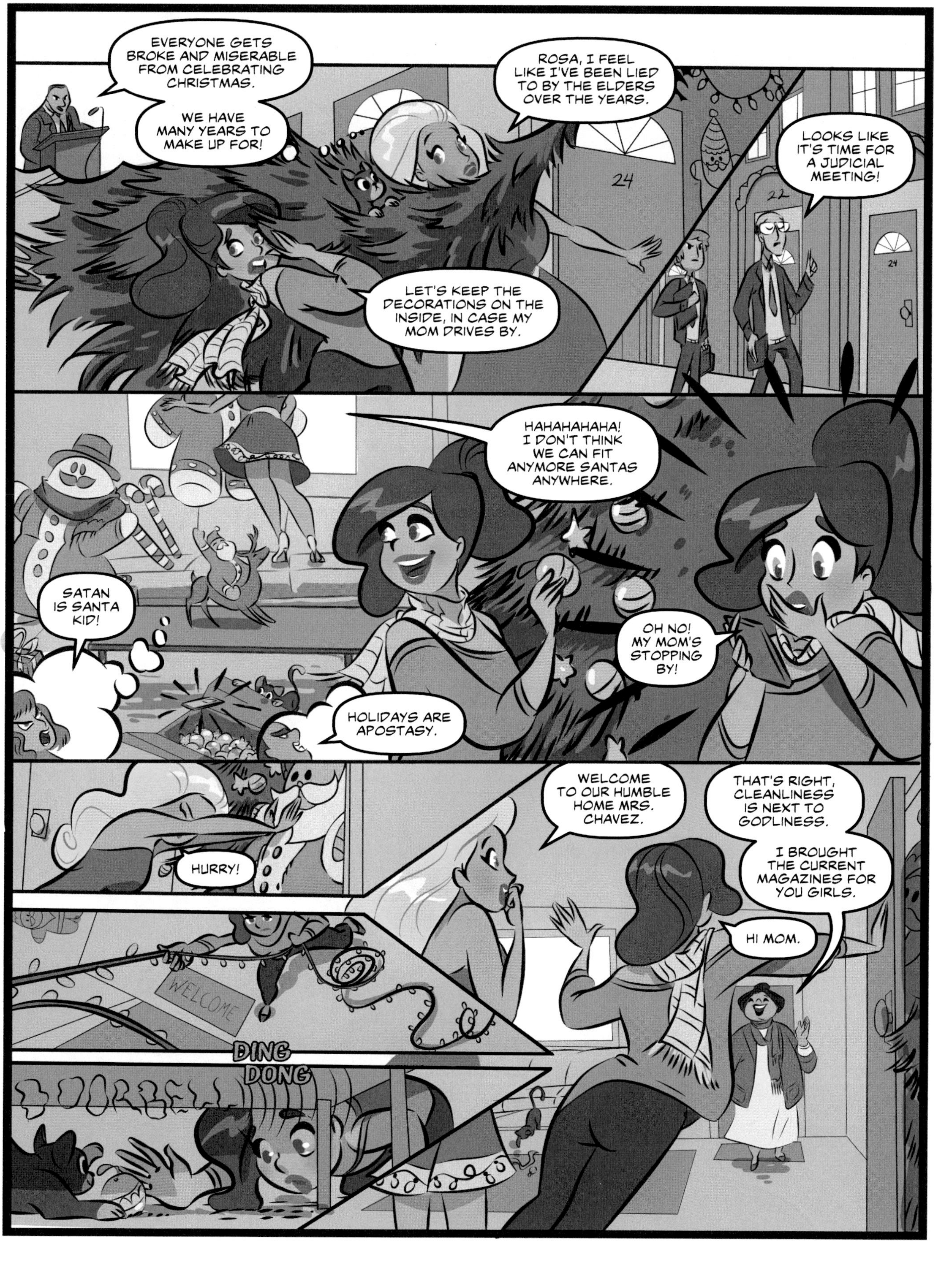
EVERYONE GETS BROKE AND MISERABLE FROM CELEBRATING CHRISTMAS.
WE HAVE MANY YEARS TO MAKE UP FOR!
ROSA, I FEEL LIKE I'VE BEEN LIED TO BY THE ELDERS OVER THE YEARS.
LET'S KEEP THE DECORATIONS ON THE INSIDE, IN CASE MY MOM DRIVES BY.
LOOKS LIKE IT'S TIME FOR A JUDICIAL MEETING!
HAHAHAHAHA! I DON'T THINK WE CAN FIT ANYMORE SANTAS ANYWHERE.
SATAN IS SANTA KID!
HOLIDAYS ARE APOSTASY.
OH NO! MY MOM'S STOPPING BY!
HURRY!
WELCOME
DING DONG
DOORBELL
WELCOME TO OUR HUMBLE HOME MRS. CHAVEZ.
HI MOM.
THAT'S RIGHT, CLEANLINESS IS NEXT TO GODLINESS.
I BROUGHT THE CURRENT MAGAZINES FOR YOU GIRLS.

FADER HOLIDAY PARTY

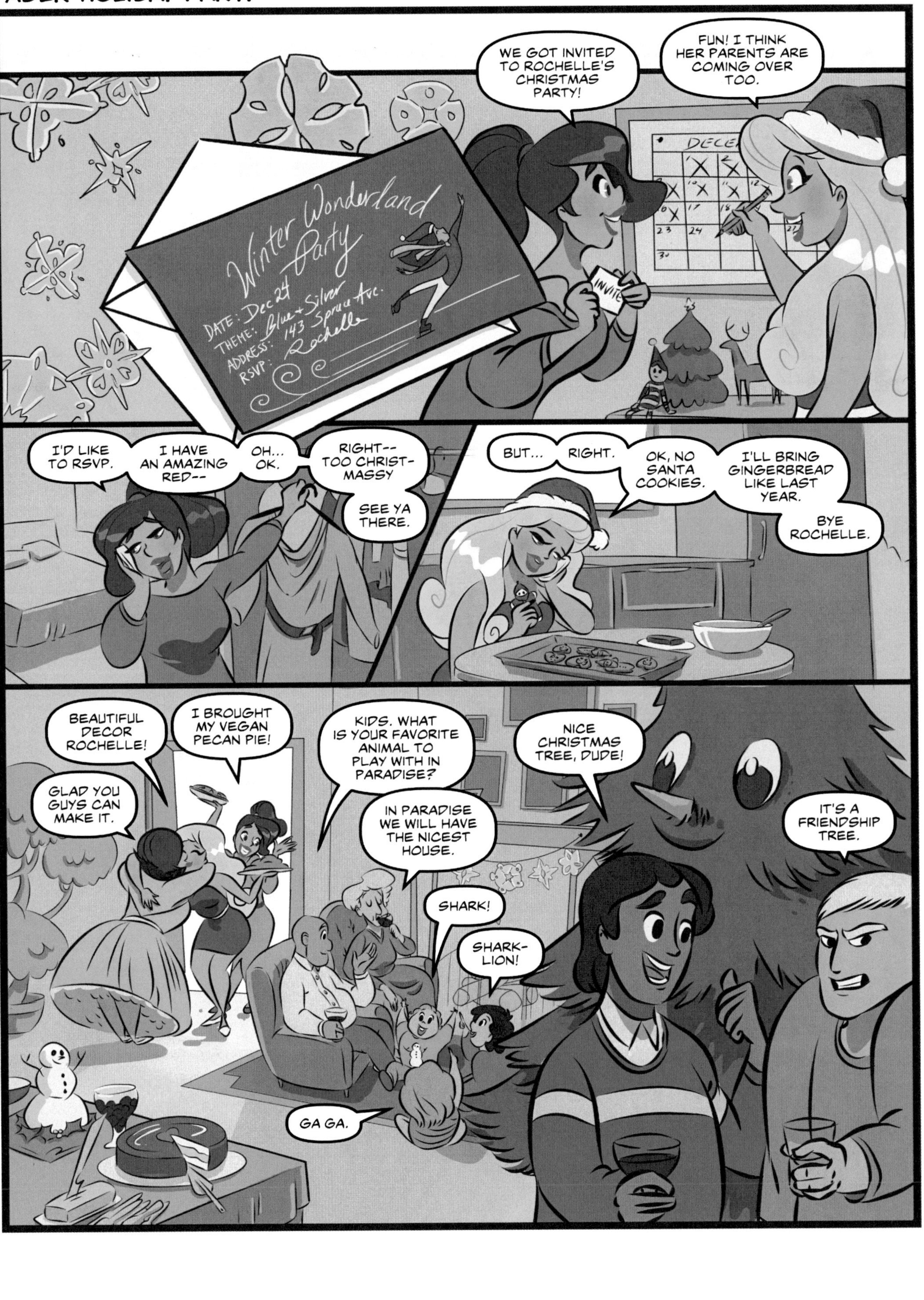

Winter Wonderland Party
DATE: Dec 24
THEME: Blue + Silver
ADDRESS: 143 Spruce Ave.
RSVP: Rochelle
INVITE
WE GOT INVITED TO ROCHELLE'S CHRISTMAS PARTY!
FUN! I THINK HER PARENTS ARE COMING OVER TOO.
I'D LIKE TO RSVP.
I HAVE AN AMAZING RED--
OH... OK.
RIGHT-- TOO CHRIST-MASSY
SEE YA THERE.
BUT...
RIGHT.
OK, NO SANTA COOKIES.
I'LL BRING GINGERBREAD LIKE LAST YEAR.
BYE ROCHELLE.
BEAUTIFUL DECOR ROCHELLE!
GLAD YOU GUYS CAN MAKE IT.
I BROUGHT MY VEGAN PECAN PIE!
KIDS. WHAT IS YOUR FAVORITE ANIMAL TO PLAY WITH IN PARADISE?
IN PARADISE WE WILL HAVE THE NICEST HOUSE.
SHARK!
SHARK-LION!
GA GA.
NICE CHRISTMAS TREE, DUDE!
IT'S A FRIENDSHIP TREE.

WE NEED TO MEET WITH YOU

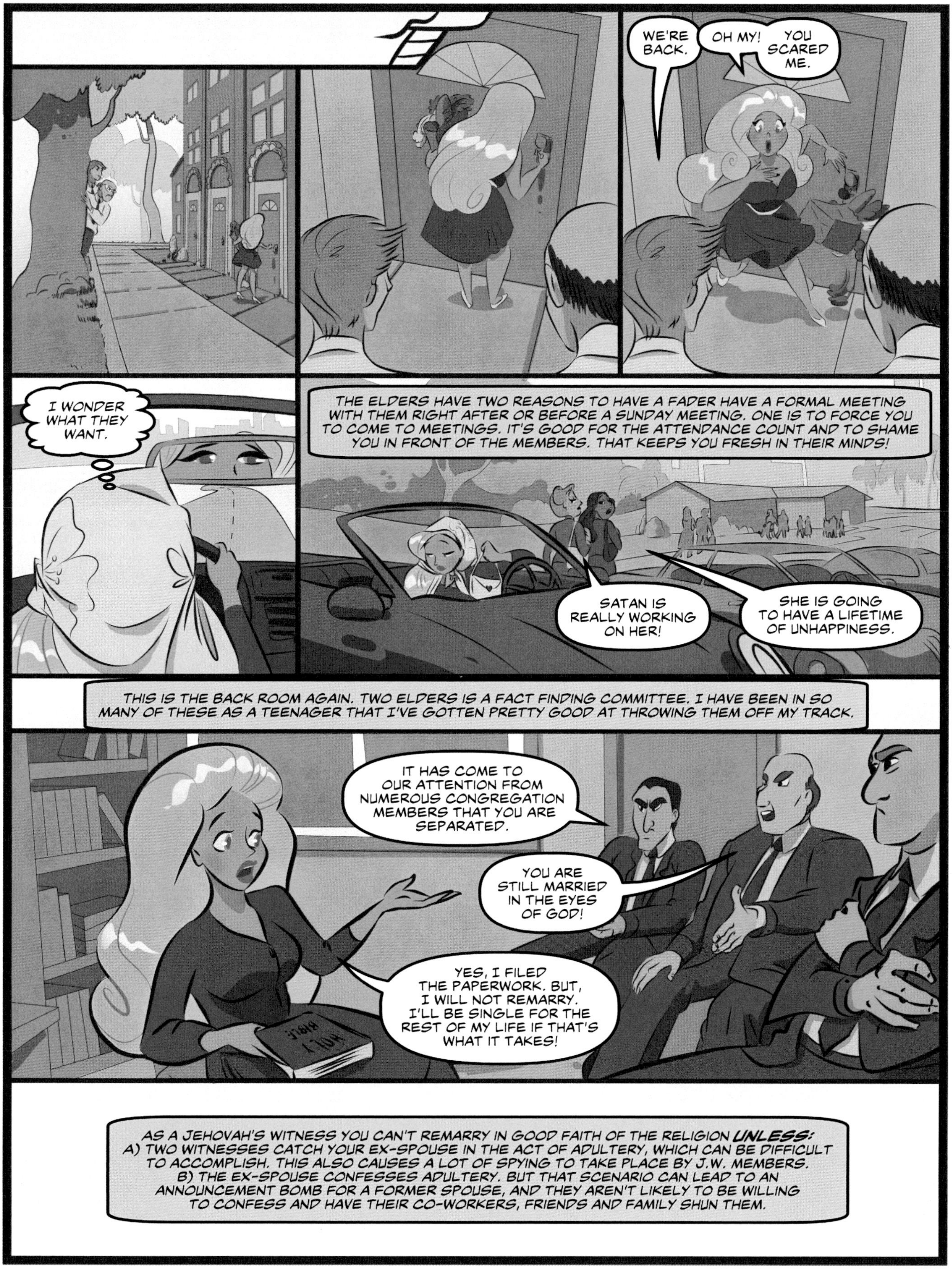

WE'RE BACK.
OH MY! YOU SCARED ME.
I WONDER WHAT THEY WANT.
THE ELDERS HAVE TWO REASONS TO HAVE A FADER HAVE A FORMAL MEETING WITH THEM RIGHT AFTER OR BEFORE A SUNDAY MEETING. ONE IS TO FORCE YOU TO COME TO MEETINGS. IT'S GOOD FOR THE ATTENDANCE COUNT AND TO SHAME YOU IN FRONT OF THE MEMBERS. THAT KEEPS YOU FRESH IN THEIR MINDS!
SATAN IS REALLY WORKING ON HER!
SHE IS GOING TO HAVE A LIFETIME OF UNHAPPINESS.
THIS IS THE BACK ROOM AGAIN. TWO ELDERS IS A FACT FINDING COMMITTEE. I HAVE BEEN IN SO MANY OF THESE AS A TEENAGER THAT I'VE GOTTEN PRETTY GOOD AT THROWING THEM OFF MY TRACK.
IT HAS COME TO OUR ATTENTION FROM NUMEROUS CONGREGATION MEMBERS THAT YOU ARE SEPARATED.
YOU ARE STILL MARRIED IN THE EYES OF GOD!
YES, I FILED THE PAPERWORK. BUT, I WILL NOT REMARRY. I'LL BE SINGLE FOR THE REST OF MY LIFE IF THAT'S WHAT IT TAKES!
HOLY BIBLE
AS A JEHOVAH'S WITNESS YOU CAN'T REMARRY IN GOOD FAITH OF THE RELIGION UNLESS:
A) TWO WITNESSES CATCH YOUR EX-SPOUSE IN THE ACT OF ADULTERY, WHICH CAN BE DIFFICULT TO ACCOMPLISH. THIS ALSO CAUSES A LOT OF SPYING TO TAKE PLACE BY J.W. MEMBERS.
B) THE EX-SPOUSE CONFESSES ADULTERY. BUT THAT SCENARIO CAN LEAD TO AN ANNOUNCEMENT BOMB FOR A FORMER SPOUSE, AND THEY AREN'T LIKELY TO BE WILLING TO CONFESS AND HAVE THEIR CO-WORKERS, FRIENDS AND FAMILY SHUN THEM.

MEANWHILE

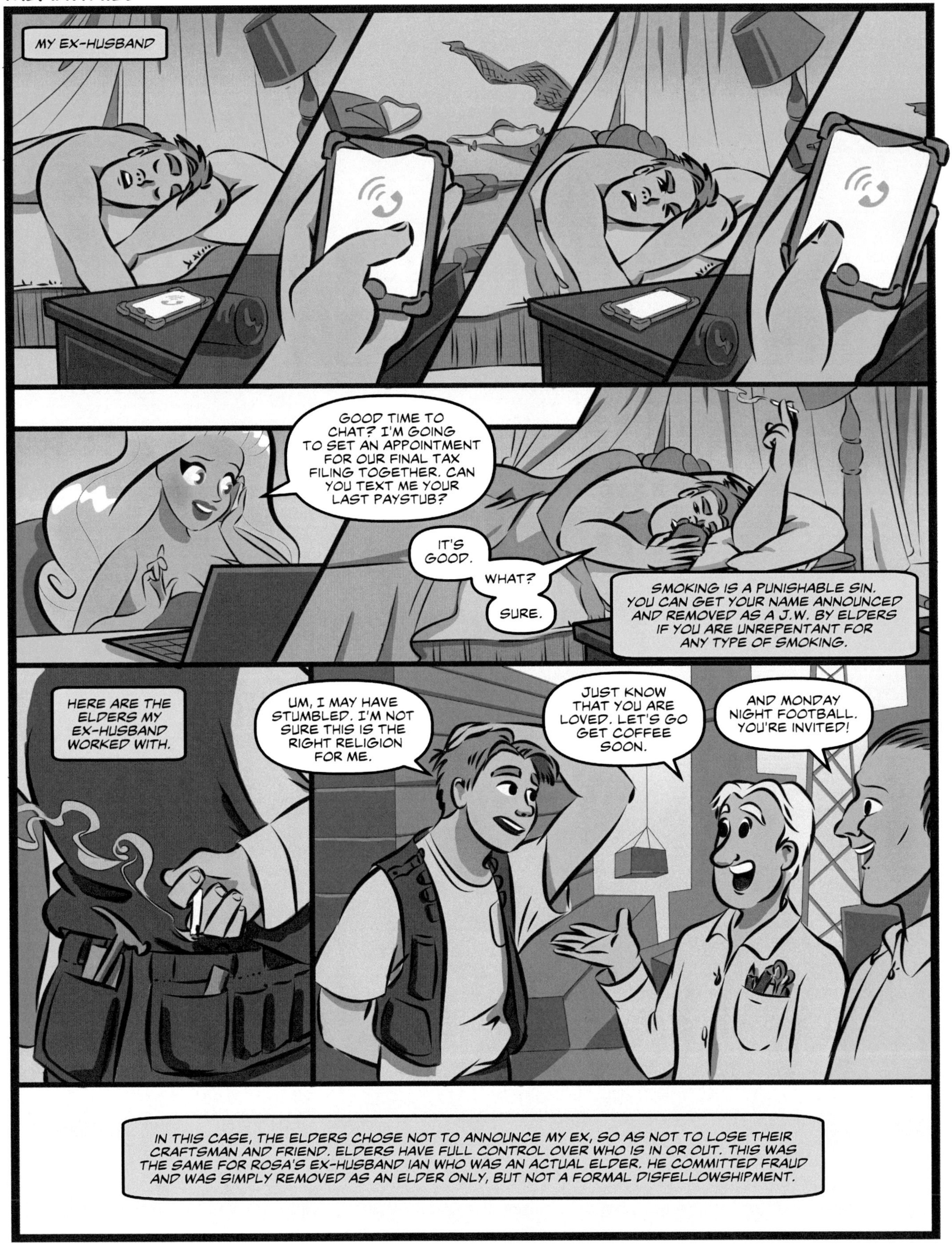

MY EX-HUSBAND
GOOD TIME TO CHAT? I'M GOING TO SET AN APPOINTMENT FOR OUR FINAL TAX FILING TOGETHER. CAN YOU TEXT ME YOUR LAST PAYSTUB?
IT'S GOOD.
WHAT?
SURE.
SMOKING IS A PUNISHABLE SIN. YOU CAN GET YOUR NAME ANNOUNCED AND REMOVED AS A J.W. BY ELDERS IF YOU ARE UNREPENTANT FOR ANY TYPE OF SMOKING.
HERE ARE THE ELDERS MY EX-HUSBAND WORKED WITH.
UM, I MAY HAVE STUMBLED. I'M NOT SURE THIS IS THE RIGHT RELIGION FOR ME.
JUST KNOW THAT YOU ARE LOVED. LET'S GO GET COFFEE SOON.
AND MONDAY NIGHT FOOTBALL. YOU'RE INVITED!
IN THIS CASE, THE ELDERS CHOSE NOT TO ANNOUNCE MY EX, SO AS NOT TO LOSE THEIR CRAFTSMAN AND FRIEND. ELDERS HAVE FULL CONTROL OVER WHO IS IN OR OUT. THIS WAS THE SAME FOR ROSA'S EX-HUSBAND IAN WHO WAS AN ACTUAL ELDER. HE COMMITTED FRAUD AND WAS SIMPLY REMOVED AS AN ELDER ONLY, BUT NOT A FORMAL DISFELLOWSHIPMENT.

TRAVEL PLANS

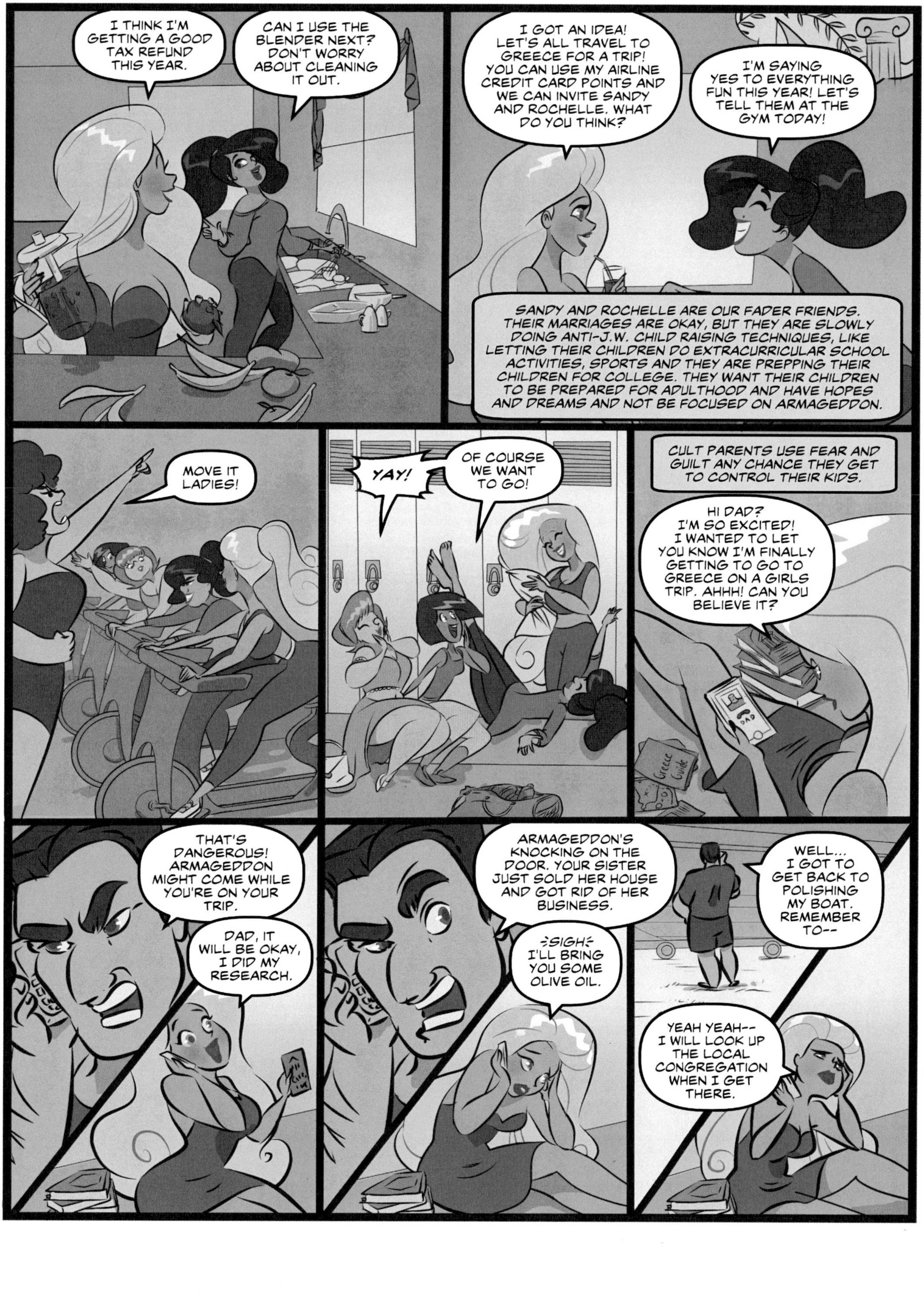
I THINK I'M GETTING A GOOD TAX REFUND THIS YEAR.
CAN I USE THE BLENDER NEXT? DON'T WORRY ABOUT CLEANING IT OUT.
I GOT AN IDEA! LET'S ALL TRAVEL TO GREECE FOR A TRIP! YOU CAN USE MY AIRLINE CREDIT CARD POINTS AND WE CAN INVITE SANDY AND ROCHELLE. WHAT DO YOU THINK?
I'M SAYING YES TO EVERYTHING FUN THIS YEAR! LET'S TELL THEM AT THE GYM TODAY!
SANDY AND ROCHELLE ARE OUR FADER FRIENDS. THEIR MARRIAGES ARE OKAY, BUT THEY ARE SLOWLY DOING ANTI-J.W. CHILD RAISING TECHNIQUES, LIKE LETTING THEIR CHILDREN DO EXTRACURRICULAR SCHOOL ACTIVITIES, SPORTS AND THEY ARE PREPPING THEIR CHILDREN FOR COLLEGE. THEY WANT THEIR CHILDREN TO BE PREPARED FOR ADULTHOOD AND HAVE HOPES AND DREAMS AND NOT BE FOCUSED ON ARMAGEDDON.
MOVE IT LADIES!
YAY!
OF COURSE WE WANT TO GO!
CULT PARENTS USE FEAR AND GUILT ANY CHANCE THEY GET TO CONTROL THEIR KIDS.
HI DAD? I'M SO EXCITED! I WANTED TO LET YOU KNOW I'M FINALLY GETTING TO GO TO GREECE ON A GIRLS TRIP. AHHH! CAN YOU BELIEVE IT?
DAD
Greece Guide
THAT'S DANGEROUS! ARMAGEDDON MIGHT COME WHILE YOU'RE ON YOUR TRIP.
DAD, IT WILL BE OKAY, I DID MY RESEARCH.
ARMAGEDDON'S KNOCKING ON THE DOOR. YOUR SISTER JUST SOLD HER HOUSE AND GOT RID OF HER BUSINESS.
SIGH I'LL BRING YOU SOME OLIVE OIL.
WELL... I GOT TO GET BACK TO POLISHING MY BOAT. REMEMBER TO--
YEAH YEAH-- I WILL LOOK UP THE LOCAL CONGREGATION WHEN I GET THERE.

GREECE

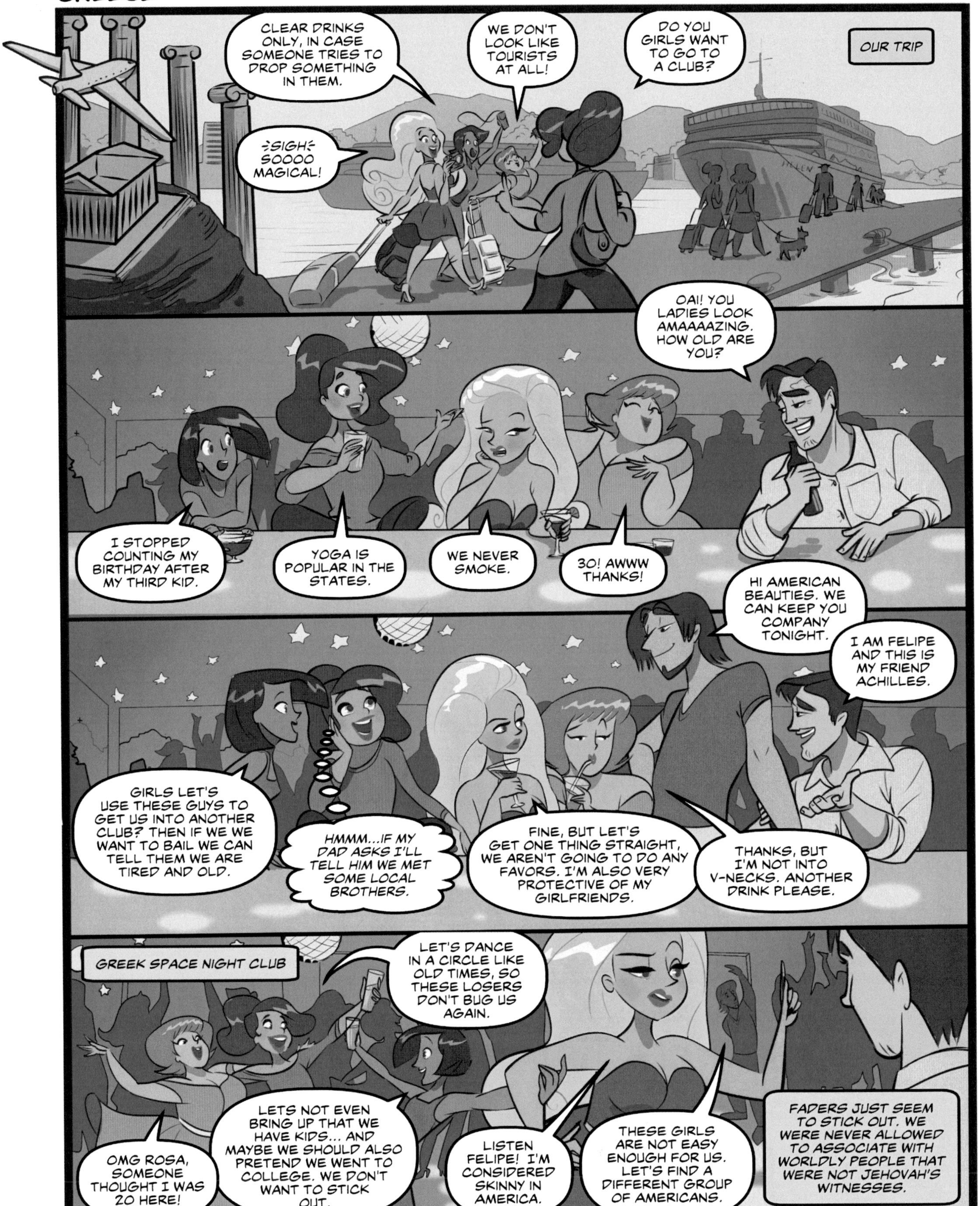
OUR TRIP
CLEAR DRINKS ONLY, IN CASE SOMEONE TRIES TO DROP SOMETHING IN THEM.
WE DON'T LOOK LIKE TOURISTS AT ALL!
DO YOU GIRLS WANT TO GO TO A CLUB?
-SIGH- SOOOO MAGICAL!
OAI! YOU LADIES LOOK AMAAAAZING. HOW OLD ARE YOU?
I STOPPED COUNTING MY BIRTHDAY AFTER MY THIRD KID.
YOGA IS POPULAR IN THE STATES.
WE NEVER SMOKE.
30! AWWW THANKS!
HI AMERICAN BEAUTIES. WE CAN KEEP YOU COMPANY TONIGHT.
I AM FELIPE AND THIS IS MY FRIEND ACHILLES.
GIRLS LET'S USE THESE GUYS TO GET US INTO ANOTHER CLUB? THEN IF WE WE WANT TO BAIL WE CAN TELL THEM WE ARE TIRED AND OLD.
HMMM...IF MY DAD ASKS I'LL TELL HIM WE MET SOME LOCAL BROTHERS.
FINE, BUT LET'S GET ONE THING STRAIGHT, WE AREN'T GOING TO DO ANY FAVORS. I'M ALSO VERY PROTECTIVE OF MY GIRLFRIENDS.
THANKS, BUT I'M NOT INTO V-NECKS. ANOTHER DRINK PLEASE.
GREEK SPACE NIGHT CLUB
LET'S DANCE IN A CIRCLE LIKE OLD TIMES, SO THESE LOSERS DON'T BUG US AGAIN.
OMG ROSA, SOMEONE THOUGHT I WAS 20 HERE!
LETS NOT EVEN BRING UP THAT WE HAVE KIDS... AND MAYBE WE SHOULD ALSO PRETEND WE WENT TO COLLEGE. WE DON'T WANT TO STICK OUT.
LISTEN FELIPE! I'M CONSIDERED SKINNY IN AMERICA.
THESE GIRLS ARE NOT EASY ENOUGH FOR US. LET'S FIND A DIFFERENT GROUP OF AMERICANS.
FADERS JUST SEEM TO STICK OUT. WE WERE NEVER ALLOWED TO ASSOCIATE WITH WORLDLY PEOPLE THAT WERE NOT JEHOVAH'S WITNESSES.

SANTORINI WAS PARADISE...

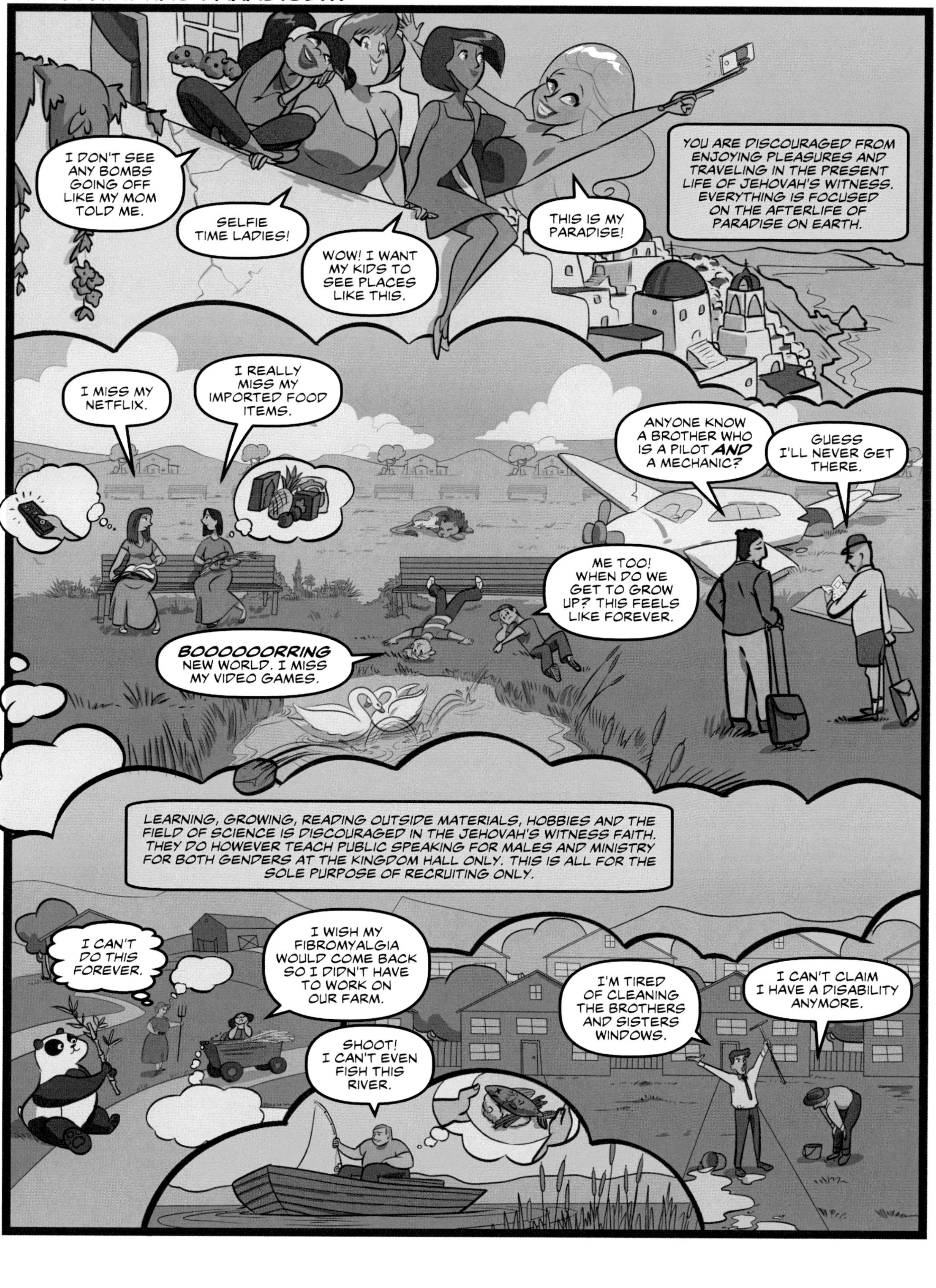
I DON'T SEE ANY BOMBS GOING OFF LIKE MY MOM TOLD ME.
SELFIE TIME LADIES!
WOW! I WANT MY KIDS TO SEE PLACES LIKE THIS.
THIS IS MY PARADISE!
YOU ARE DISCOURAGED FROM ENJOYING PLEASURES AND TRAVELING IN THE PRESENT LIFE OF JEHOVAH'S WITNESS. EVERYTHING IS FOCUSED ON THE AFTERLIFE OF PARADISE ON EARTH.
I MISS MY NETFLIX.
I REALLY MISS MY IMPORTED FOOD ITEMS.
ANYONE KNOW A BROTHER WHO IS A PILOT AND A MECHANIC?
GUESS I'LL NEVER GET THERE.
ME TOO! WHEN DO WE GET TO GROW UP? THIS FEELS LIKE FOREVER.
BOOOOOORRING NEW WORLD. I MISS MY VIDEO GAMES.
LEARNING, GROWING, READING OUTSIDE MATERIALS, HOBBIES AND THE FIELD OF SCIENCE IS DISCOURAGED IN THE JEHOVAH'S WITNESS FAITH. THEY DO HOWEVER TEACH PUBLIC SPEAKING FOR MALES AND MINISTRY FOR BOTH GENDERS AT THE KINGDOM HALL ONLY. THIS IS ALL FOR THE SOLE PURPOSE OF RECRUITING ONLY.
I CAN'T DO THIS FOREVER.
I WISH MY FIBROMYALGIA WOULD COME BACK SO I DIDN'T HAVE TO WORK ON OUR FARM.
SHOOT! I CAN'T EVEN FISH THIS RIVER.
I'M TIRED OF CLEANING THE BROTHERS AND SISTERS WINDOWS.
I CAN'T CLAIM I HAVE A DISABILITY ANYMORE.

VIEWS ON HOMOSEXUALITY

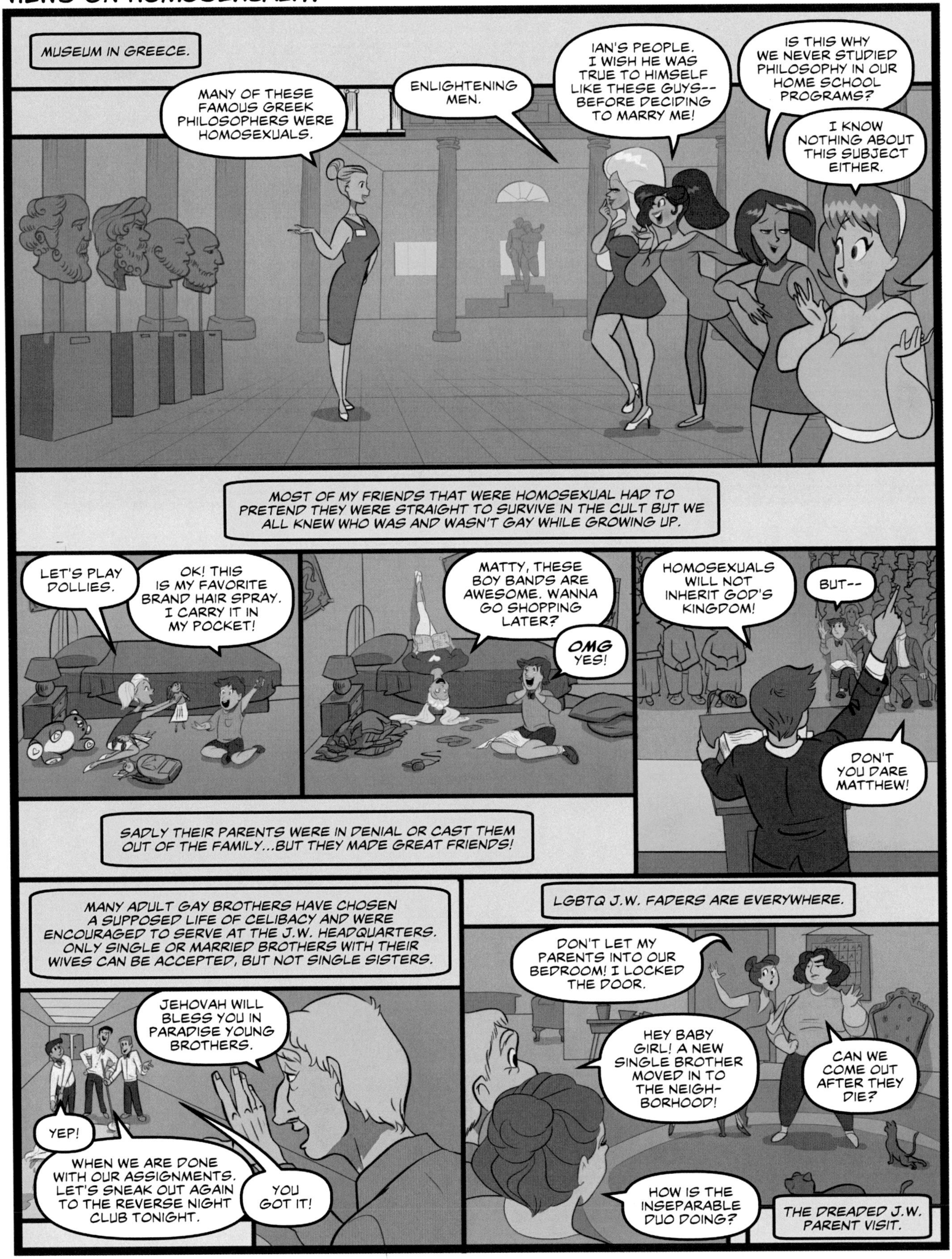

MUSEUM IN GREECE.
MANY OF THESE FAMOUS GREEK PHILOSOPHERS WERE HOMOSEXUALS.
ENLIGHTENING MEN.
IAN'S PEOPLE. I WISH HE WAS TRUE TO HIMSELF LIKE THESE GUYS-- BEFORE DECIDING TO MARRY ME!
IS THIS WHY WE NEVER STUDIED PHILOSOPHY IN OUR HOME SCHOOL PROGRAMS?
I KNOW NOTHING ABOUT THIS SUBJECT EITHER.
MOST OF MY FRIENDS THAT WERE HOMOSEXUAL HAD TO PRETEND THEY WERE STRAIGHT TO SURVIVE IN THE CULT BUT WE ALL KNEW WHO WAS AND WASN'T GAY WHILE GROWING UP.
LET'S PLAY DOLLIES.
OK! THIS IS MY FAVORITE BRAND HAIR SPRAY. I CARRY IT IN MY POCKET!
MATTY, THESE BOY BANDS ARE AWESOME. WANNA GO SHOPPING LATER?
OMG YES!
HOMOSEXUALS WILL NOT INHERIT GOD'S KINGDOM!
BUT--
DON'T YOU DARE MATTHEW!
SADLY THEIR PARENTS WERE IN DENIAL OR CAST THEM OUT OF THE FAMILY...BUT THEY MADE GREAT FRIENDS!
MANY ADULT GAY BROTHERS HAVE CHOSEN A SUPPOSED LIFE OF CELIBACY AND WERE ENCOURAGED TO SERVE AT THE J.W. HEADQUARTERS. ONLY SINGLE OR MARRIED BROTHERS WITH THEIR WIVES CAN BE ACCEPTED, BUT NOT SINGLE SISTERS.
JEHOVAH WILL BLESS YOU IN PARADISE YOUNG BROTHERS.
YEP!
WHEN WE ARE DONE WITH OUR ASSIGNMENTS. LET'S SNEAK OUT AGAIN TO THE REVERSE NIGHT CLUB TONIGHT.
YOU GOT IT!
LGBTQ J.W. FADERS ARE EVERYWHERE.
DON'T LET MY PARENTS INTO OUR BEDROOM! I LOCKED THE DOOR.
HEY BABY GIRL! A NEW SINGLE BROTHER MOVED IN TO THE NEIGH-BORHOOD!
CAN WE COME OUT AFTER THEY DIE?
HOW IS THE INSEPARABLE DUO DOING?
THE DREADED J.W. PARENT VISIT.

MEN ARE BETTER THAN WOMEN

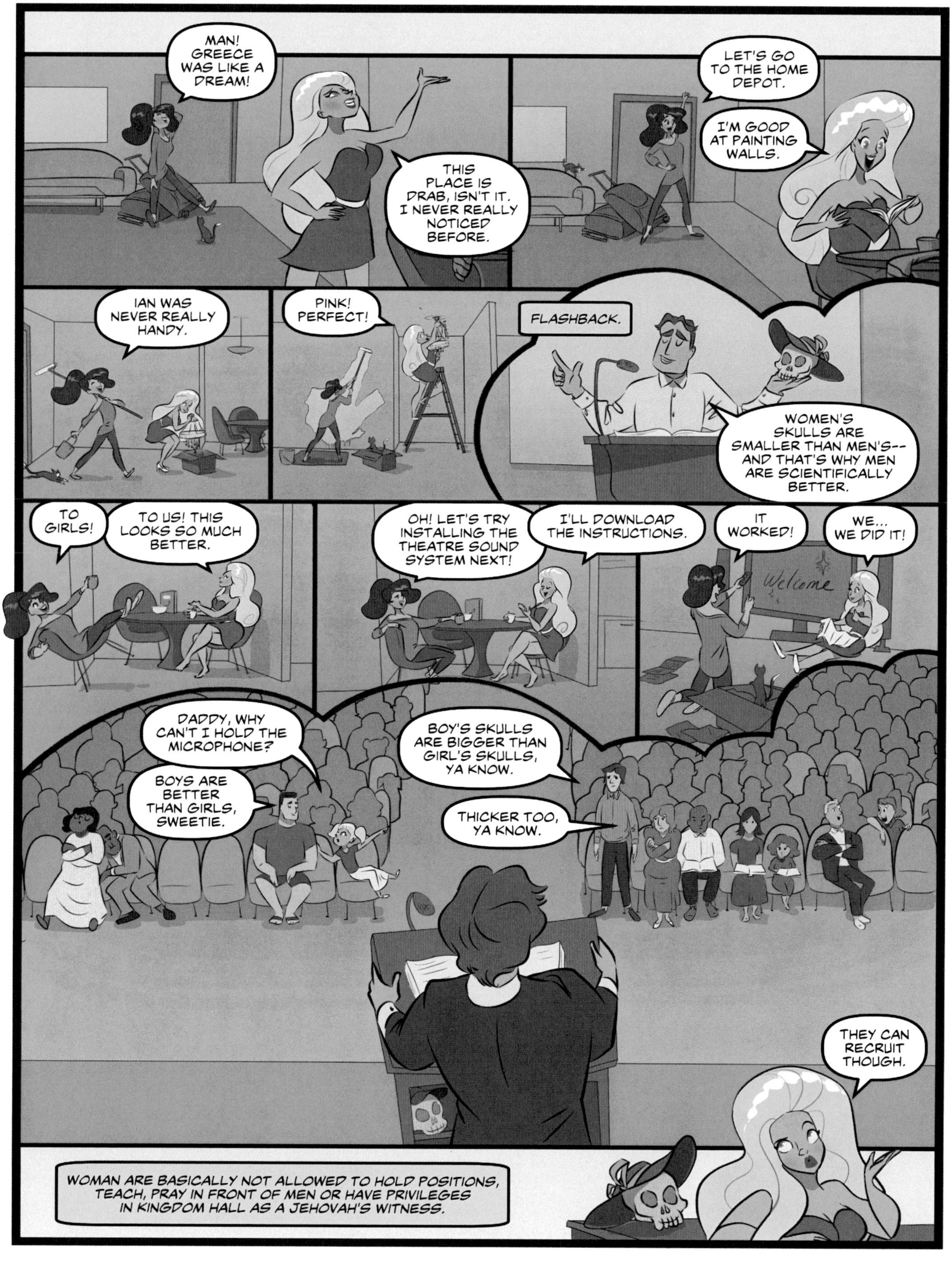

MAN! GREECE WAS LIKE A DREAM!
THIS PLACE IS DRAB, ISN'T IT. I NEVER REALLY NOTICED BEFORE.
LET'S GO TO THE HOME DEPOT.
I'M GOOD AT PAINTING WALLS.
IAN WAS NEVER REALLY HANDY.
PINK! PERFECT!
FLASHBACK.
WOMEN'S SKULLS ARE SMALLER THAN MEN'S-- AND THAT'S WHY MEN ARE SCIENTIFICALLY BETTER.
TO GIRLS!
TO US! THIS LOOKS SO MUCH BETTER.
OH! LET'S TRY INSTALLING THE THEATRE SOUND SYSTEM NEXT!
I'LL DOWNLOAD THE INSTRUCTIONS.
IT WORKED!
WE... WE DID IT!
Welcome
DADDY, WHY CAN'T I HOLD THE MICROPHONE?
BOYS ARE BETTER THAN GIRLS, SWEETIE.
BOY'S SKULLS ARE BIGGER THAN GIRL'S SKULLS, YA KNOW.
THICKER TOO, YA KNOW.
THEY CAN RECRUIT THOUGH.
WOMAN ARE BASICALLY NOT ALLOWED TO HOLD POSITIONS, TEACH, PRAY IN FRONT OF MEN OR HAVE PRIVILEGES IN KINGDOM HALL AS A JEHOVAH'S WITNESS.

LIFE IN REVERSE

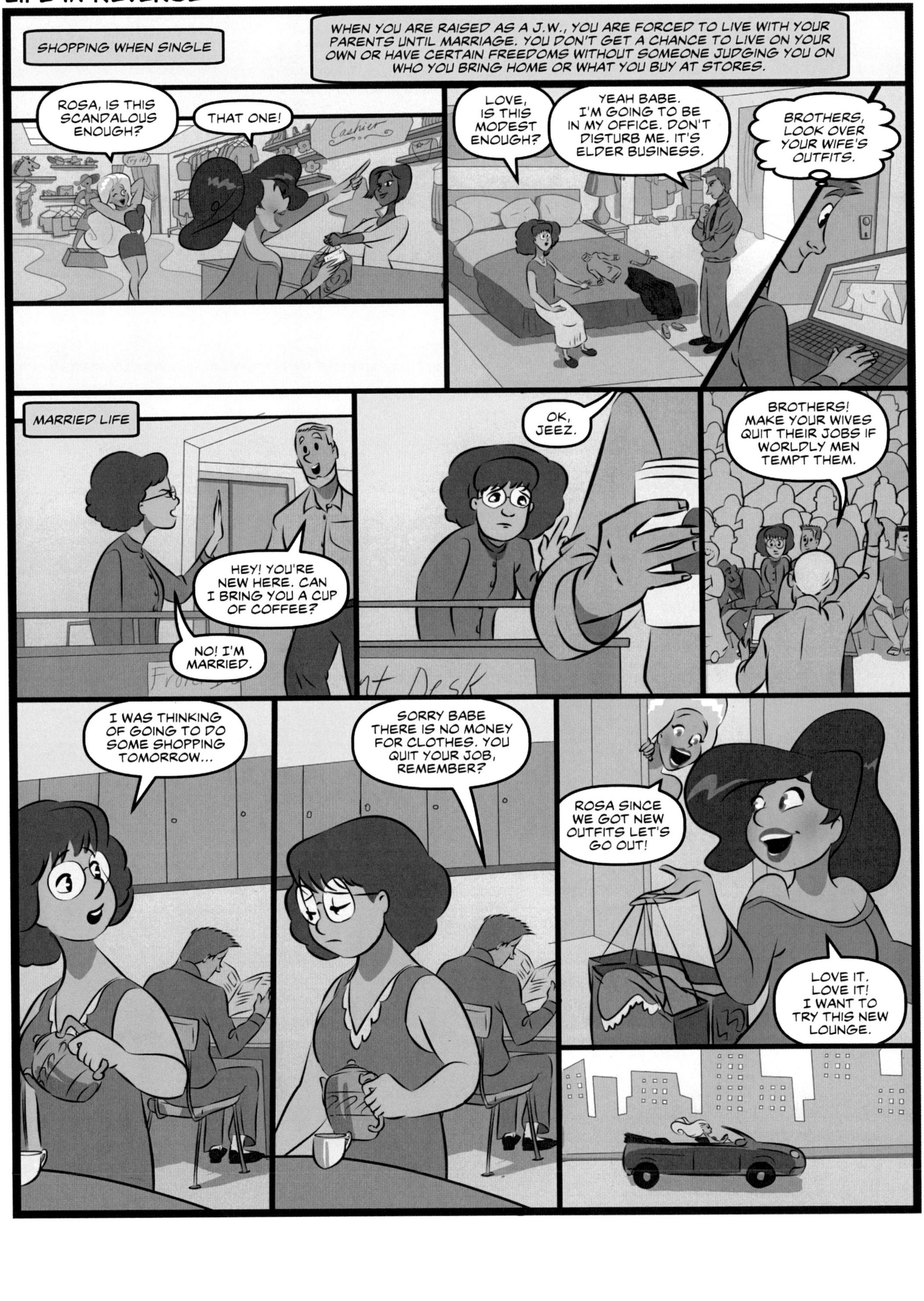

SHOPPING WHEN SINGLE
WHEN YOU ARE RAISED AS A J.W., YOU ARE FORCED TO LIVE WITH YOUR PARENTS UNTIL MARRIAGE. YOU DON'T GET A CHANCE TO LIVE ON YOUR OWN OR HAVE CERTAIN FREEDOMS WITHOUT SOMEONE JUDGING YOU ON WHO YOU BRING HOME OR WHAT YOU BUY AT STORES.
ROSA, IS THIS SCANDALOUS ENOUGH?
THAT ONE!
Cashier
LOVE, IS THIS MODEST ENOUGH?
YEAH BABE. I'M GOING TO BE IN MY OFFICE. DON'T DISTURB ME. IT'S ELDER BUSINESS.
BROTHERS, LOOK OVER YOUR WIFE'S OUTFITS.
MARRIED LIFE
HEY! YOU'RE NEW HERE. CAN I BRING YOU A CUP OF COFFEE?
NO! I'M MARRIED.
OK, JEEZ.
BROTHERS! MAKE YOUR WIVES QUIT THEIR JOBS IF WORLDLY MEN TEMPT THEM.
I WAS THINKING OF GOING TO DO SOME SHOPPING TOMORROW...
SORRY BABE THERE IS NO MONEY FOR CLOTHES. YOU QUIT YOUR JOB, REMEMBER?
ROSA SINCE WE GOT NEW OUTFITS LET'S GO OUT!
LOVE IT. LOVE IT! I WANT TO TRY THIS NEW LOUNGE.

WORLDLY MEN

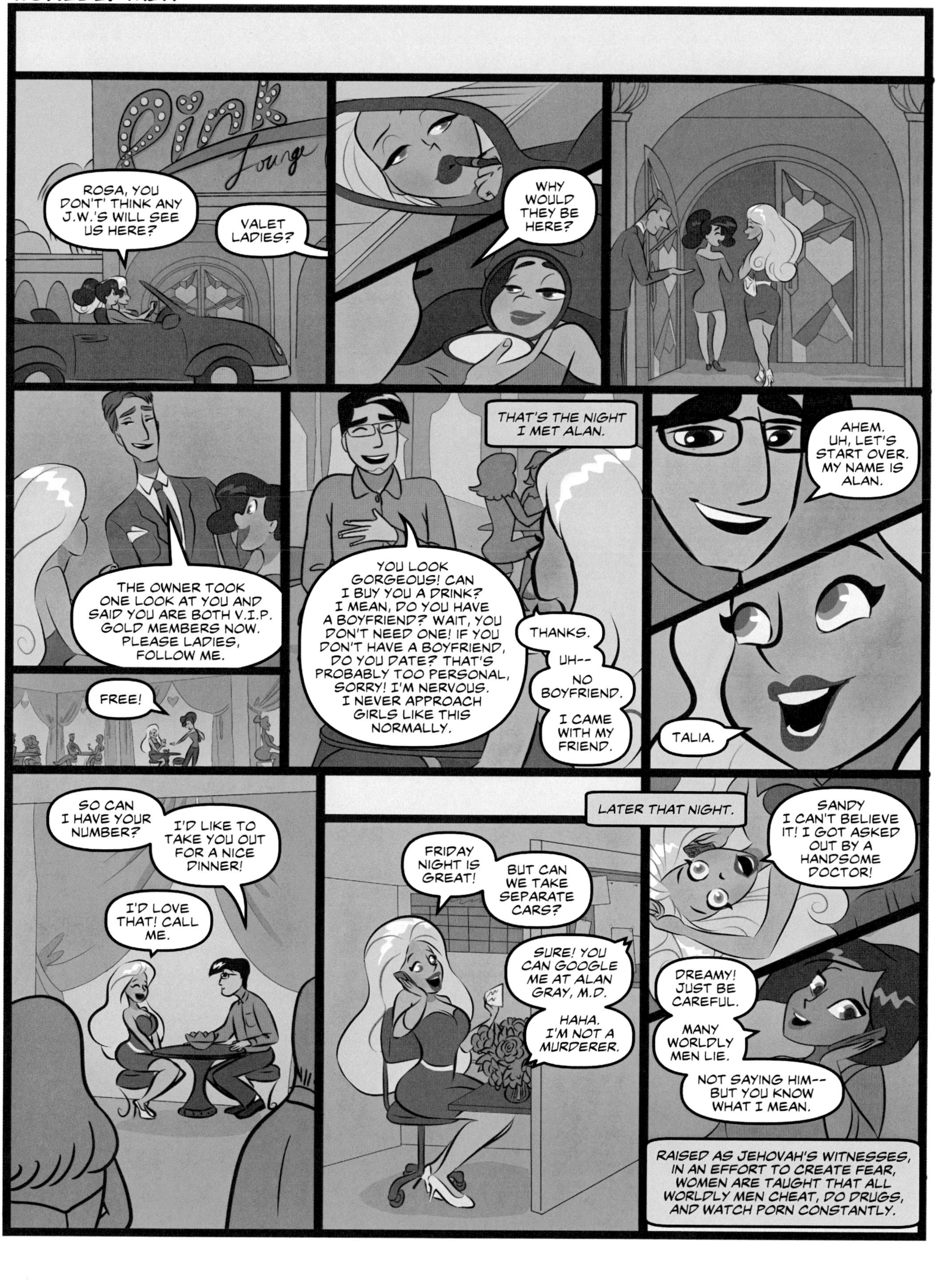

ROSA, YOU DON'T' THINK ANY J.W.'S WILL SEE US HERE?
VALET LADIES?
WHY WOULD THEY BE HERE?
THE OWNER TOOK ONE LOOK AT YOU AND SAID YOU ARE BOTH V.I.P. GOLD MEMBERS NOW. PLEASE LADIES, FOLLOW ME.
FREE!
THAT'S THE NIGHT I MET ALAN.
YOU LOOK GORGEOUS! CAN I BUY YOU A DRINK? I MEAN, DO YOU HAVE A BOYFRIEND? WAIT, YOU DON'T NEED ONE! IF YOU DON'T HAVE A BOYFRIEND, DO YOU DATE? THAT'S PROBABLY TOO PERSONAL, SORRY! I'M NERVOUS. I NEVER APPROACH GIRLS LIKE THIS NORMALLY.
THANKS.
UH--
NO BOYFRIEND.
I CAME WITH MY FRIEND.
AHEM. UH, LET'S START OVER. MY NAME IS ALAN.
TALIA.
SO CAN I HAVE YOUR NUMBER?
I'D LIKE TO TAKE YOU OUT FOR A NICE DINNER!
I'D LOVE THAT! CALL ME.
FRIDAY NIGHT IS GREAT!
BUT CAN WE TAKE SEPARATE CARS?
SURE! YOU CAN GOOGLE ME AT ALAN GRAY, M.D.
HAHA. I'M NOT A MURDERER.
LATER THAT NIGHT.
SANDY I CAN'T BELIEVE IT! I GOT ASKED OUT BY A HANDSOME DOCTOR!
DREAMY! JUST BE CAREFUL.
MANY WORLDLY MEN LIE.
NOT SAYING HIM-- BUT YOU KNOW WHAT I MEAN.
RAISED AS JEHOVAH'S WITNESSES, IN AN EFFORT TO CREATE FEAR, WOMEN ARE TAUGHT THAT ALL WORLDLY MEN CHEAT, DO DRUGS, AND WATCH PORN CONSTANTLY.

FRIDAY NIGHT

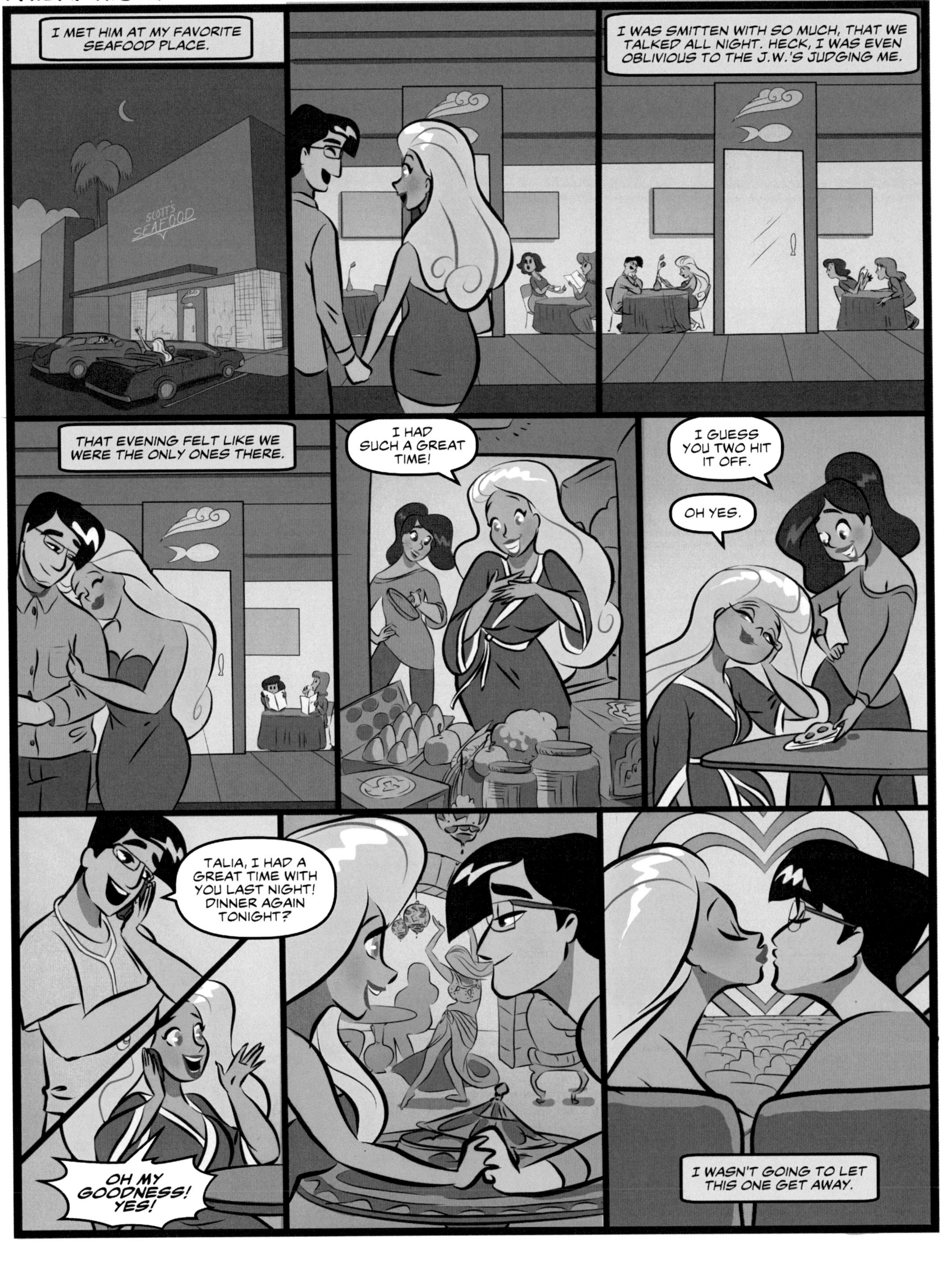
I MET HIM AT MY FAVORITE SEAFOOD PLACE.
SCOTT'S SEAFOOD
I WAS SMITTEN WITH SO MUCH, THAT WE TALKED ALL NIGHT. HECK, I WAS EVEN OBLIVIOUS TO THE J.W.'S JUDGING ME.
THAT EVENING FELT LIKE WE WERE THE ONLY ONES THERE.
I HAD SUCH A GREAT TIME!
I GUESS YOU TWO HIT IT OFF.
OH YES.
TALIA, I HAD A GREAT TIME WITH YOU LAST NIGHT! DINNER AGAIN TONIGHT?
OH MY GOODNESS! YES!
I WASN'T GOING TO LET THIS ONE GET AWAY.

THE MEMORIAL

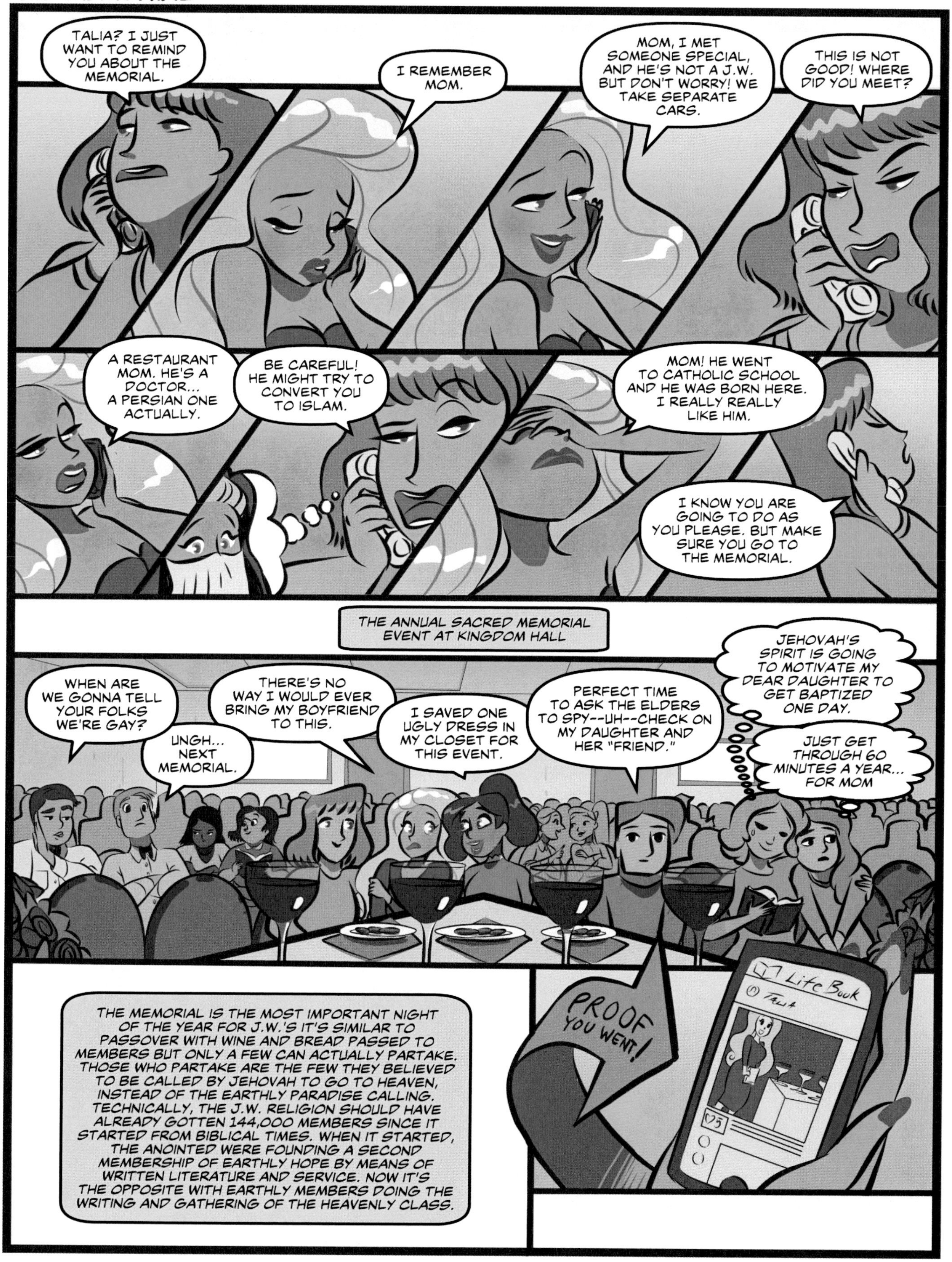
TALIA? I JUST WANT TO REMIND YOU ABOUT THE MEMORIAL.
I REMEMBER MOM.
MOM, I MET SOMEONE SPECIAL, AND HE'S NOT A J.W. BUT DON'T WORRY! WE TAKE SEPARATE CARS.
THIS IS NOT GOOD! WHERE DID YOU MEET?
A RESTAURANT MOM. HE'S A DOCTOR... A PERSIAN ONE ACTUALLY.
BE CAREFUL! HE MIGHT TRY TO CONVERT YOU TO ISLAM.
MOM! HE WENT TO CATHOLIC SCHOOL AND HE WAS BORN HERE. I REALLY REALLY LIKE HIM.
I KNOW YOU ARE GOING TO DO AS YOU PLEASE. BUT MAKE SURE YOU GO TO THE MEMORIAL.
THE ANNUAL SACRED MEMORIAL EVENT AT KINGDOM HALL
WHEN ARE WE GONNA TELL YOUR FOLKS WE'RE GAY?
UNGH... NEXT MEMORIAL.
THERE'S NO WAY I WOULD EVER BRING MY BOYFRIEND TO THIS.
I SAVED ONE UGLY DRESS IN MY CLOSET FOR THIS EVENT.
PERFECT TIME TO ASK THE ELDERS TO SPY--UH--CHECK ON MY DAUGHTER AND HER "FRIEND."
JEHOVAH'S SPIRIT IS GOING TO MOTIVATE MY DEAR DAUGHTER TO GET BAPTIZED ONE DAY.
JUST GET THROUGH 60 MINUTES A YEAR... FOR MOM
THE MEMORIAL IS THE MOST IMPORTANT NIGHT OF THE YEAR FOR J.W.'S IT'S SIMILAR TO PASSOVER WITH WINE AND BREAD PASSED TO MEMBERS BUT ONLY A FEW CAN ACTUALLY PARTAKE. THOSE WHO PARTAKE ARE THE FEW THEY BELIEVED TO BE CALLED BY JEHOVAH TO GO TO HEAVEN, INSTEAD OF THE EARTHLY PARADISE CALLING. TECHNICALLY, THE J.W. RELIGION SHOULD HAVE ALREADY GOTTEN 144,000 MEMBERS SINCE IT STARTED FROM BIBLICAL TIMES. WHEN IT STARTED, THE ANOINTED WERE FOUNDING A SECOND MEMBERSHIP OF EARTHLY HOPE BY MEANS OF WRITTEN LITERATURE AND SERVICE. NOW IT'S THE OPPOSITE WITH EARTHLY MEMBERS DOING THE WRITING AND GATHERING OF THE HEAVENLY CLASS.
PROOF YOU WENT!
Life Book

CERTIFIED MAIL FROM ELDERS

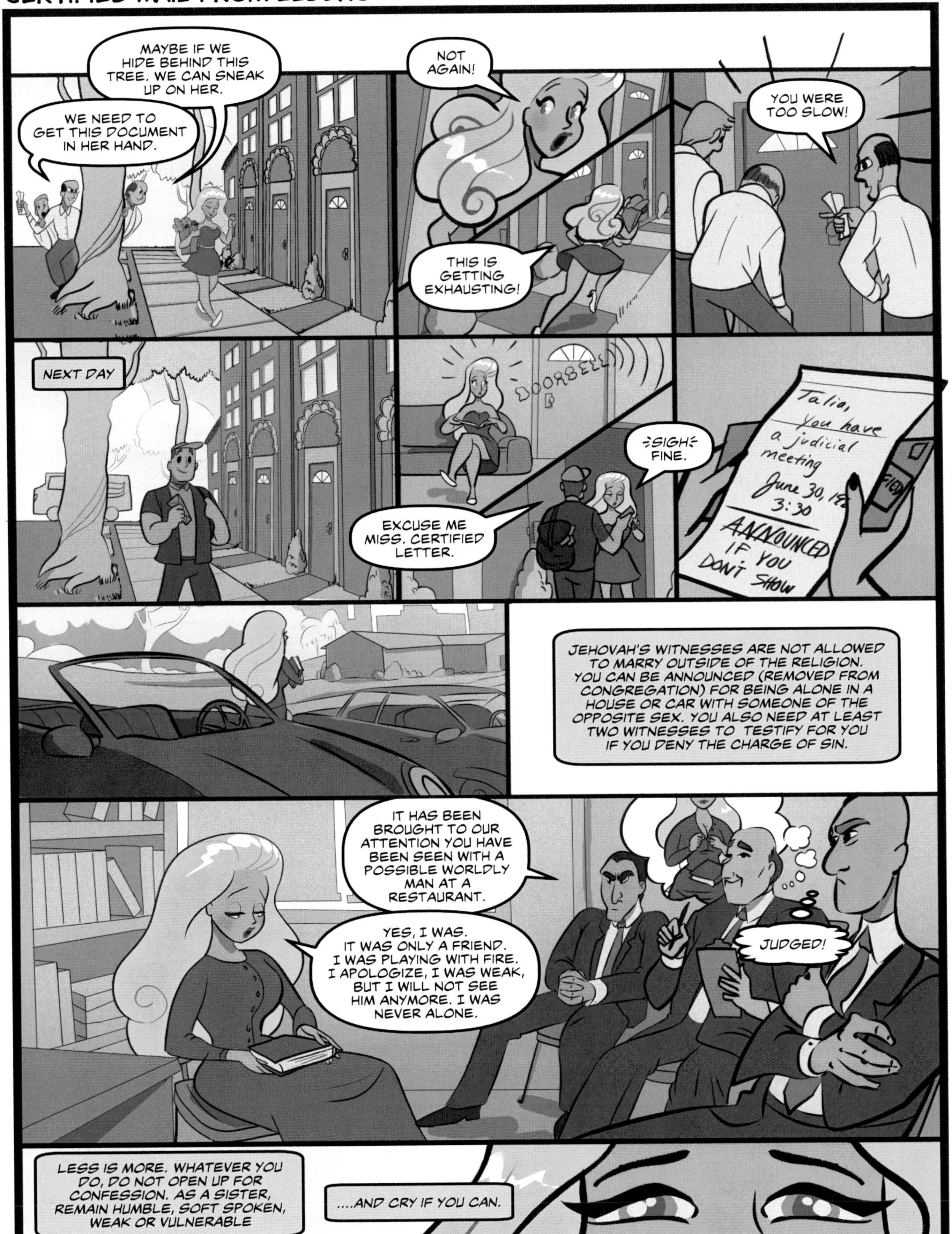

MAYBE IF WE HIDE BEHIND THIS TREE. WE CAN SNEAK UP ON HER.
WE NEED TO GET THIS DOCUMENT IN HER HAND.
NOT AGAIN!
THIS IS GETTING EXHAUSTING!
YOU WERE TOO SLOW!
NEXT DAY
DOORBELL
EXCUSE ME MISS. CERTIFIED LETTER.
SIGH FINE.
Talia, you have a judicial meeting June 30, 19
3:30
ANNOUNCED IF YOU DON'T SHOW
JEHOVAH'S WITNESSES ARE NOT ALLOWED TO MARRY OUTSIDE OF THE RELIGION. YOU CAN BE ANNOUNCED (REMOVED FROM CONGREGATION) FOR BEING ALONE IN A HOUSE OR CAR WITH SOMEONE OF THE OPPOSITE SEX. YOU ALSO NEED AT LEAST TWO WITNESSES TO TESTIFY FOR YOU IF YOU DENY THE CHARGE OF SIN.
IT HAS BEEN BROUGHT TO OUR ATTENTION YOU HAVE BEEN SEEN WITH A POSSIBLE WORLDLY MAN AT A RESTAURANT.
YES, I WAS. IT WAS ONLY A FRIEND. I WAS PLAYING WITH FIRE. I APOLOGIZE, I WAS WEAK, BUT I WILL NOT SEE HIM ANYMORE. I WAS NEVER ALONE.
JUDGED!
LESS IS MORE. WHATEVER YOU DO, DO NOT OPEN UP FOR CONFESSION. AS A SISTER, REMAIN HUMBLE, SOFT SPOKEN, WEAK OR VULNERABLE
....AND CRY IF YOU CAN.

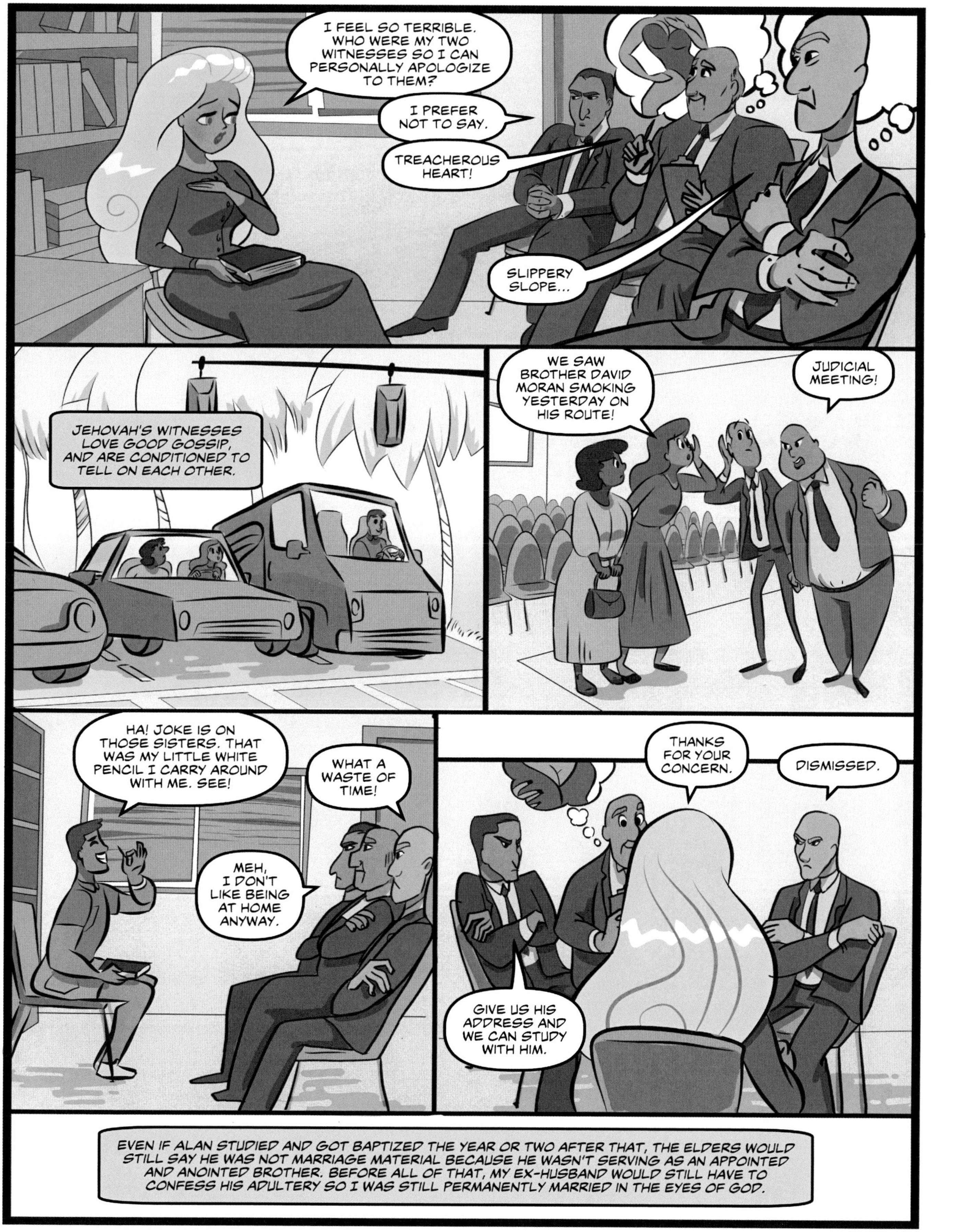
I FEEL SO TERRIBLE. WHO WERE MY TWO WITNESSES SO I CAN PERSONALLY APOLOGIZE TO THEM?
I PREFER NOT TO SAY.
TREACHEROUS HEART!
SLIPPERY SLOPE...
JEHOVAH'S WITNESSES LOVE GOOD GOSSIP, AND ARE CONDITIONED TO TELL ON EACH OTHER.
WE SAW BROTHER DAVID MORAN SMOKING YESTERDAY ON HIS ROUTE!
JUDICIAL MEETING!
HA! JOKE IS ON THOSE SISTERS. THAT WAS MY LITTLE WHITE PENCIL I CARRY AROUND WITH ME. SEE!
WHAT A WASTE OF TIME!
MEH, I DON'T LIKE BEING AT HOME ANYWAY.
THANKS FOR YOUR CONCERN.
DISMISSED.
GIVE US HIS ADDRESS AND WE CAN STUDY WITH HIM.
EVEN IF ALAN STUDIED AND GOT BAPTIZED THE YEAR OR TWO AFTER THAT, THE ELDERS WOULD STILL SAY HE WAS NOT MARRIAGE MATERIAL BECAUSE HE WASN'T SERVING AS AN APPOINTED AND ANOINTED BROTHER. BEFORE ALL OF THAT, MY EX-HUSBAND WOULD STILL HAVE TO CONFESS HIS ADULTERY SO I WAS STILL PERMANENTLY MARRIED IN THE EYES OF GOD.

A VISIT FROM DAD (IF YOU CAN CALL IT THAT)

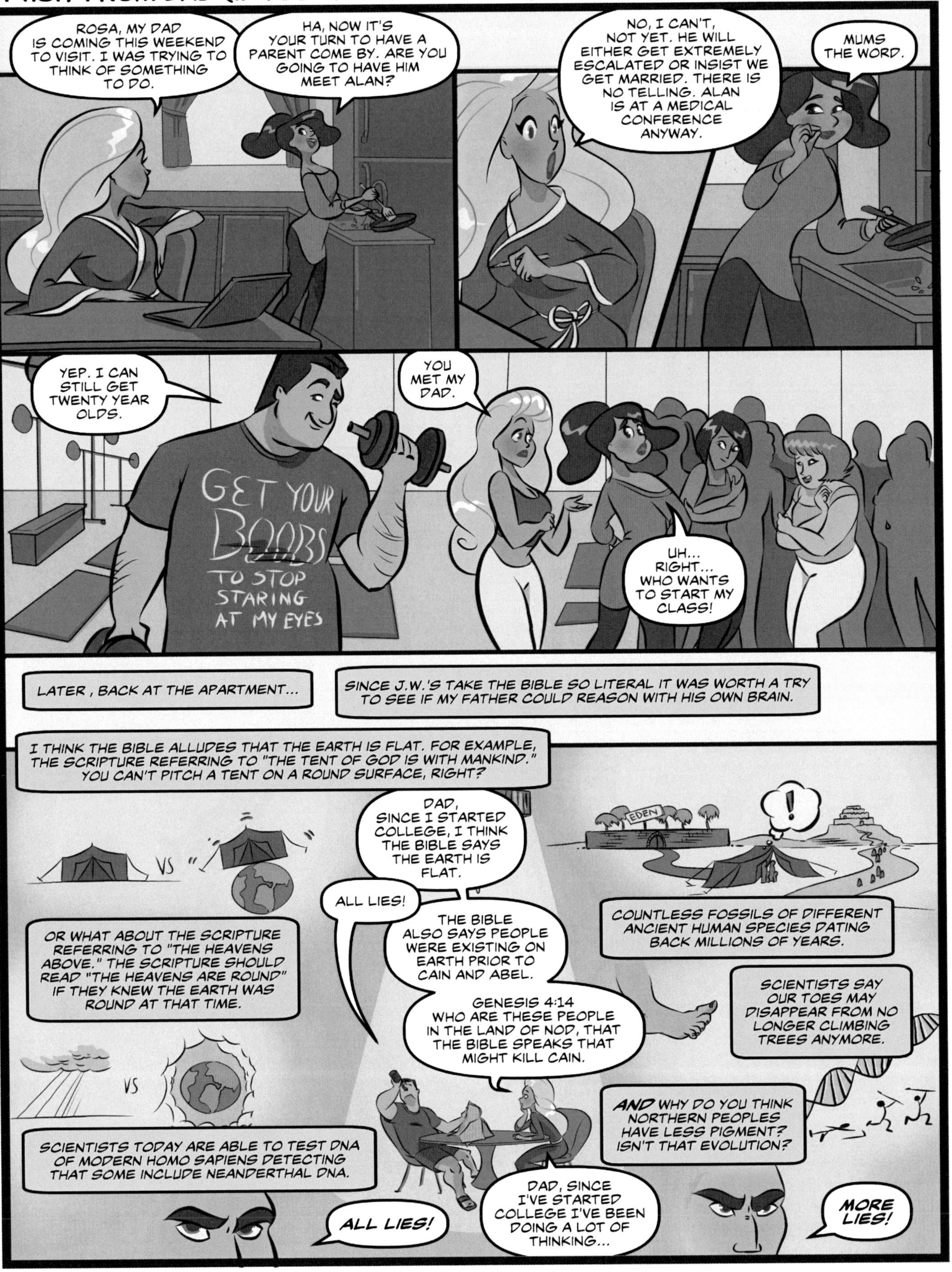
ROSA, MY DAD IS COMING THIS WEEKEND TO VISIT. I WAS TRYING TO THINK OF SOMETHING TO DO.
HA, NOW IT'S YOUR TURN TO HAVE A PARENT COME BY. ARE YOU GOING TO HAVE HIM MEET ALAN?
NO, I CAN'T, NOT YET. HE WILL EITHER GET EXTREMELY ESCALATED OR INSIST WE GET MARRIED. THERE IS NO TELLING. ALAN IS AT A MEDICAL CONFERENCE ANYWAY.
MUMS THE WORD.
YEP. I CAN STILL GET TWENTY YEAR OLDS.
GET YOUR BOOBS TO STOP STARING AT MY EYES
YOU MET MY DAD.
UH... RIGHT... WHO WANTS TO START MY CLASS!
LATER , BACK AT THE APARTMENT...
SINCE J.W.'S TAKE THE BIBLE SO LITERAL IT WAS WORTH A TRY TO SEE IF MY FATHER COULD REASON WITH HIS OWN BRAIN.
I THINK THE BIBLE ALLUDES THAT THE EARTH IS FLAT. FOR EXAMPLE, THE SCRIPTURE REFERRING TO "THE TENT OF GOD IS WITH MANKIND." YOU CAN'T PITCH A TENT ON A ROUND SURFACE, RIGHT?
VS
DAD, SINCE I STARTED COLLEGE, I THINK THE BIBLE SAYS THE EARTH IS FLAT.
ALL LIES!
EDEN
!
OR WHAT ABOUT THE SCRIPTURE REFERRING TO "THE HEAVENS ABOVE." THE SCRIPTURE SHOULD READ "THE HEAVENS ARE ROUND" IF THEY KNEW THE EARTH WAS ROUND AT THAT TIME.
THE BIBLE ALSO SAYS PEOPLE WERE EXISTING ON EARTH PRIOR TO CAIN AND ABEL.
GENESIS 4:14 WHO ARE THESE PEOPLE IN THE LAND OF NOD, THAT THE BIBLE SPEAKS THAT MIGHT KILL CAIN.
COUNTLESS FOSSILS OF DIFFERENT ANCIENT HUMAN SPECIES DATING BACK MILLIONS OF YEARS.
SCIENTISTS SAY OUR TOES MAY DISAPPEAR FROM NO LONGER CLIMBING TREES ANYMORE.
VS
AND WHY DO YOU THINK NORTHERN PEOPLES HAVE LESS PIGMENT? ISN'T THAT EVOLUTION?
SCIENTISTS TODAY ARE ABLE TO TEST DNA OF MODERN HOMO SAPIENS DETECTING THAT SOME INCLUDE NEANDERTHAL DNA.
ALL LIES!
DAD, SINCE I'VE STARTED COLLEGE I'VE BEEN DOING A LOT OF THINKING...
MORE LIES!

STILL TRYING TO DEBATE WITH DAD

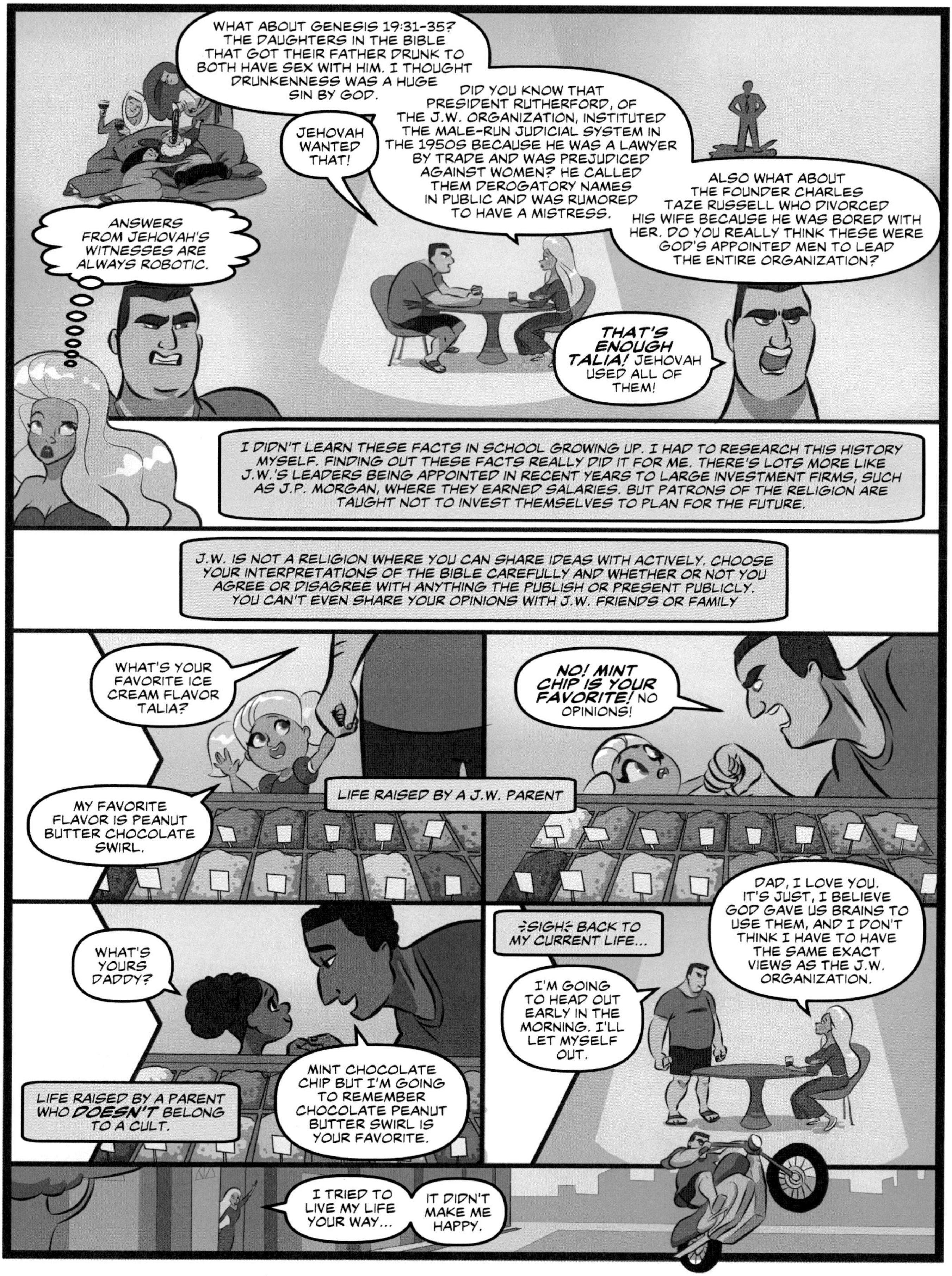

WHAT ABOUT GENESIS 19:31-35? THE DAUGHTERS IN THE BIBLE THAT GOT THEIR FATHER DRUNK TO BOTH HAVE SEX WITH HIM. I THOUGHT DRUNKENNESS WAS A HUGE SIN BY GOD.
JEHOVAH WANTED THAT!
DID YOU KNOW THAT PRESIDENT RUTHERFORD, OF THE J.W. ORGANIZATION, INSTITUTED THE MALE-RUN JUDICIAL SYSTEM IN THE 1950S BECAUSE HE WAS A LAWYER BY TRADE AND WAS PREJUDICED AGAINST WOMEN? HE CALLED THEM DEROGATORY NAMES IN PUBLIC AND WAS RUMORED TO HAVE A MISTRESS.
ALSO WHAT ABOUT THE FOUNDER CHARLES TAZE RUSSELL WHO DIVORCED HIS WIFE BECAUSE HE WAS BORED WITH HER. DO YOU REALLY THINK THESE WERE GOD'S APPOINTED MEN TO LEAD THE ENTIRE ORGANIZATION?
ANSWERS FROM JEHOVAH'S WITNESSES ARE ALWAYS ROBOTIC.
THAT'S ENOUGH TALIA! JEHOVAH USED ALL OF THEM!
I DIDN'T LEARN THESE FACTS IN SCHOOL GROWING UP. I HAD TO RESEARCH THIS HISTORY MYSELF. FINDING OUT THESE FACTS REALLY DID IT FOR ME. THERE'S LOTS MORE LIKE J.W.'S LEADERS BEING APPOINTED IN RECENT YEARS TO LARGE INVESTMENT FIRMS, SUCH AS J.P. MORGAN, WHERE THEY EARNED SALARIES. BUT PATRONS OF THE RELIGION ARE TAUGHT NOT TO INVEST THEMSELVES TO PLAN FOR THE FUTURE.
J.W. IS NOT A RELIGION WHERE YOU CAN SHARE IDEAS WITH ACTIVELY. CHOOSE YOUR INTERPRETATIONS OF THE BIBLE CAREFULLY AND WHETHER OR NOT YOU AGREE OR DISAGREE WITH ANYTHING THE PUBLISH OR PRESENT PUBLICLY. YOU CAN'T EVEN SHARE YOUR OPINIONS WITH J.W. FRIENDS OR FAMILY
WHAT'S YOUR FAVORITE ICE CREAM FLAVOR TALIA?
MY FAVORITE FLAVOR IS PEANUT BUTTER CHOCOLATE SWIRL.
LIFE RAISED BY A J.W. PARENT
NO! MINT CHIP IS YOUR FAVORITE! NO OPINIONS!
WHAT'S YOURS DADDY?
MINT CHOCOLATE CHIP BUT I'M GOING TO REMEMBER CHOCOLATE PEANUT BUTTER SWIRL IS YOUR FAVORITE.
LIFE RAISED BY A PARENT WHO DOESN'T BELONG TO A CULT.
-SIGH- BACK TO MY CURRENT LIFE...
DAD, I LOVE YOU. IT'S JUST, I BELIEVE GOD GAVE US BRAINS TO USE THEM, AND I DON'T THINK I HAVE TO HAVE THE SAME EXACT VIEWS AS THE J.W. ORGANIZATION.
I'M GOING TO HEAD OUT EARLY IN THE MORNING. I'LL LET MYSELF OUT.
I TRIED TO LIVE MY LIFE YOUR WAY...
IT DIDN'T MAKE ME HAPPY.

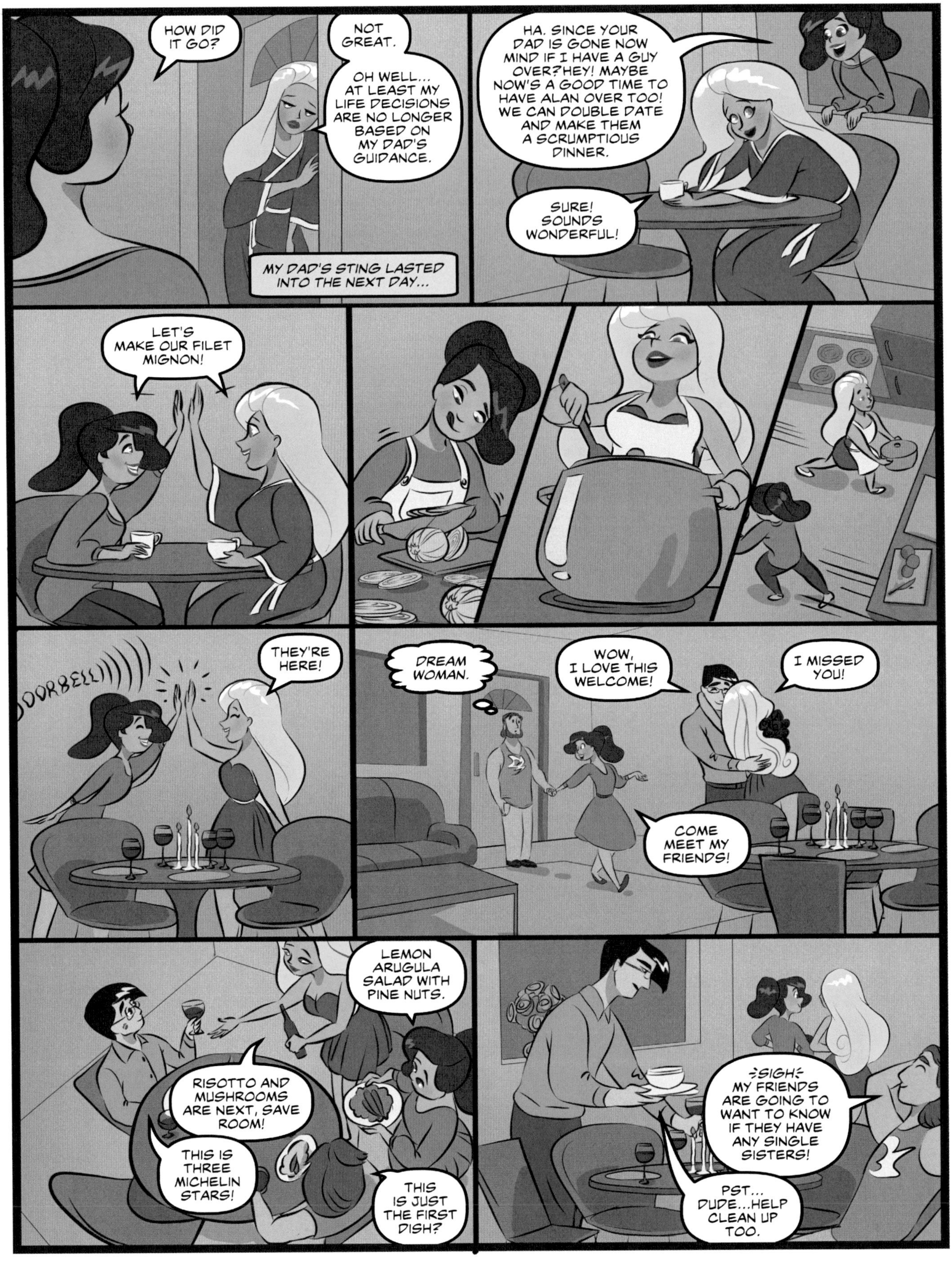
HOW DID IT GO?
NOT GREAT.
OH WELL... AT LEAST MY LIFE DECISIONS ARE NO LONGER BASED ON MY DAD'S GUIDANCE.
MY DAD'S STING LASTED INTO THE NEXT DAY...
HA. SINCE YOUR DAD IS GONE NOW MIND IF I HAVE A GUY OVER? HEY! MAYBE NOW'S A GOOD TIME TO HAVE ALAN OVER TOO! WE CAN DOUBLE DATE AND MAKE THEM A SCRUMPTIOUS DINNER.
SURE! SOUNDS WONDERFUL!
LET'S MAKE OUR FILET MIGNON!
DOORBELL
THEY'RE HERE!
DREAM WOMAN.
WOW, I LOVE THIS WELCOME!
I MISSED YOU!
COME MEET MY FRIENDS!
LEMON ARUGULA SALAD WITH PINE NUTS.
RISOTTO AND MUSHROOMS ARE NEXT, SAVE ROOM!
THIS IS THREE MICHELIN STARS!
THIS IS JUST THE FIRST DISH?
SIGH MY FRIENDS ARE GOING TO WANT TO KNOW IF THEY HAVE ANY SINGLE SISTERS!
PST... DUDE...HELP CLEAN UP TOO.

MAKING FRIENDS FROM WORK

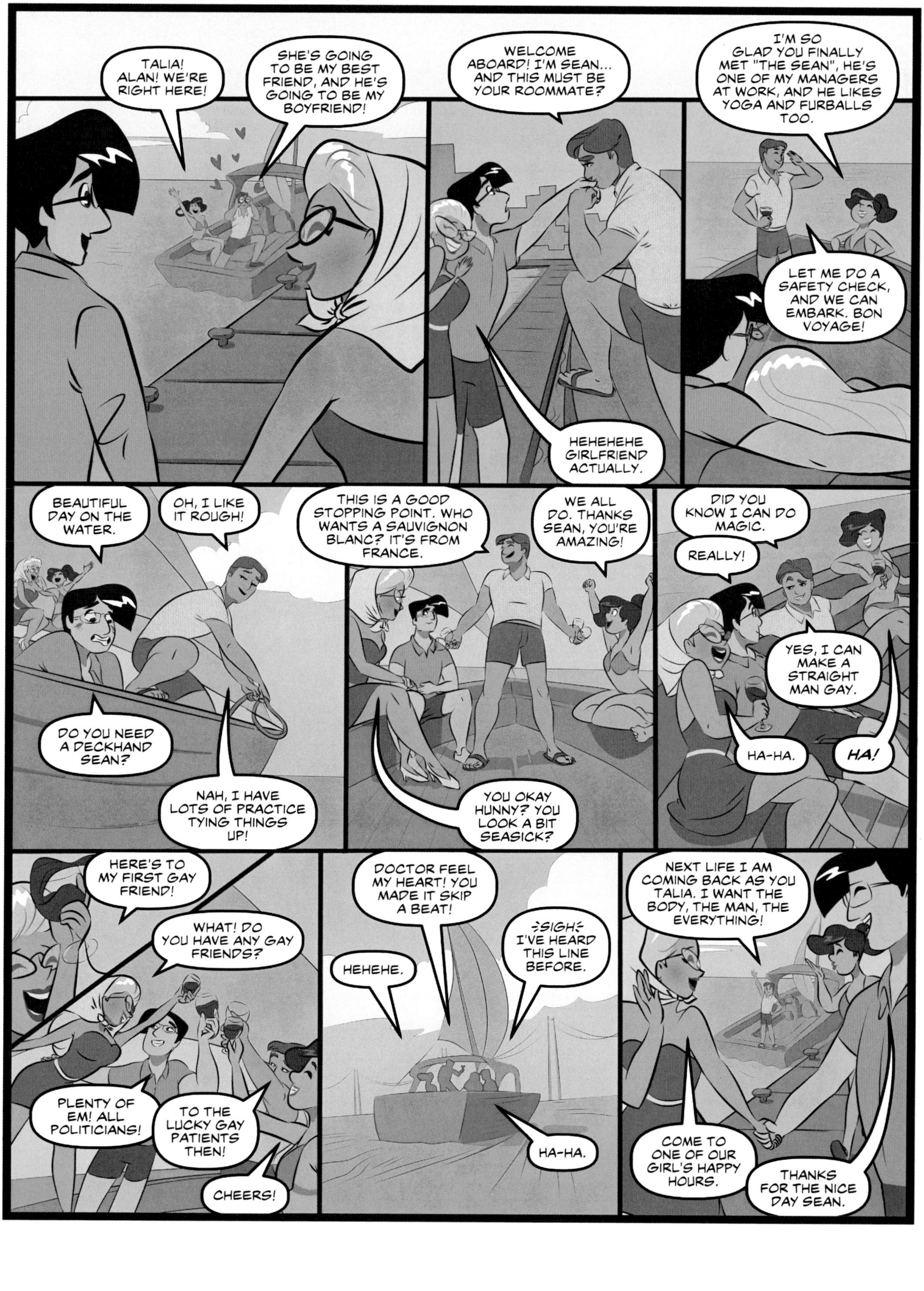

TALIA! ALAN! WE'RE RIGHT HERE!
SHE'S GOING TO BE MY BEST FRIEND, AND HE'S GOING TO BE MY BOYFRIEND!
WELCOME ABOARD! I'M SEAN... AND THIS MUST BE YOUR ROOMMATE?
HEHEHEHE GIRLFRIEND ACTUALLY.
I'M SO GLAD YOU FINALLY MET "THE SEAN", HE'S ONE OF MY MANAGERS AT WORK, AND HE LIKES YOGA AND FURBALLS TOO.
LET ME DO A SAFETY CHECK, AND WE CAN EMBARK. BON VOYAGE!
BEAUTIFUL DAY ON THE WATER.
OH, I LIKE IT ROUGH!
DO YOU NEED A DECKHAND SEAN?
NAH, I HAVE LOTS OF PRACTICE TYING THINGS UP!
THIS IS A GOOD STOPPING POINT. WHO WANTS A SAUVIGNON BLANC? IT'S FROM FRANCE.
WE ALL DO. THANKS SEAN, YOU'RE AMAZING!
YOU OKAY HUNNY? YOU LOOK A BIT SEASICK?
DID YOU KNOW I CAN DO MAGIC.
REALLY!
YES, I CAN MAKE A STRAIGHT MAN GAY.
HA-HA.
HA!
HERE'S TO MY FIRST GAY FRIEND!
WHAT! DO YOU HAVE ANY GAY FRIENDS?
PLENTY OF EM! ALL POLITICIANS!
TO THE LUCKY GAY PATIENTS THEN!
CHEERS!
DOCTOR FEEL MY HEART! YOU MADE IT SKIP A BEAT!
HEHEHE.
SIGH I'VE HEARD THIS LINE BEFORE.
HA-HA.
NEXT LIFE I AM COMING BACK AS YOU TALIA. I WANT THE BODY, THE MAN, THE EVERYTHING!
COME TO ONE OF OUR GIRL'S HAPPY HOURS.
THANKS FOR THE NICE DAY SEAN.

FIRST EVER VALENTINE'S DAY

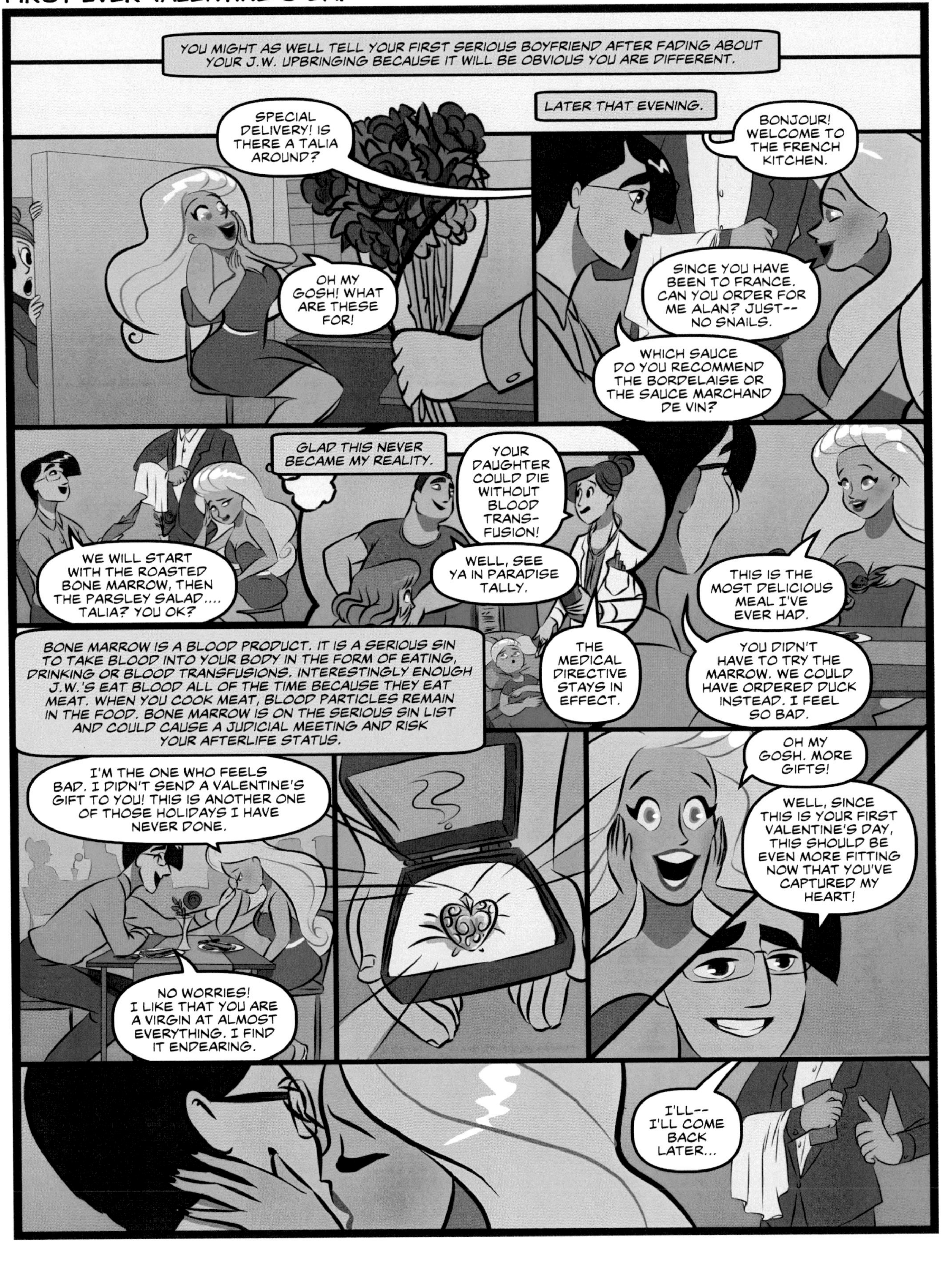

YOU MIGHT AS WELL TELL YOUR FIRST SERIOUS BOYFRIEND AFTER FADING ABOUT YOUR J.W. UPBRINGING BECAUSE IT WILL BE OBVIOUS YOU ARE DIFFERENT.
SPECIAL DELIVERY! IS THERE A TALIA AROUND?
OH MY GOSH! WHAT ARE THESE FOR!
LATER THAT EVENING.
BONJOUR! WELCOME TO THE FRENCH KITCHEN.
SINCE YOU HAVE BEEN TO FRANCE. CAN YOU ORDER FOR ME ALAN? JUST-- NO SNAILS.
WHICH SAUCE DO YOU RECOMMEND THE BORDELAISE OR THE SAUCE MARCHAND DE VIN?
WE WILL START WITH THE ROASTED BONE MARROW, THEN THE PARSLEY SALAD.... TALIA? YOU OK?
GLAD THIS NEVER BECAME MY REALITY.
YOUR DAUGHTER COULD DIE WITHOUT BLOOD TRANS-FUSION!
WELL, SEE YA IN PARADISE TALLY.
THE MEDICAL DIRECTIVE STAYS IN EFFECT.
BONE MARROW IS A BLOOD PRODUCT. IT IS A SERIOUS SIN TO TAKE BLOOD INTO YOUR BODY IN THE FORM OF EATING, DRINKING OR BLOOD TRANSFUSIONS. INTERESTINGLY ENOUGH J.W.'S EAT BLOOD ALL OF THE TIME BECAUSE THEY EAT MEAT. WHEN YOU COOK MEAT, BLOOD PARTICLES REMAIN IN THE FOOD. BONE MARROW IS ON THE SERIOUS SIN LIST AND COULD CAUSE A JUDICIAL MEETING AND RISK YOUR AFTERLIFE STATUS.
THIS IS THE MOST DELICIOUS MEAL I'VE EVER HAD.
YOU DIDN'T HAVE TO TRY THE MARROW. WE COULD HAVE ORDERED DUCK INSTEAD. I FEEL SO BAD.
I'M THE ONE WHO FEELS BAD. I DIDN'T SEND A VALENTINE'S GIFT TO YOU! THIS IS ANOTHER ONE OF THOSE HOLIDAYS I HAVE NEVER DONE.
NO WORRIES! I LIKE THAT YOU ARE A VIRGIN AT ALMOST EVERYTHING. I FIND IT ENDEARING.
OH MY GOSH. MORE GIFTS!
WELL, SINCE THIS IS YOUR FIRST VALENTINE'S DAY, THIS SHOULD BE EVEN MORE FITTING NOW THAT YOU'VE CAPTURED MY HEART!
I'LL-- I'LL COME BACK LATER...

R-RATED MOVIES

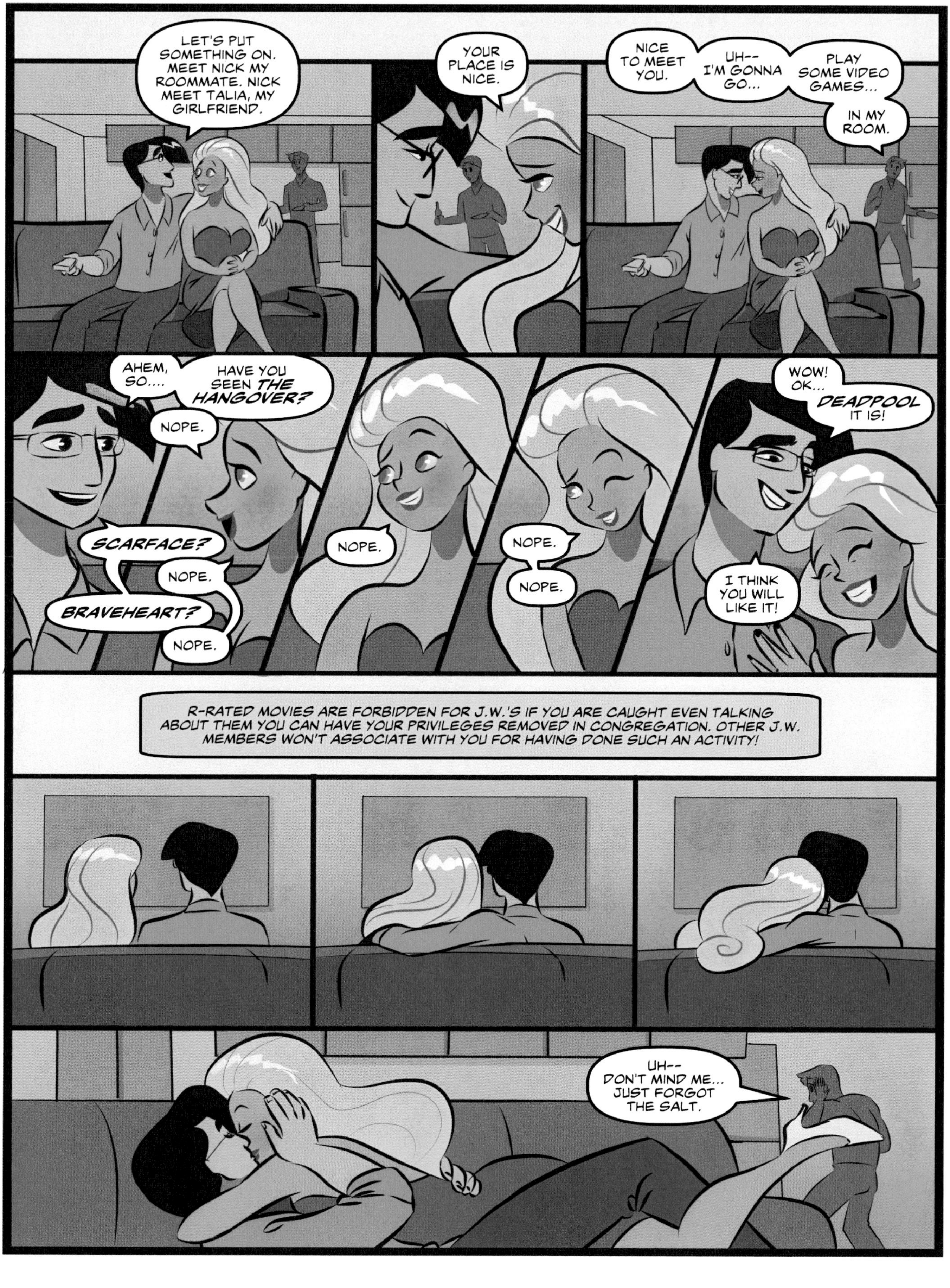

LET'S PUT SOMETHING ON. MEET NICK MY ROOMMATE. NICK MEET TALIA, MY GIRLFRIEND.
YOUR PLACE IS NICE.
NICE TO MEET YOU.
UH-- I'M GONNA GO...
PLAY SOME VIDEO GAMES...
IN MY ROOM.
AHEM, SO....
HAVE YOU SEEN *THE HANGOVER?*
NOPE.
SCARFACE?
NOPE.
BRAVEHEART?
NOPE.
NOPE.
NOPE.
NOPE.
WOW! OK... *DEADPOOL* IT IS!
I THINK YOU WILL LIKE IT!
R-RATED MOVIES ARE FORBIDDEN FOR J.W.'S IF YOU ARE CAUGHT EVEN TALKING ABOUT THEM YOU CAN HAVE YOUR PRIVILEGES REMOVED IN CONGREGATION. OTHER J.W. MEMBERS WON'T ASSOCIATE WITH YOU FOR HAVING DONE SUCH AN ACTIVITY!
UH-- DON'T MIND ME... JUST FORGOT THE SALT.

POLITICS

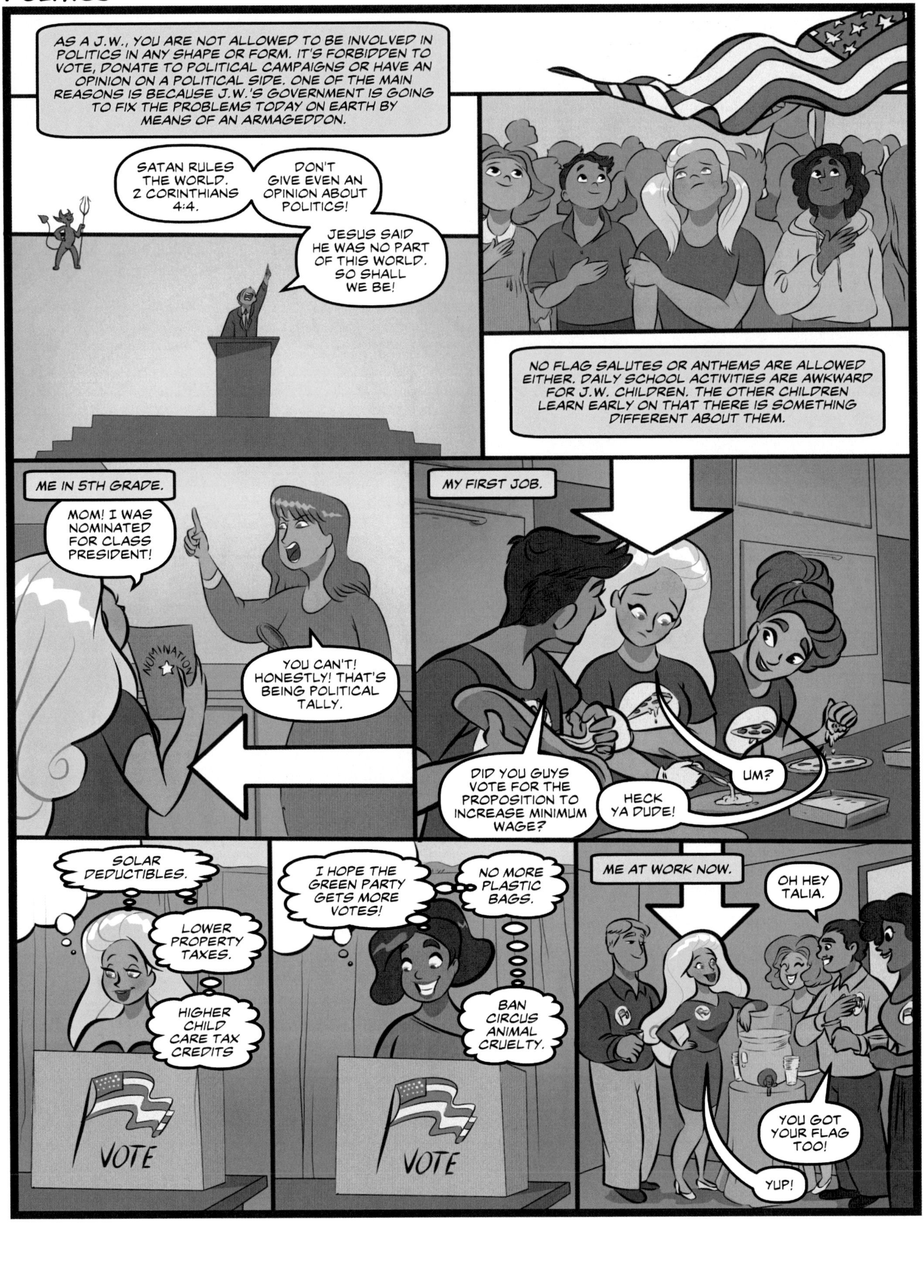
AS A J.W., YOU ARE NOT ALLOWED TO BE INVOLVED IN POLITICS IN ANY SHAPE OR FORM. IT'S FORBIDDEN TO VOTE, DONATE TO POLITICAL CAMPAIGNS OR HAVE AN OPINION ON A POLITICAL SIDE. ONE OF THE MAIN REASONS IS BECAUSE J.W.'S GOVERNMENT IS GOING TO FIX THE PROBLEMS TODAY ON EARTH BY MEANS OF AN ARMAGEDDON.
SATAN RULES THE WORLD. 2 CORINTHIANS 4:4.
DON'T GIVE EVEN AN OPINION ABOUT POLITICS!
JESUS SAID HE WAS NO PART OF THIS WORLD. SO SHALL WE BE!
NO FLAG SALUTES OR ANTHEMS ARE ALLOWED EITHER. DAILY SCHOOL ACTIVITIES ARE AWKWARD FOR J.W. CHILDREN. THE OTHER CHILDREN LEARN EARLY ON THAT THERE IS SOMETHING DIFFERENT ABOUT THEM.
ME IN 5TH GRADE.
MOM! I WAS NOMINATED FOR CLASS PRESIDENT!
NOMINATION
YOU CAN'T! HONESTLY! THAT'S BEING POLITICAL TALLY.
MY FIRST JOB.
DID YOU GUYS VOTE FOR THE PROPOSITION TO INCREASE MINIMUM WAGE?
HECK YA DUDE!
UM?
SOLAR DEDUCTIBLES.
LOWER PROPERTY TAXES.
HIGHER CHILD CARE TAX CREDITS
VOTE
I HOPE THE GREEN PARTY GETS MORE VOTES!
NO MORE PLASTIC BAGS.
BAN CIRCUS ANIMAL CRUELTY.
VOTE
ME AT WORK NOW.
OH HEY TALIA.
YOU GOT YOUR FLAG TOO!
YUP!

NEUTRALITY

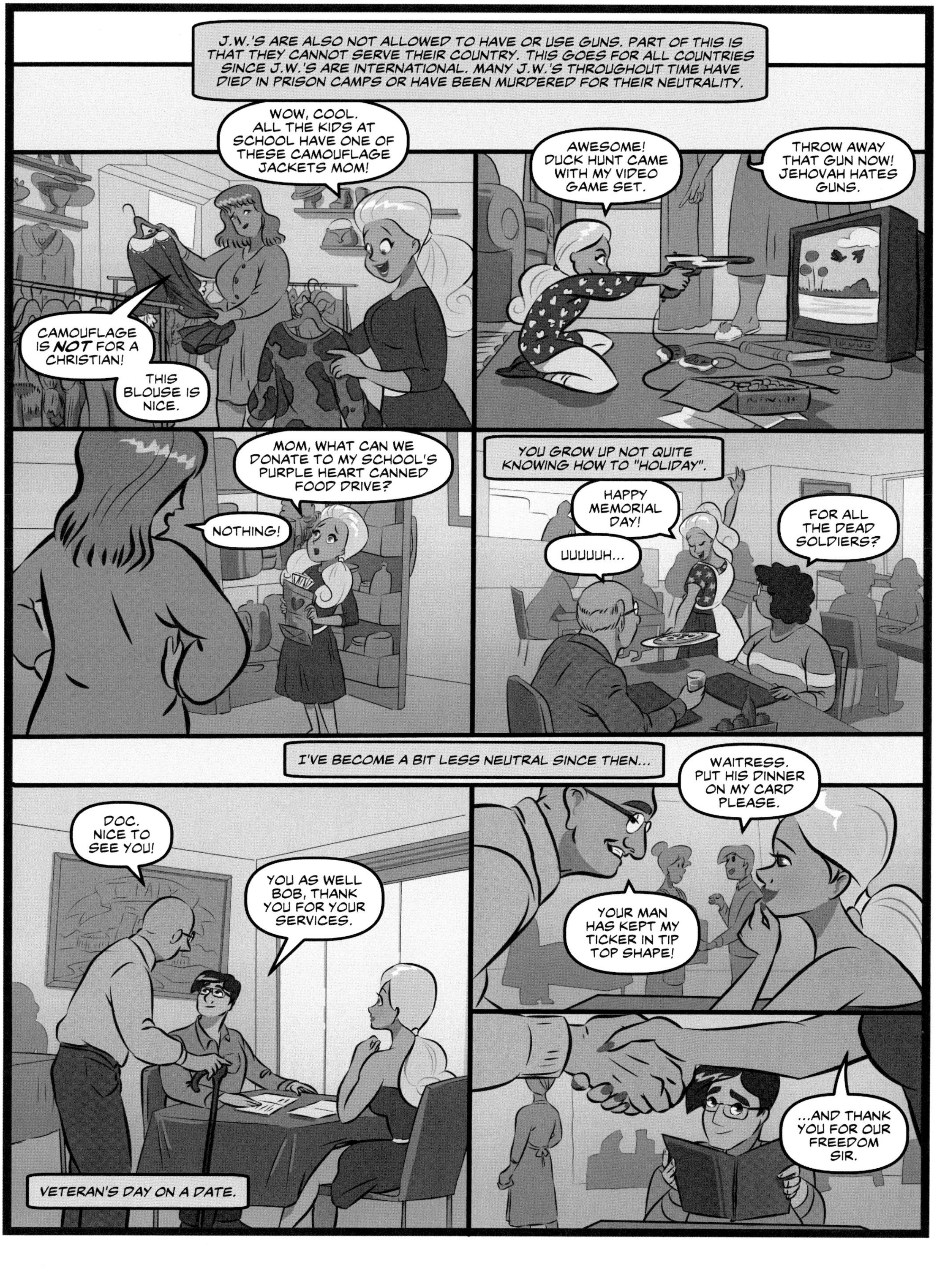
J.W.'S ARE ALSO NOT ALLOWED TO HAVE OR USE GUNS. PART OF THIS IS THAT THEY CANNOT SERVE THEIR COUNTRY. THIS GOES FOR ALL COUNTRIES SINCE J.W.'S ARE INTERNATIONAL. MANY J.W.'S THROUGHOUT TIME HAVE DIED IN PRISON CAMPS OR HAVE BEEN MURDERED FOR THEIR NEUTRALITY.
WOW, COOL. ALL THE KIDS AT SCHOOL HAVE ONE OF THESE CAMOUFLAGE JACKETS MOM!
CAMOUFLAGE IS NOT FOR A CHRISTIAN!
THIS BLOUSE IS NICE.
AWESOME! DUCK HUNT CAME WITH MY VIDEO GAME SET.
THROW AWAY THAT GUN NOW! JEHOVAH HATES GUNS.
MOM, WHAT CAN WE DONATE TO MY SCHOOL'S PURPLE HEART CANNED FOOD DRIVE?
NOTHING!
YOU GROW UP NOT QUITE KNOWING HOW TO "HOLIDAY".
HAPPY MEMORIAL DAY!
UUUUUH...
FOR ALL THE DEAD SOLDIERS?
I'VE BECOME A BIT LESS NEUTRAL SINCE THEN...
DOC. NICE TO SEE YOU!
YOU AS WELL BOB, THANK YOU FOR YOUR SERVICES.
VETERAN'S DAY ON A DATE.
WAITRESS. PUT HIS DINNER ON MY CARD PLEASE.
YOUR MAN HAS KEPT MY TICKER IN TIP TOP SHAPE!
...AND THANK YOU FOR OUR FREEDOM SIR.

J.W.S & RACIAL DISCRIMINATION

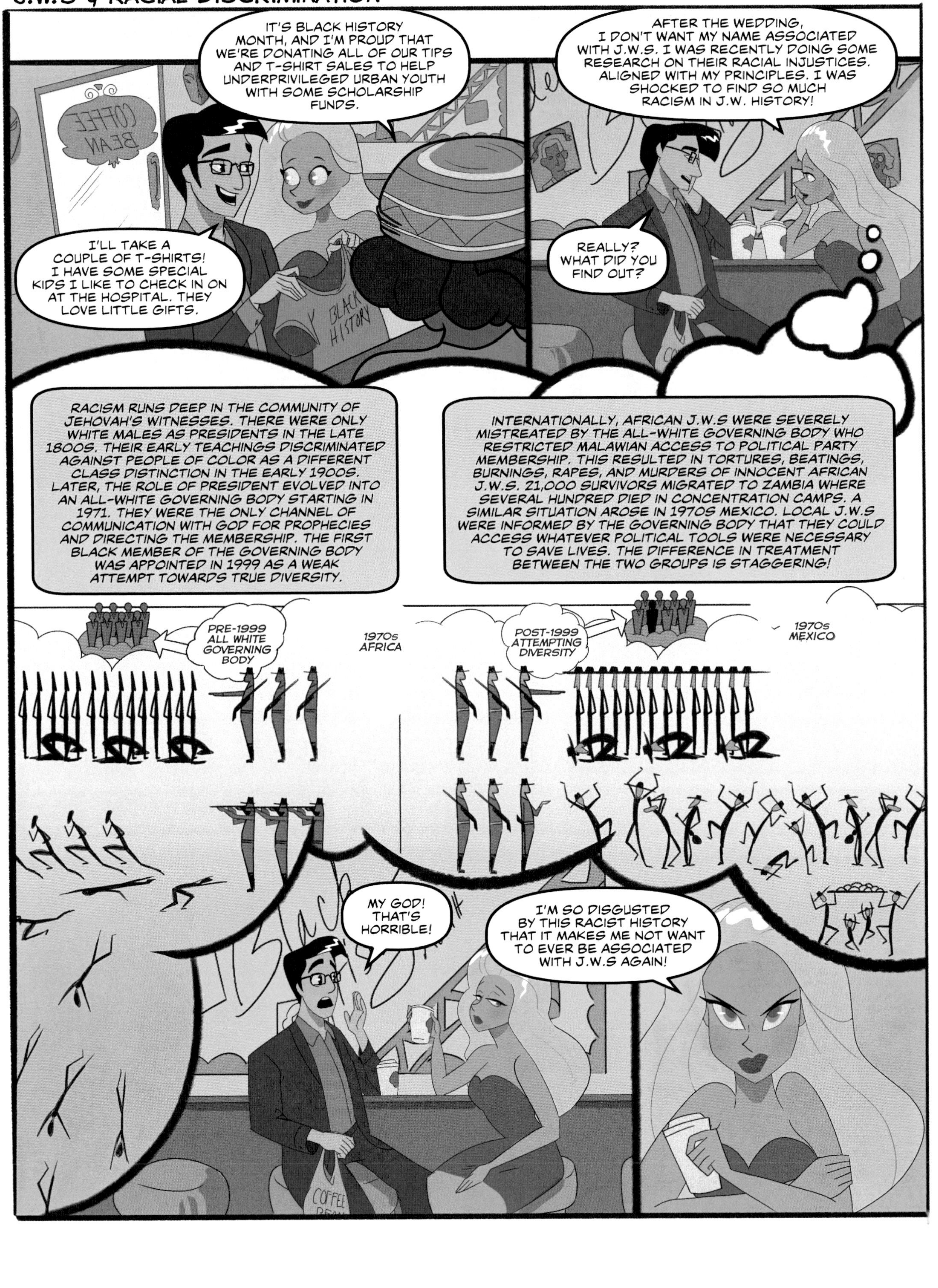

IT'S BLACK HISTORY MONTH, AND I'M PROUD THAT WE'RE DONATING ALL OF OUR TIPS AND T-SHIRT SALES TO HELP UNDERPRIVILEGED URBAN YOUTH WITH SOME SCHOLARSHIP FUNDS.
COFFEE BEAN
I'LL TAKE A COUPLE OF T-SHIRTS! I HAVE SOME SPECIAL KIDS I LIKE TO CHECK IN ON AT THE HOSPITAL. THEY LOVE LITTLE GIFTS.
BLACK HISTORY
AFTER THE WEDDING, I DON'T WANT MY NAME ASSOCIATED WITH J.W.S. I WAS RECENTLY DOING SOME RESEARCH ON THEIR RACIAL INJUSTICES. ALIGNED WITH MY PRINCIPLES. I WAS SHOCKED TO FIND SO MUCH RACISM IN J.W. HISTORY!
REALLY? WHAT DID YOU FIND OUT?
RACISM RUNS DEEP IN THE COMMUNITY OF JEHOVAH'S WITNESSES. THERE WERE ONLY WHITE MALES AS PRESIDENTS IN THE LATE 1800S. THEIR EARLY TEACHINGS DISCRIMINATED AGAINST PEOPLE OF COLOR AS A DIFFERENT CLASS DISTINCTION IN THE EARLY 1900S. LATER, THE ROLE OF PRESIDENT EVOLVED INTO AN ALL-WHITE GOVERNING BODY STARTING IN 1971. THEY WERE THE ONLY CHANNEL OF COMMUNICATION WITH GOD FOR PROPHECIES AND DIRECTING THE MEMBERSHIP. THE FIRST BLACK MEMBER OF THE GOVERNING BODY WAS APPOINTED IN 1999 AS A WEAK ATTEMPT TOWARDS TRUE DIVERSITY.
INTERNATIONALLY, AFRICAN J.W.S WERE SEVERELY MISTREATED BY THE ALL-WHITE GOVERNING BODY WHO RESTRICTED MALAWIAN ACCESS TO POLITICAL PARTY MEMBERSHIP. THIS RESULTED IN TORTURES, BEATINGS, BURNINGS, RAPES, AND MURDERS OF INNOCENT AFRICAN J.W.S. 21,000 SURVIVORS MIGRATED TO ZAMBIA WHERE SEVERAL HUNDRED DIED IN CONCENTRATION CAMPS. A SIMILAR SITUATION AROSE IN 1970S MEXICO. LOCAL J.W.S WERE INFORMED BY THE GOVERNING BODY THAT THEY COULD ACCESS WHATEVER POLITICAL TOOLS WERE NECESSARY TO SAVE LIVES. THE DIFFERENCE IN TREATMENT BETWEEN THE TWO GROUPS IS STAGGERING!
PRE-1999 ALL WHITE GOVERNING BODY
1970s AFRICA
POST-1999 ATTEMPTING DIVERSITY
1970s MEXICO
MY GOD! THAT'S HORRIBLE!
I'M SO DISGUSTED BY THIS RACIST HISTORY THAT IT MAKES ME NOT WANT TO EVER BE ASSOCIATED WITH J.W.S AGAIN!
COFFEE BEAN

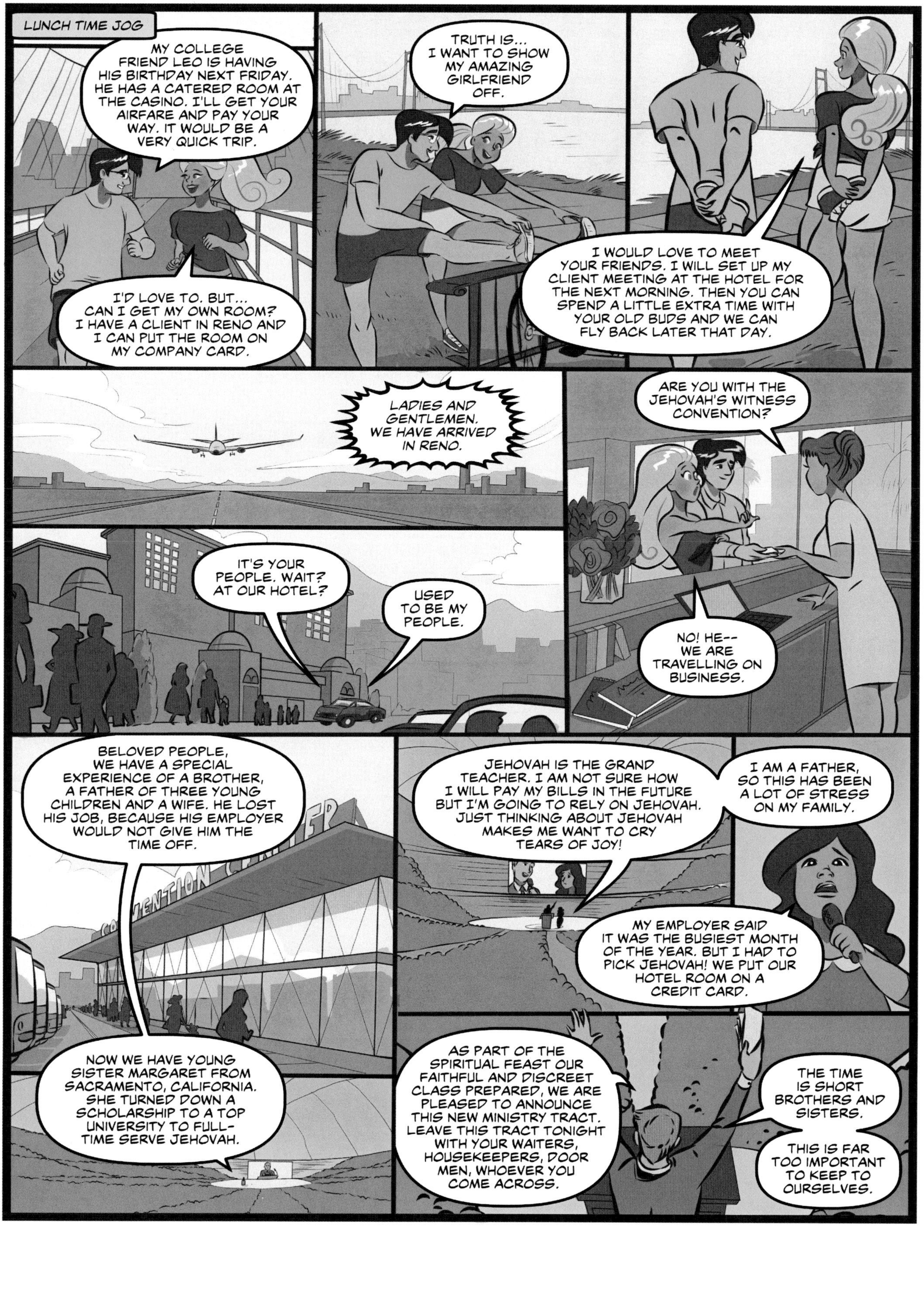
LUNCH TIME JOG
MY COLLEGE FRIEND LEO IS HAVING HIS BIRTHDAY NEXT FRIDAY. HE HAS A CATERED ROOM AT THE CASINO. I'LL GET YOUR AIRFARE AND PAY YOUR WAY. IT WOULD BE A VERY QUICK TRIP.
I'D LOVE TO. BUT... CAN I GET MY OWN ROOM? I HAVE A CLIENT IN RENO AND I CAN PUT THE ROOM ON MY COMPANY CARD.
TRUTH IS... I WANT TO SHOW MY AMAZING GIRLFRIEND OFF.
I WOULD LOVE TO MEET YOUR FRIENDS. I WILL SET UP MY CLIENT MEETING AT THE HOTEL FOR THE NEXT MORNING. THEN YOU CAN SPEND A LITTLE EXTRA TIME WITH YOUR OLD BUDS AND WE CAN FLY BACK LATER THAT DAY.
LADIES AND GENTLEMEN. WE HAVE ARRIVED IN RENO.
ARE YOU WITH THE JEHOVAH'S WITNESS CONVENTION?
NO! HE-- WE ARE TRAVELLING ON BUSINESS.
IT'S YOUR PEOPLE. WAIT? AT OUR HOTEL?
USED TO BE MY PEOPLE.
BELOVED PEOPLE, WE HAVE A SPECIAL EXPERIENCE OF A BROTHER, A FATHER OF THREE YOUNG CHILDREN AND A WIFE. HE LOST HIS JOB, BECAUSE HIS EMPLOYER WOULD NOT GIVE HIM THE TIME OFF.
JEHOVAH IS THE GRAND TEACHER. I AM NOT SURE HOW I WILL PAY MY BILLS IN THE FUTURE BUT I'M GOING TO RELY ON JEHOVAH. JUST THINKING ABOUT JEHOVAH MAKES ME WANT TO CRY TEARS OF JOY!
I AM A FATHER, SO THIS HAS BEEN A LOT OF STRESS ON MY FAMILY.
NOW WE HAVE YOUNG SISTER MARGARET FROM SACRAMENTO, CALIFORNIA. SHE TURNED DOWN A SCHOLARSHIP TO A TOP UNIVERSITY TO FULL-TIME SERVE JEHOVAH.
MY EMPLOYER SAID IT WAS THE BUSIEST MONTH OF THE YEAR. BUT I HAD TO PICK JEHOVAH! WE PUT OUR HOTEL ROOM ON A CREDIT CARD.
AS PART OF THE SPIRITUAL FEAST OUR FAITHFUL AND DISCREET CLASS PREPARED, WE ARE PLEASED TO ANNOUNCE THIS NEW MINISTRY TRACT. LEAVE THIS TRACT TONIGHT WITH YOUR WAITERS, HOUSEKEEPERS, DOOR MEN, WHOEVER YOU COME ACROSS.
THE TIME IS SHORT BROTHERS AND SISTERS.
THIS IS FAR TOO IMPORTANT TO KEEP TO OURSELVES.

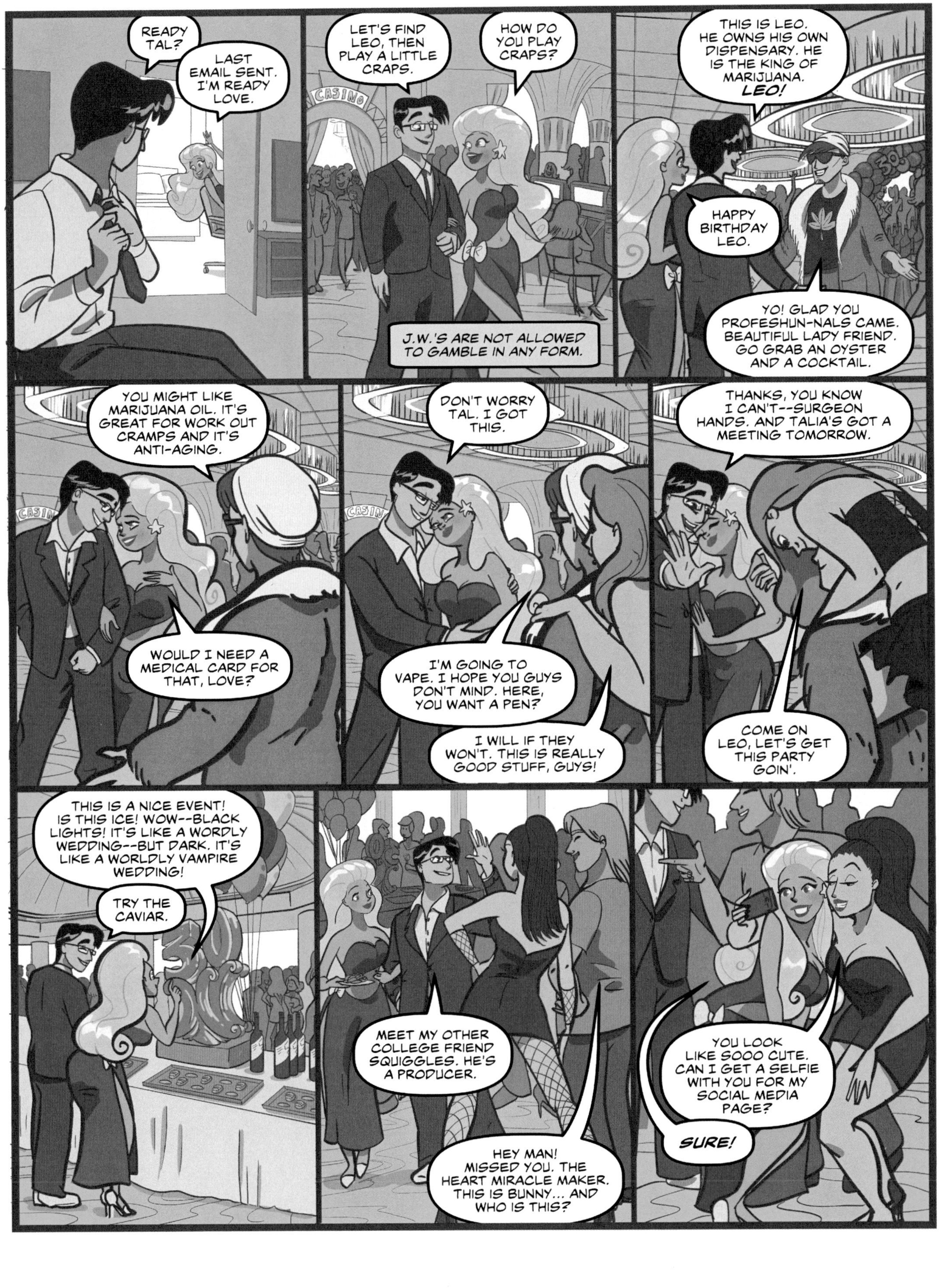
READY TAL?
LAST EMAIL SENT. I'M READY LOVE.
LET'S FIND LEO, THEN PLAY A LITTLE CRAPS.
HOW DO YOU PLAY CRAPS?
CASINO
J.W.'S ARE NOT ALLOWED TO GAMBLE IN ANY FORM.
THIS IS LEO. HE OWNS HIS OWN DISPENSARY. HE IS THE KING OF MARIJUANA. LEO!
HAPPY BIRTHDAY LEO.
YO! GLAD YOU PROFESHUN-NALS CAME. BEAUTIFUL LADY FRIEND. GO GRAB AN OYSTER AND A COCKTAIL.
YOU MIGHT LIKE MARIJUANA OIL. IT'S GREAT FOR WORK OUT CRAMPS AND IT'S ANTI-AGING.
WOULD I NEED A MEDICAL CARD FOR THAT, LOVE?
DON'T WORRY TAL. I GOT THIS.
I'M GOING TO VAPE. I HOPE YOU GUYS DON'T MIND. HERE, YOU WANT A PEN?
I WILL IF THEY WON'T. THIS IS REALLY GOOD STUFF, GUYS!
THANKS, YOU KNOW I CAN'T--SURGEON HANDS. AND TALIA'S GOT A MEETING TOMORROW.
COME ON LEO, LET'S GET THIS PARTY GOIN'.
THIS IS A NICE EVENT! IS THIS ICE! WOW--BLACK LIGHTS! IT'S LIKE A WORDLY WEDDING--BUT DARK. IT'S LIKE A WORLDLY VAMPIRE WEDDING!
TRY THE CAVIAR.
MEET MY OTHER COLLEGE FRIEND SQUIGGLES. HE'S A PRODUCER.
HEY MAN! MISSED YOU. THE HEART MIRACLE MAKER. THIS IS BUNNY... AND WHO IS THIS?
YOU LOOK LIKE SOOO CUTE. CAN I GET A SELFIE WITH YOU FOR MY SOCIAL MEDIA PAGE?
SURE!

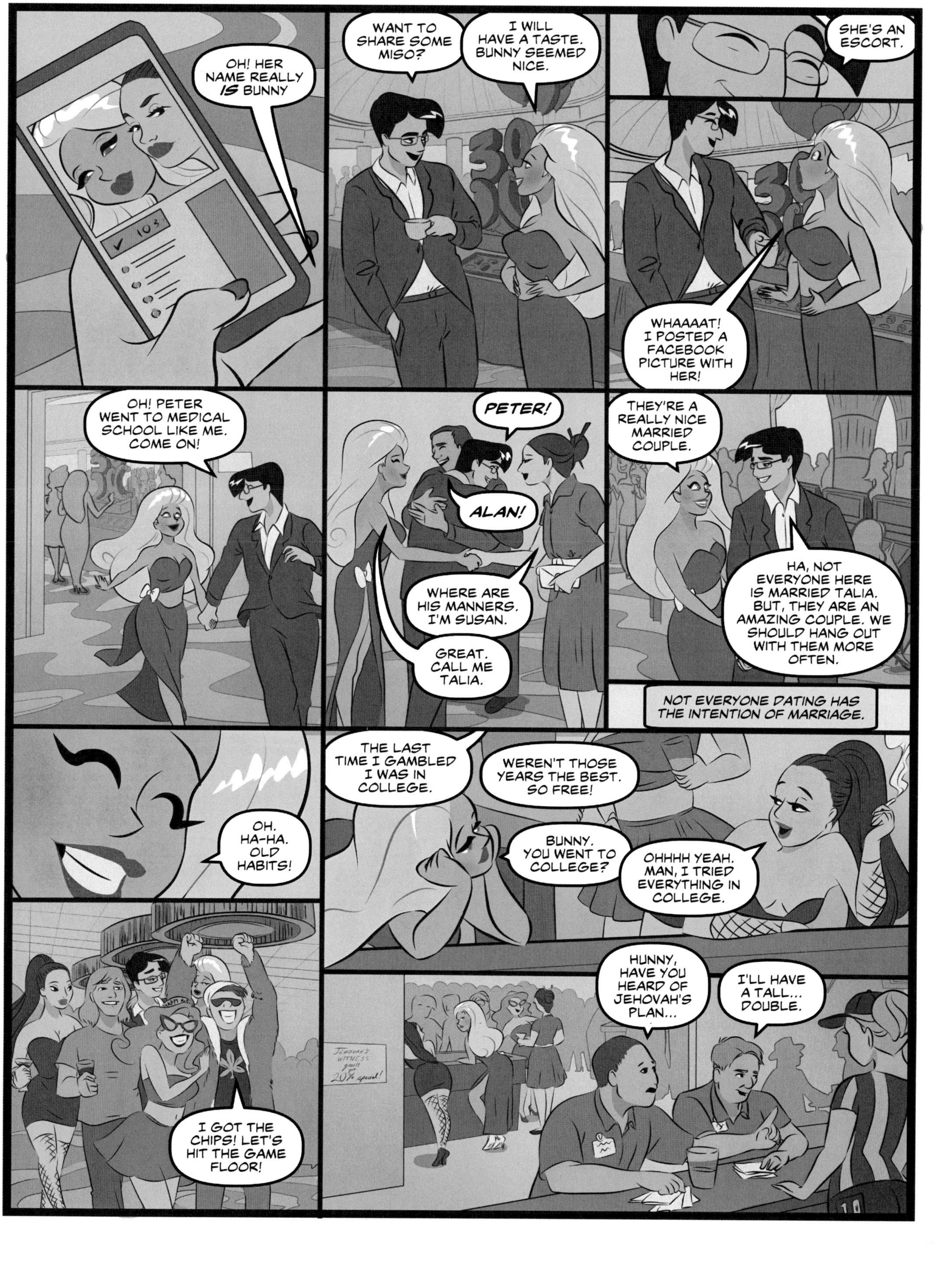

OH! HER NAME REALLY IS BUNNY
WANT TO SHARE SOME MISO?
I WILL HAVE A TASTE. BUNNY SEEMED NICE.
SHE'S AN ESCORT.
WHAAAAT! I POSTED A FACEBOOK PICTURE WITH HER!
OH! PETER WENT TO MEDICAL SCHOOL LIKE ME. COME ON!
PETER!
ALAN!
WHERE ARE HIS MANNERS. I'M SUSAN.
GREAT. CALL ME TALIA.
THEY'RE A REALLY NICE MARRIED COUPLE.
HA, NOT EVERYONE HERE IS MARRIED TALIA. BUT, THEY ARE AN AMAZING COUPLE. WE SHOULD HANG OUT WITH THEM MORE OFTEN.
NOT EVERYONE DATING HAS THE INTENTION OF MARRIAGE.
OH. HA-HA. OLD HABITS!
THE LAST TIME I GAMBLED I WAS IN COLLEGE.
WEREN'T THOSE YEARS THE BEST. SO FREE!
BUNNY. YOU WENT TO COLLEGE?
OHHHH YEAH. MAN, I TRIED EVERYTHING IN COLLEGE.
I GOT THE CHIPS! LET'S HIT THE GAME FLOOR!
HUNNY, HAVE YOU HEARD OF JEHOVAH'S PLAN...
I'LL HAVE A TALL... DOUBLE.

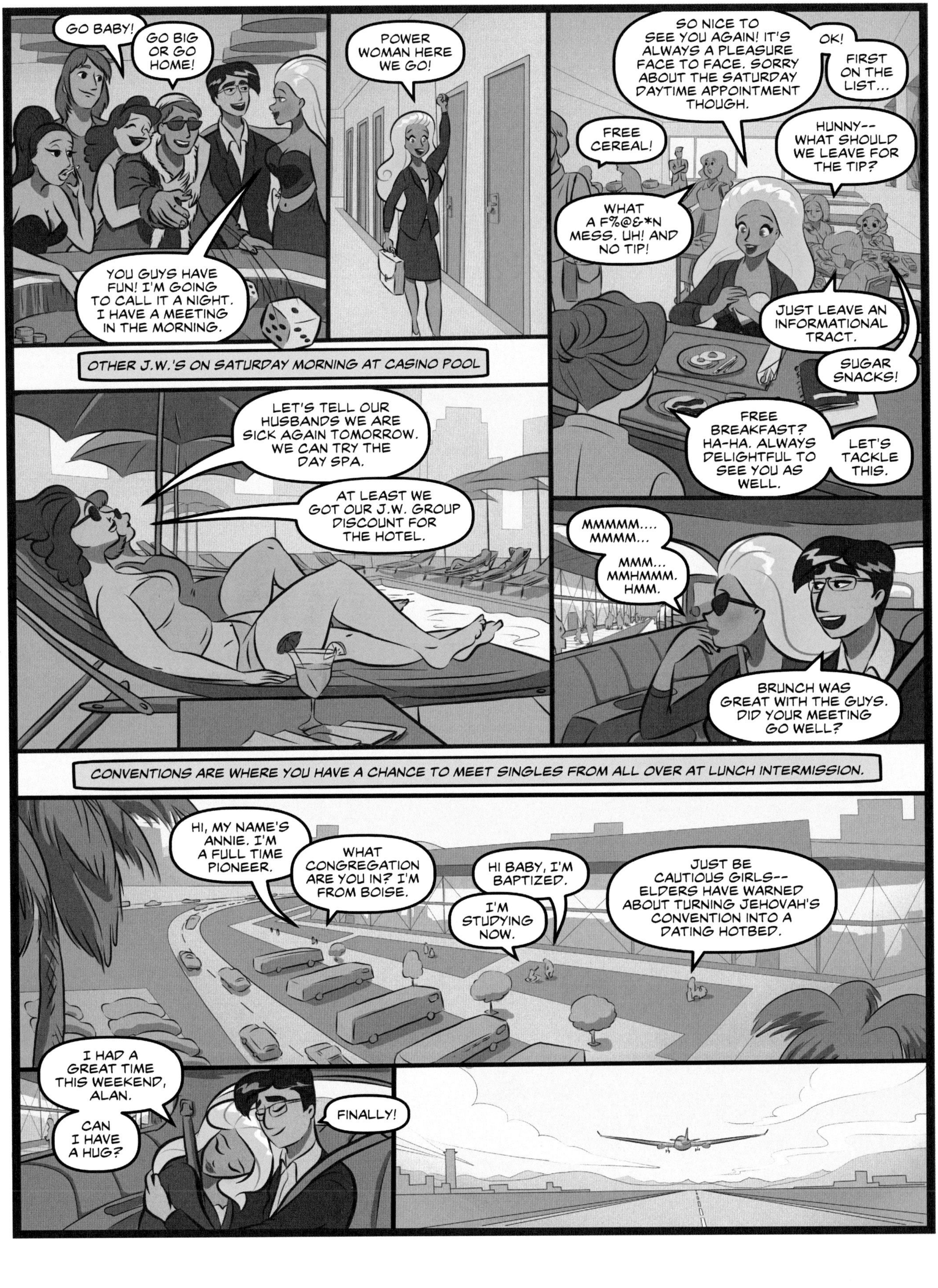
GO BABY!
GO BIG OR GO HOME!
YOU GUYS HAVE FUN! I'M GOING TO CALL IT A NIGHT. I HAVE A MEETING IN THE MORNING.
POWER WOMAN HERE WE GO!
SO NICE TO SEE YOU AGAIN! IT'S ALWAYS A PLEASURE FACE TO FACE. SORRY ABOUT THE SATURDAY DAYTIME APPOINTMENT THOUGH.
OK!
FIRST ON THE LIST...
FREE CEREAL!
HUNNY-- WHAT SHOULD WE LEAVE FOR THE TIP?
WHAT A F%@&*N MESS. UH! AND NO TIP!
JUST LEAVE AN INFORMATIONAL TRACT.
SUGAR SNACKS!
FREE BREAKFAST? HA-HA. ALWAYS DELIGHTFUL TO SEE YOU AS WELL.
LET'S TACKLE THIS.
OTHER J.W.'S ON SATURDAY MORNING AT CASINO POOL
LET'S TELL OUR HUSBANDS WE ARE SICK AGAIN TOMORROW. WE CAN TRY THE DAY SPA.
AT LEAST WE GOT OUR J.W. GROUP DISCOUNT FOR THE HOTEL.
MMMMM.... MMMM...
MMM... MMHMMM. HMM.
BRUNCH WAS GREAT WITH THE GUYS. DID YOUR MEETING GO WELL?
CONVENTIONS ARE WHERE YOU HAVE A CHANCE TO MEET SINGLES FROM ALL OVER AT LUNCH INTERMISSION.
HI, MY NAME'S ANNIE. I'M A FULL TIME PIONEER.
WHAT CONGREGATION ARE YOU IN? I'M FROM BOISE.
HI BABY, I'M BAPTIZED.
I'M STUDYING NOW.
JUST BE CAUTIOUS GIRLS-- ELDERS HAVE WARNED ABOUT TURNING JEHOVAH'S CONVENTION INTO A DATING HOTBED.
I HAD A GREAT TIME THIS WEEKEND, ALAN.
CAN I HAVE A HUG?
FINALLY!

ORPHAN SYNDROME

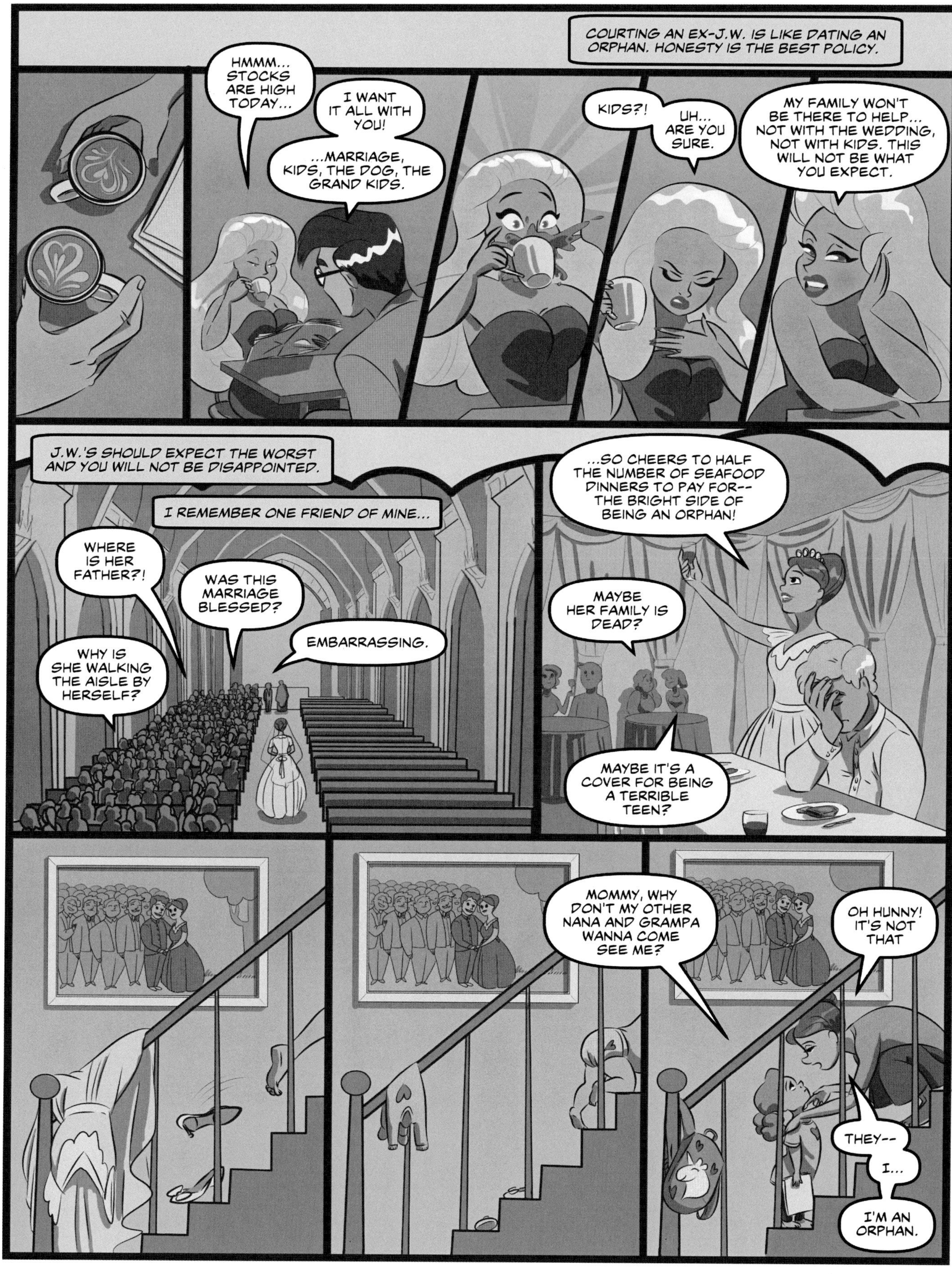

COURTING AN EX-J.W. IS LIKE DATING AN ORPHAN. HONESTY IS THE BEST POLICY.
HMMM... STOCKS ARE HIGH TODAY...
I WANT IT ALL WITH YOU!
...MARRIAGE, KIDS, THE DOG, THE GRAND KIDS.
KIDS?!
UH... ARE YOU SURE.
MY FAMILY WON'T BE THERE TO HELP... NOT WITH THE WEDDING, NOT WITH KIDS. THIS WILL NOT BE WHAT YOU EXPECT.
J.W.'S SHOULD EXPECT THE WORST AND YOU WILL NOT BE DISAPPOINTED.
I REMEMBER ONE FRIEND OF MINE...
WHERE IS HER FATHER?!
WAS THIS MARRIAGE BLESSED?
EMBARRASSING.
WHY IS SHE WALKING THE AISLE BY HERSELF?
...SO CHEERS TO HALF THE NUMBER OF SEAFOOD DINNERS TO PAY FOR-- THE BRIGHT SIDE OF BEING AN ORPHAN!
MAYBE HER FAMILY IS DEAD?
MAYBE IT'S A COVER FOR BEING A TERRIBLE TEEN?
MOMMY, WHY DON'T MY OTHER NANA AND GRAMPA WANNA COME SEE ME?
OH HUNNY! IT'S NOT THAT
THEY--
I...
I'M AN ORPHAN.

PARENTS & J.W.'S

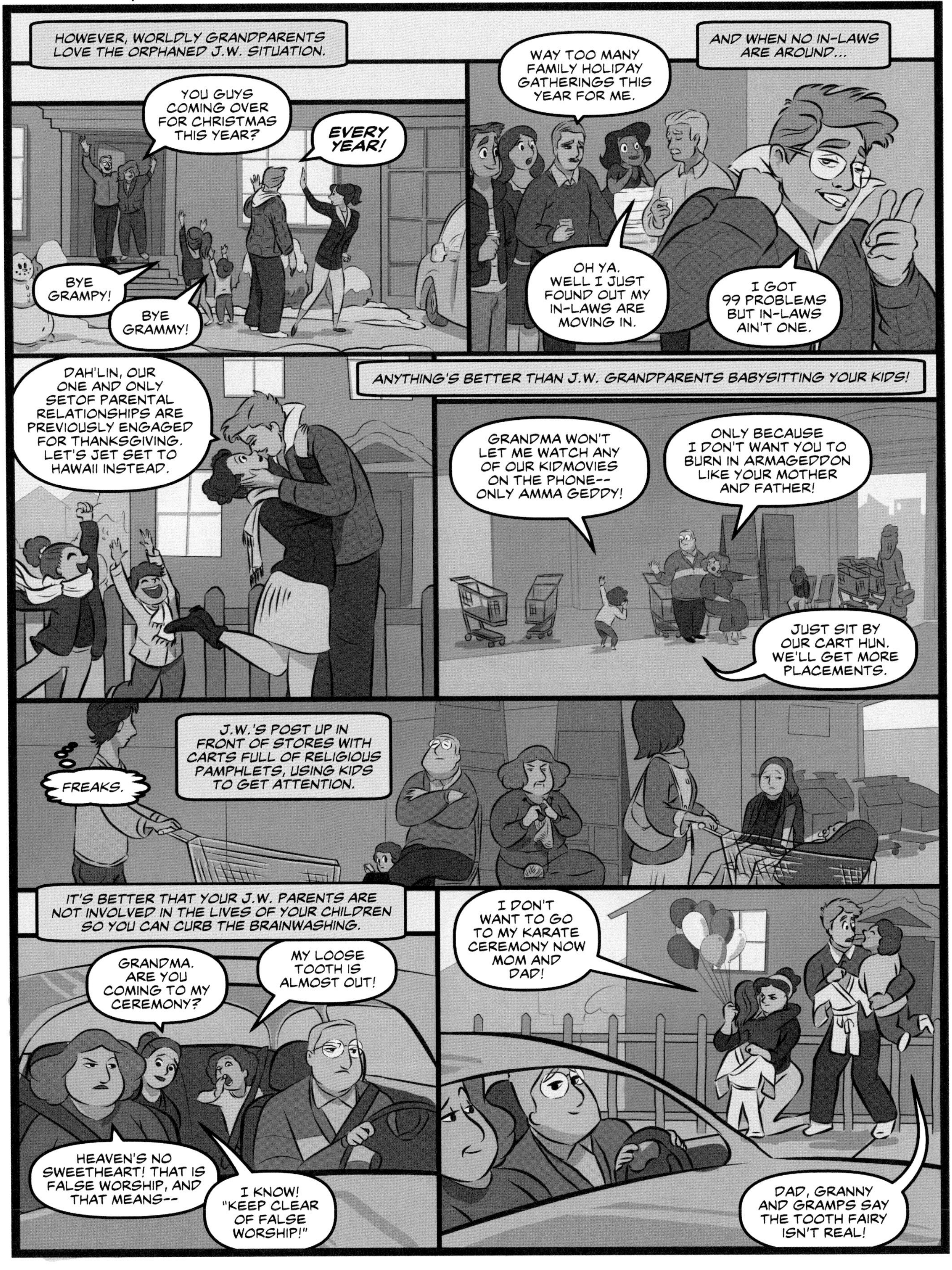
HOWEVER, WORLDLY GRANDPARENTS LOVE THE ORPHANED J.W. SITUATION.
YOU GUYS COMING OVER FOR CHRISTMAS THIS YEAR?
EVERY YEAR!
BYE GRAMPY!
BYE GRAMMY!
AND WHEN NO IN-LAWS ARE AROUND...
WAY TOO MANY FAMILY HOLIDAY GATHERINGS THIS YEAR FOR ME.
OH YA. WELL I JUST FOUND OUT MY IN-LAWS ARE MOVING IN.
I GOT 99 PROBLEMS BUT IN-LAWS AIN'T ONE.
DAH'LIN, OUR ONE AND ONLY SETOF PARENTAL RELATIONSHIPS ARE PREVIOUSLY ENGAGED FOR THANKSGIVING. LET'S JET SET TO HAWAII INSTEAD.
ANYTHING'S BETTER THAN J.W. GRANDPARENTS BABYSITTING YOUR KIDS!
GRANDMA WON'T LET ME WATCH ANY OF OUR KIDMOVIES ON THE PHONE-- ONLY AMMA GEDDY!
ONLY BECAUSE I DON'T WANT YOU TO BURN IN ARMAGEDDON LIKE YOUR MOTHER AND FATHER!
JUST SIT BY OUR CART HUN. WE'LL GET MORE PLACEMENTS.
FREAKS.
J.W.'S POST UP IN FRONT OF STORES WITH CARTS FULL OF RELIGIOUS PAMPHLETS, USING KIDS TO GET ATTENTION.
IT'S BETTER THAT YOUR J.W. PARENTS ARE NOT INVOLVED IN THE LIVES OF YOUR CHILDREN SO YOU CAN CURB THE BRAINWASHING.
GRANDMA. ARE YOU COMING TO MY CEREMONY?
MY LOOSE TOOTH IS ALMOST OUT!
HEAVEN'S NO SWEETHEART! THAT IS FALSE WORSHIP, AND THAT MEANS--
I KNOW! "KEEP CLEAR OF FALSE WORSHIP!"
I DON'T WANT TO GO TO MY KARATE CEREMONY NOW MOM AND DAD!
DAD, GRANNY AND GRAMPS SAY THE TOOTH FAIRY ISN'T REAL!

MEETING WORLDLY PARENTS

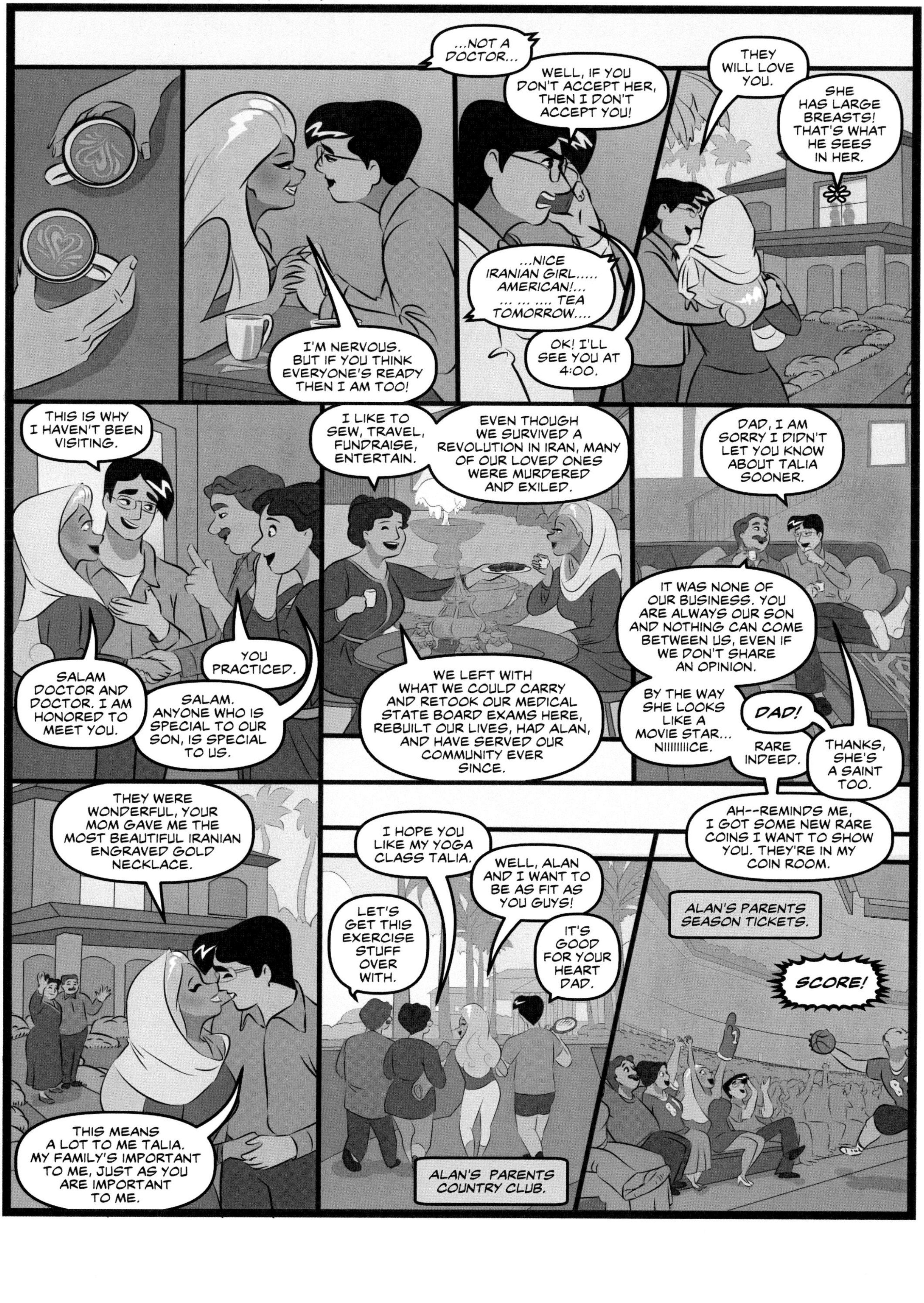

I'M NERVOUS. BUT IF YOU THINK EVERYONE'S READY THEN I AM TOO!
...NOT A DOCTOR...
WELL, IF YOU DON'T ACCEPT HER, THEN I DON'T ACCEPT YOU!
...NICE IRANIAN GIRL..... AMERICAN!... ... ... TEA TOMORROW....
OK! I'LL SEE YOU AT 4:00.
THEY WILL LOVE YOU.
SHE HAS LARGE BREASTS! THAT'S WHAT HE SEES IN HER.
THIS IS WHY I HAVEN'T BEEN VISITING.
SALAM DOCTOR AND DOCTOR. I AM HONORED TO MEET YOU.
YOU PRACTICED.
SALAM. ANYONE WHO IS SPECIAL TO OUR SON, IS SPECIAL TO US.
I LIKE TO SEW, TRAVEL, FUNDRAISE, ENTERTAIN.
EVEN THOUGH WE SURVIVED A REVOLUTION IN IRAN, MANY OF OUR LOVED ONES WERE MURDERED AND EXILED.
WE LEFT WITH WHAT WE COULD CARRY AND RETOOK OUR MEDICAL STATE BOARD EXAMS HERE, REBUILT OUR LIVES, HAD ALAN, AND HAVE SERVED OUR COMMUNITY EVER SINCE.
DAD, I AM SORRY I DIDN'T LET YOU KNOW ABOUT TALIA SOONER.
IT WAS NONE OF OUR BUSINESS. YOU ARE ALWAYS OUR SON AND NOTHING CAN COME BETWEEN US, EVEN IF WE DON'T SHARE AN OPINION.
BY THE WAY SHE LOOKS LIKE A MOVIE STAR... NIIIIIIICE.
DAD!
RARE INDEED.
THANKS, SHE'S A SAINT TOO.
THEY WERE WONDERFUL, YOUR MOM GAVE ME THE MOST BEAUTIFUL IRANIAN ENGRAVED GOLD NECKLACE.
THIS MEANS A LOT TO ME TALIA. MY FAMILY'S IMPORTANT TO ME, JUST AS YOU ARE IMPORTANT TO ME.
I HOPE YOU LIKE MY YOGA CLASS TALIA.
WELL, ALAN AND I WANT TO BE AS FIT AS YOU GUYS!
LET'S GET THIS EXERCISE STUFF OVER WITH.
IT'S GOOD FOR YOUR HEART DAD.
ALAN'S PARENTS COUNTRY CLUB.
AH--REMINDS ME, I GOT SOME NEW RARE COINS I WANT TO SHOW YOU. THEY'RE IN MY COIN ROOM.
ALAN'S PARENTS SEASON TICKETS.
SCORE!

ESCAPEE CULT GIRLS MEET UP

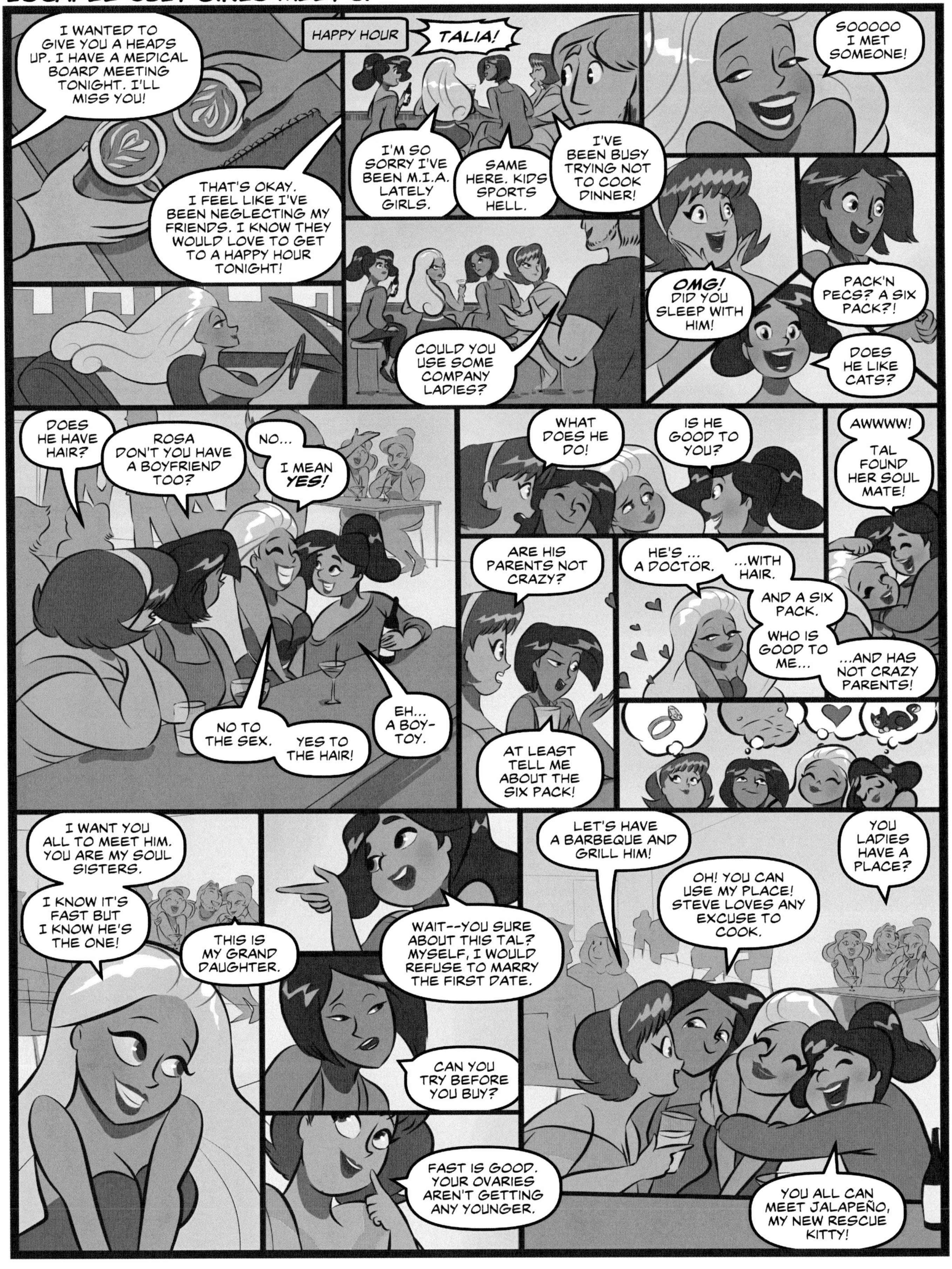
I WANTED TO GIVE YOU A HEADS UP. I HAVE A MEDICAL BOARD MEETING TONIGHT. I'LL MISS YOU!
THAT'S OKAY. I FEEL LIKE I'VE BEEN NEGLECTING MY FRIENDS. I KNOW THEY WOULD LOVE TO GET TO A HAPPY HOUR TONIGHT!
HAPPY HOUR
TALIA!
I'M SO SORRY I'VE BEEN M.I.A. LATELY GIRLS.
SAME HERE. KIDS SPORTS HELL.
I'VE BEEN BUSY TRYING NOT TO COOK DINNER!
COULD YOU USE SOME COMPANY LADIES?
SOOOOO I MET SOMEONE!
OMG! DID YOU SLEEP WITH HIM!
PACK'N PECS? A SIX PACK?!
DOES HE LIKE CATS?
DOES HE HAVE HAIR?
ROSA DON'T YOU HAVE A BOYFRIEND TOO?
NO...
I MEAN YES!
NO TO THE SEX.
YES TO THE HAIR!
EH... A BOY-TOY.
WHAT DOES HE DO!
IS HE GOOD TO YOU?
AWWWW!
TAL FOUND HER SOUL MATE!
ARE HIS PARENTS NOT CRAZY?
AT LEAST TELL ME ABOUT THE SIX PACK!
HE'S ... A DOCTOR.
...WITH HAIR.
AND A SIX PACK.
WHO IS GOOD TO ME...
...AND HAS NOT CRAZY PARENTS!
I WANT YOU ALL TO MEET HIM. YOU ARE MY SOUL SISTERS.
I KNOW IT'S FAST BUT I KNOW HE'S THE ONE!
THIS IS MY GRAND DAUGHTER.
WAIT--YOU SURE ABOUT THIS TAL? MYSELF, I WOULD REFUSE TO MARRY THE FIRST DATE.
CAN YOU TRY BEFORE YOU BUY?
FAST IS GOOD. YOUR OVARIES AREN'T GETTING ANY YOUNGER.
LET'S HAVE A BARBEQUE AND GRILL HIM!
YOU LADIES HAVE A PLACE?
OH! YOU CAN USE MY PLACE! STEVE LOVES ANY EXCUSE TO COOK.
YOU ALL CAN MEET JALAPEÑO, MY NEW RESCUE KITTY!

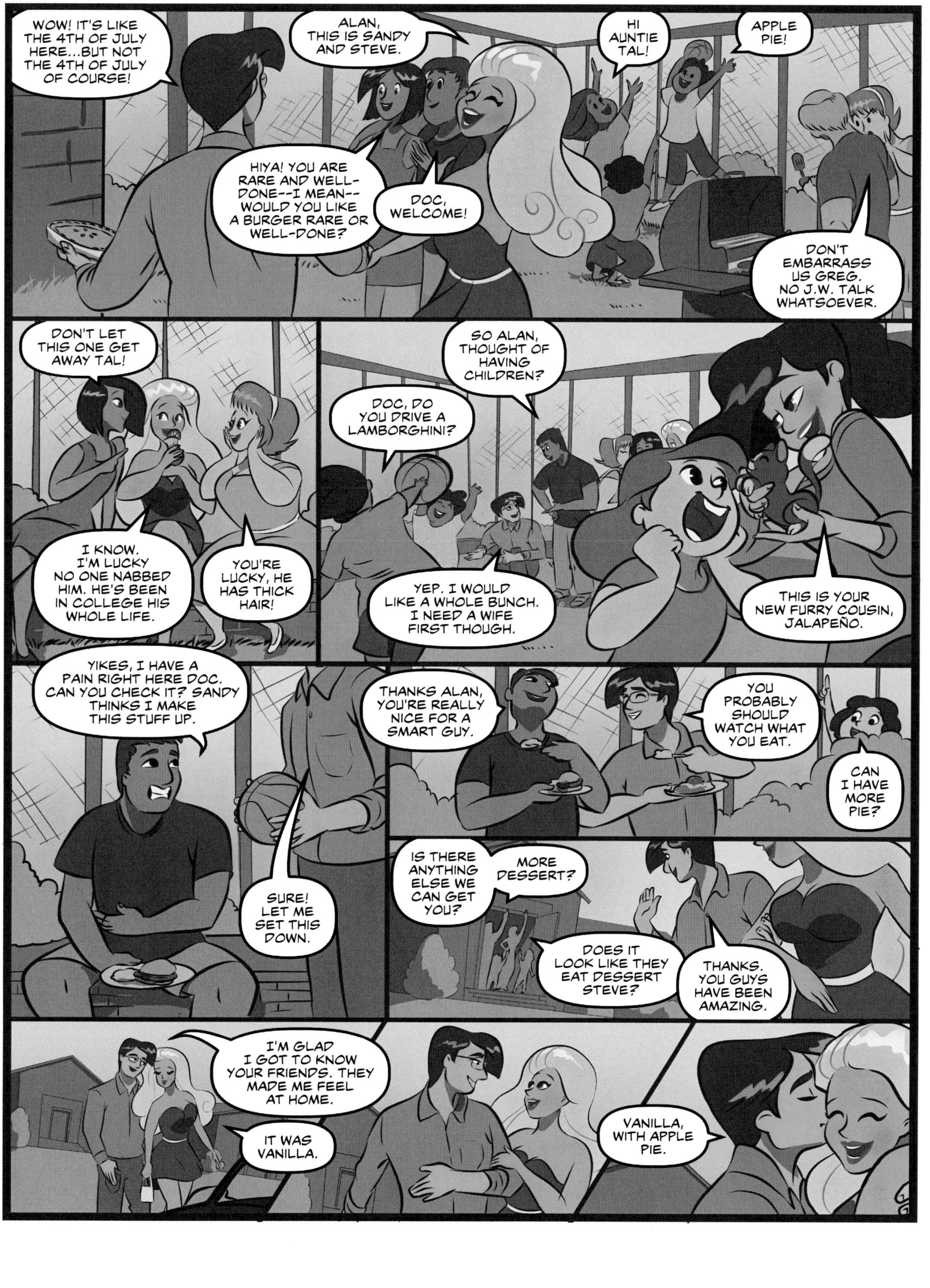
WOW! IT'S LIKE THE 4TH OF JULY HERE...BUT NOT THE 4TH OF JULY OF COURSE!
ALAN, THIS IS SANDY AND STEVE.
HIYA! YOU ARE RARE AND WELL-DONE--I MEAN--WOULD YOU LIKE A BURGER RARE OR WELL-DONE?
DOC, WELCOME!
HI AUNTIE TAL!
APPLE PIE!
DON'T EMBARRASS US GREG. NO J.W. TALK WHATSOEVER.
DON'T LET THIS ONE GET AWAY TAL!
I KNOW. I'M LUCKY NO ONE NABBED HIM. HE'S BEEN IN COLLEGE HIS WHOLE LIFE.
YOU'RE LUCKY, HE HAS THICK HAIR!
SO ALAN, THOUGHT OF HAVING CHILDREN?
DOC, DO YOU DRIVE A LAMBORGHINI?
YEP. I WOULD LIKE A WHOLE BUNCH. I NEED A WIFE FIRST THOUGH.
THIS IS YOUR NEW FURRY COUSIN, JALAPEÑO.
YIKES, I HAVE A PAIN RIGHT HERE DOC. CAN YOU CHECK IT? SANDY THINKS I MAKE THIS STUFF UP.
SURE! LET ME SET THIS DOWN.
THANKS ALAN, YOU'RE REALLY NICE FOR A SMART GUY.
YOU PROBABLY SHOULD WATCH WHAT YOU EAT.
CAN I HAVE MORE PIE?
IS THERE ANYTHING ELSE WE CAN GET YOU?
MORE DESSERT?
DOES IT LOOK LIKE THEY EAT DESSERT STEVE?
THANKS. YOU GUYS HAVE BEEN AMAZING.
I'M GLAD I GOT TO KNOW YOUR FRIENDS. THEY MADE ME FEEL AT HOME.
IT WAS VANILLA.
VANILLA, WITH APPLE PIE.

BREAKING THE CYCLE – 3RD GENERATION

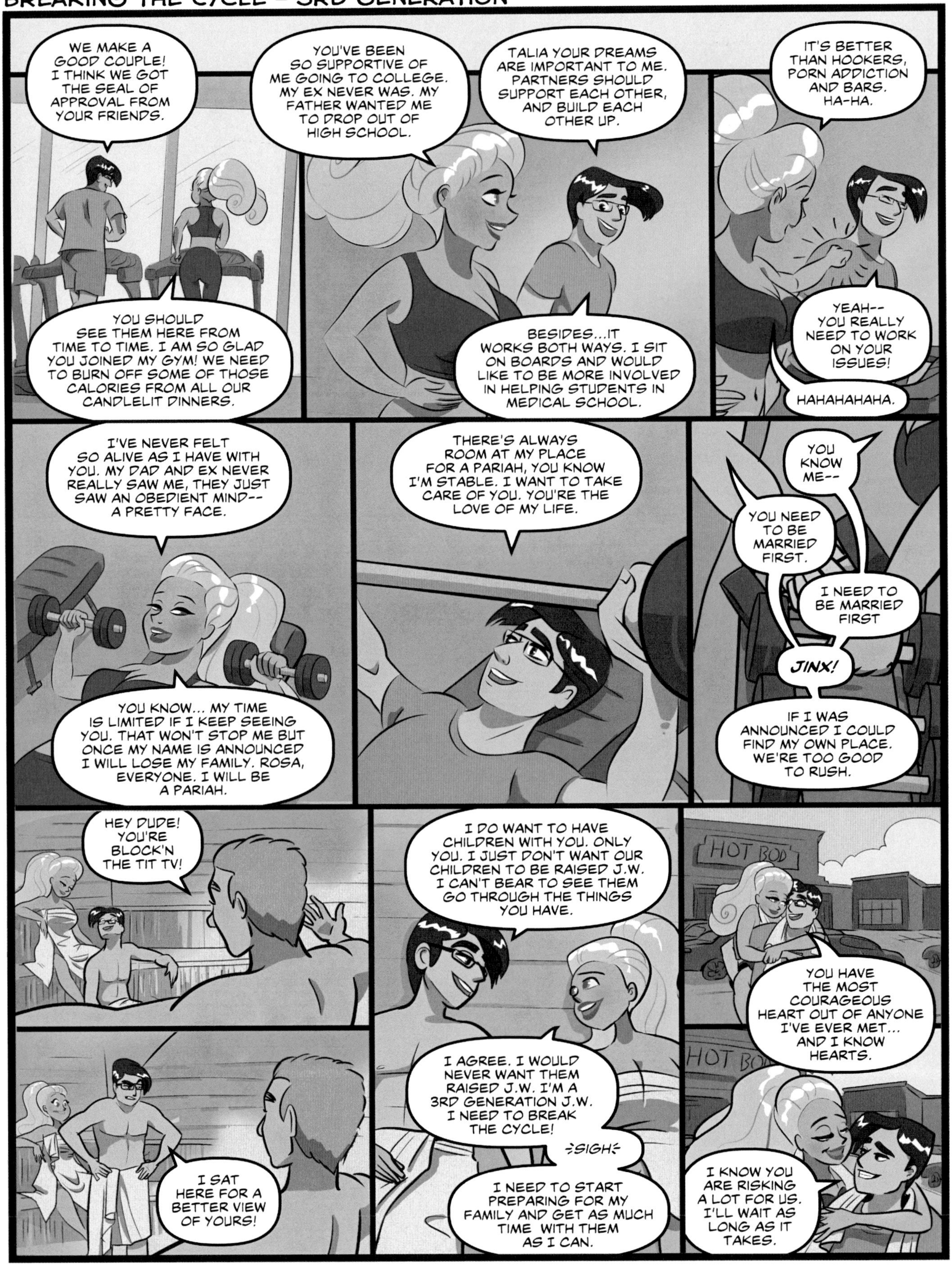

WE MAKE A GOOD COUPLE! I THINK WE GOT THE SEAL OF APPROVAL FROM YOUR FRIENDS.
YOU SHOULD SEE THEM HERE FROM TIME TO TIME. I AM SO GLAD YOU JOINED MY GYM! WE NEED TO BURN OFF SOME OF THOSE CALORIES FROM ALL OUR CANDLELIT DINNERS.
YOU'VE BEEN SO SUPPORTIVE OF ME GOING TO COLLEGE. MY EX NEVER WAS. MY FATHER WANTED ME TO DROP OUT OF HIGH SCHOOL.
TALIA YOUR DREAMS ARE IMPORTANT TO ME. PARTNERS SHOULD SUPPORT EACH OTHER, AND BUILD EACH OTHER UP.
BESIDES...IT WORKS BOTH WAYS. I SIT ON BOARDS AND WOULD LIKE TO BE MORE INVOLVED IN HELPING STUDENTS IN MEDICAL SCHOOL.
IT'S BETTER THAN HOOKERS, PORN ADDICTION AND BARS. HA-HA.
YEAH-- YOU REALLY NEED TO WORK ON YOUR ISSUES!
HAHAHAHAHA.
I'VE NEVER FELT SO ALIVE AS I HAVE WITH YOU. MY DAD AND EX NEVER REALLY SAW ME, THEY JUST SAW AN OBEDIENT MIND-- A PRETTY FACE.
YOU KNOW... MY TIME IS LIMITED IF I KEEP SEEING YOU. THAT WON'T STOP ME BUT ONCE MY NAME IS ANNOUNCED I WILL LOSE MY FAMILY. ROSA, EVERYONE. I WILL BE A PARIAH.
THERE'S ALWAYS ROOM AT MY PLACE FOR A PARIAH, YOU KNOW I'M STABLE. I WANT TO TAKE CARE OF YOU. YOU'RE THE LOVE OF MY LIFE.
YOU KNOW ME--
YOU NEED TO BE MARRIED FIRST.
I NEED TO BE MARRIED FIRST
JINX!
IF I WAS ANNOUNCED I COULD FIND MY OWN PLACE. WE'RE TOO GOOD TO RUSH.
HEY DUDE! YOU'RE BLOCK'N THE TIT TV!
I SAT HERE FOR A BETTER VIEW OF YOURS!
I DO WANT TO HAVE CHILDREN WITH YOU. ONLY YOU. I JUST DON'T WANT OUR CHILDREN TO BE RAISED J.W. I CAN'T BEAR TO SEE THEM GO THROUGH THE THINGS YOU HAVE.
I AGREE. I WOULD NEVER WANT THEM RAISED J.W. I'M A 3RD GENERATION J.W. I NEED TO BREAK THE CYCLE!
SIGH
I NEED TO START PREPARING FOR MY FAMILY AND GET AS MUCH TIME WITH THEM AS I CAN.
HOT BOD
YOU HAVE THE MOST COURAGEOUS HEART OUT OF ANYONE I'VE EVER MET... AND I KNOW HEARTS.
I KNOW YOU ARE RISKING A LOT FOR US. I'LL WAIT AS LONG AS IT TAKES.

SISTER VISIT

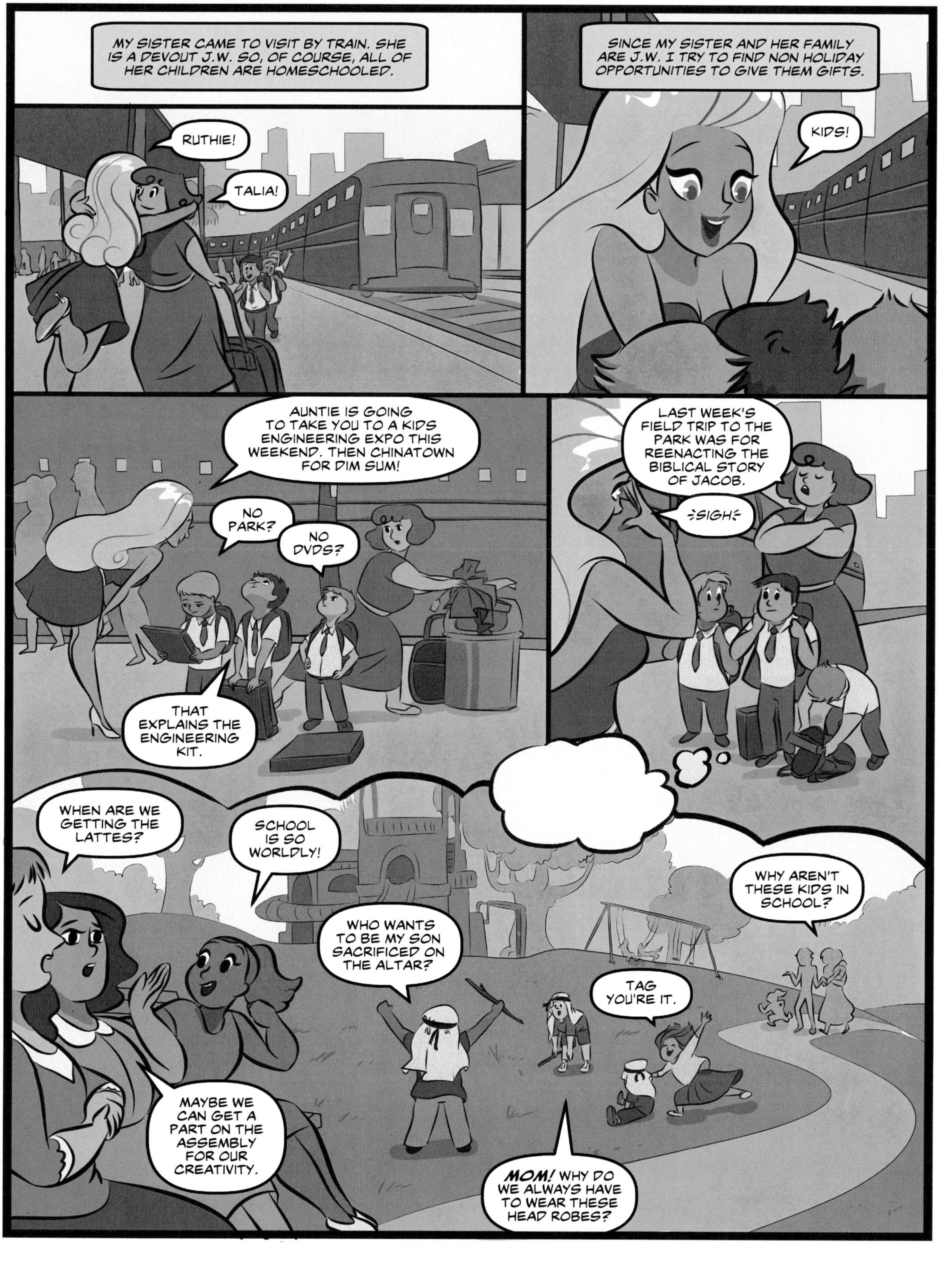
MY SISTER CAME TO VISIT BY TRAIN. SHE IS A DEVOUT J.W. SO, OF COURSE, ALL OF HER CHILDREN ARE HOMESCHOOLED.
RUTHIE!
TALIA!
SINCE MY SISTER AND HER FAMILY ARE J.W. I TRY TO FIND NON HOLIDAY OPPORTUNITIES TO GIVE THEM GIFTS.
KIDS!
AUNTIE IS GOING TO TAKE YOU TO A KIDS ENGINEERING EXPO THIS WEEKEND. THEN CHINATOWN FOR DIM SUM!
NO PARK?
NO DVDS?
THAT EXPLAINS THE ENGINEERING KIT.
LAST WEEK'S FIELD TRIP TO THE PARK WAS FOR REENACTING THE BIBLICAL STORY OF JACOB.
SIGH
WHEN ARE WE GETTING THE LATTES?
SCHOOL IS SO WORLDLY!
MAYBE WE CAN GET A PART ON THE ASSEMBLY FOR OUR CREATIVITY.
WHO WANTS TO BE MY SON SACRIFICED ON THE ALTAR?
TAG YOU'RE IT.
WHY AREN'T THESE KIDS IN SCHOOL?
MOM! WHY DO WE ALWAYS HAVE TO WEAR THESE HEAD ROBES?

CHINATOWN

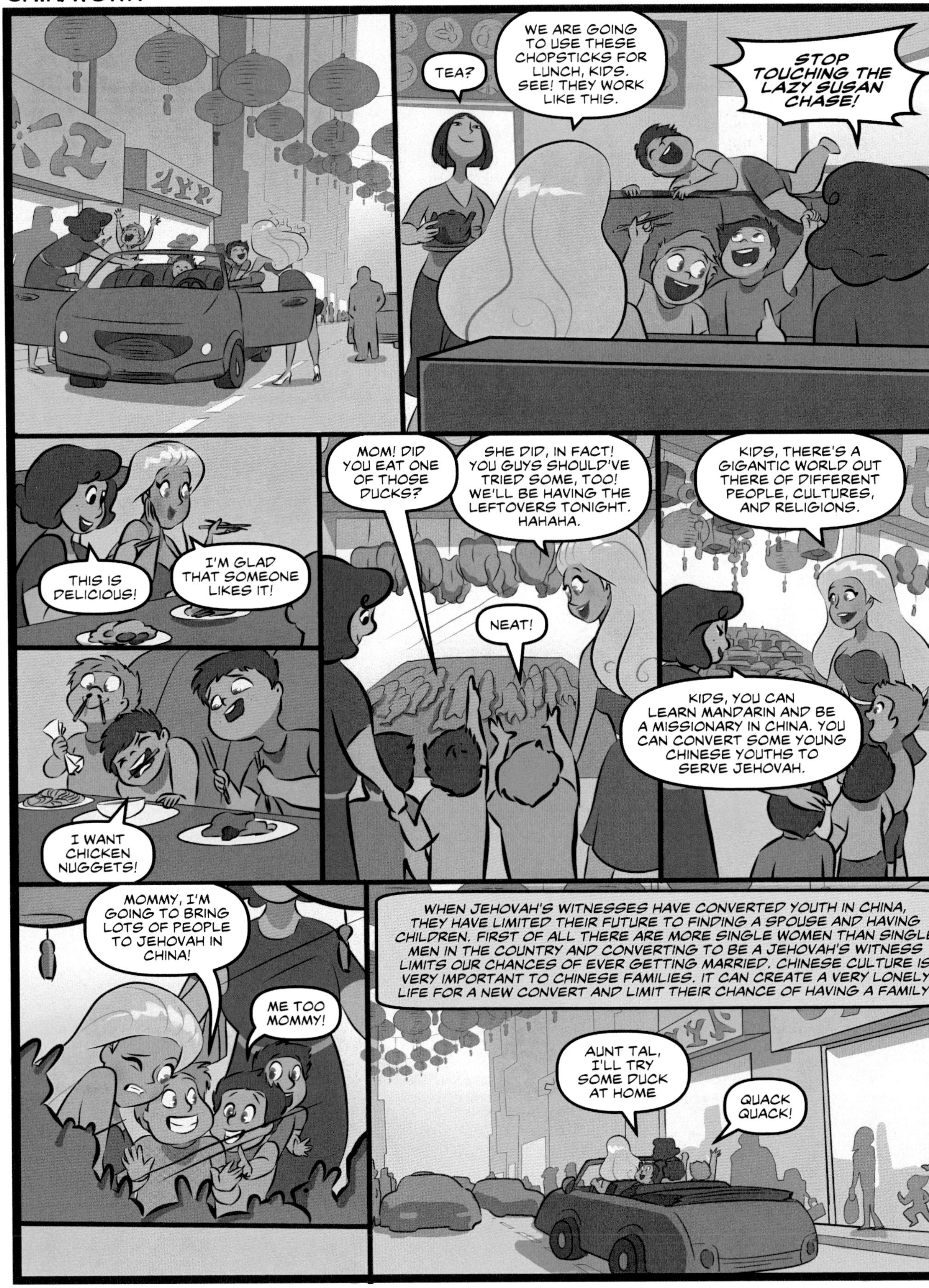
TEA?
WE ARE GOING TO USE THESE CHOPSTICKS FOR LUNCH, KIDS. SEE! THEY WORK LIKE THIS.
STOP TOUCHING THE LAZY SUSAN CHASE!
THIS IS DELICIOUS!
I'M GLAD THAT SOMEONE LIKES IT!
I WANT CHICKEN NUGGETS!
MOM! DID YOU EAT ONE OF THOSE DUCKS?
SHE DID, IN FACT! YOU GUYS SHOULD'VE TRIED SOME, TOO! WE'LL BE HAVING THE LEFTOVERS TONIGHT. HAHAHA.
NEAT!
KIDS, THERE'S A GIGANTIC WORLD OUT THERE OF DIFFERENT PEOPLE, CULTURES, AND RELIGIONS.
KIDS, YOU CAN LEARN MANDARIN AND BE A MISSIONARY IN CHINA. YOU CAN CONVERT SOME YOUNG CHINESE YOUTHS TO SERVE JEHOVAH.
MOMMY, I'M GOING TO BRING LOTS OF PEOPLE TO JEHOVAH IN CHINA!
ME TOO MOMMY!
WHEN JEHOVAH'S WITNESSES HAVE CONVERTED YOUTH IN CHINA, THEY HAVE LIMITED THEIR FUTURE TO FINDING A SPOUSE AND HAVING CHILDREN. FIRST OF ALL THERE ARE MORE SINGLE WOMEN THAN SINGLE MEN IN THE COUNTRY AND CONVERTING TO BE A JEHOVAH'S WITNESS LIMITS OUR CHANCES OF EVER GETTING MARRIED. CHINESE CULTURE IS VERY IMPORTANT TO CHINESE FAMILIES. IT CAN CREATE A VERY LONELY LIFE FOR A NEW CONVERT AND LIMIT THEIR CHANCE OF HAVING A FAMILY.
AUNT TAL, I'LL TRY SOME DUCK AT HOME
QUACK QUACK!

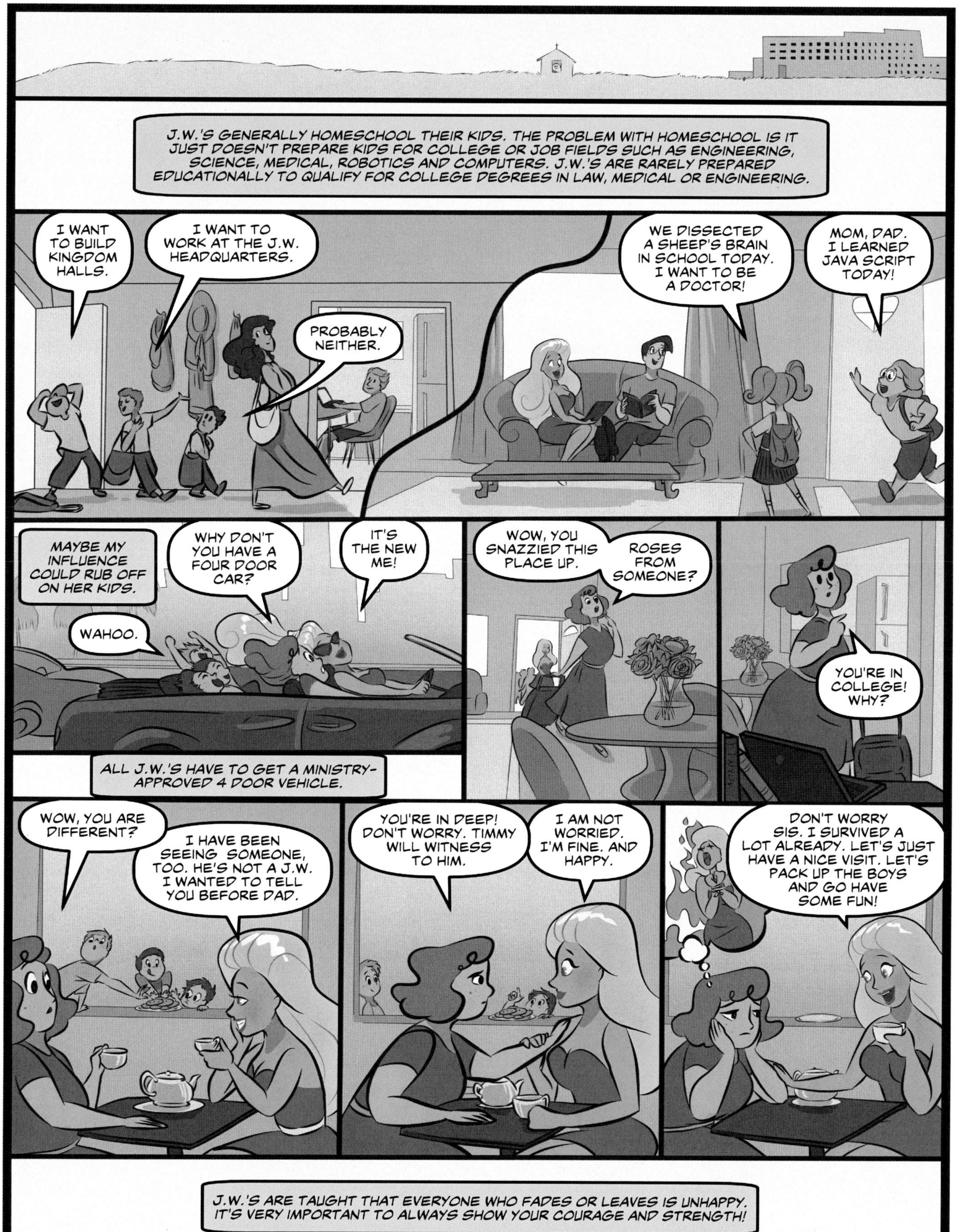
J.W.'S GENERALLY HOMESCHOOL THEIR KIDS. THE PROBLEM WITH HOMESCHOOL IS IT JUST DOESN'T PREPARE KIDS FOR COLLEGE OR JOB FIELDS SUCH AS ENGINEERING, SCIENCE, MEDICAL, ROBOTICS AND COMPUTERS. J.W.'S ARE RARELY PREPARED EDUCATIONALLY TO QUALIFY FOR COLLEGE DEGREES IN LAW, MEDICAL OR ENGINEERING.
I WANT TO BUILD KINGDOM HALLS.
I WANT TO WORK AT THE J.W. HEADQUARTERS.
PROBABLY NEITHER.
WE DISSECTED A SHEEP'S BRAIN IN SCHOOL TODAY. I WANT TO BE A DOCTOR!
MOM, DAD. I LEARNED JAVA SCRIPT TODAY!
MAYBE MY INFLUENCE COULD RUB OFF ON HER KIDS.
WHY DON'T YOU HAVE A FOUR DOOR CAR?
IT'S THE NEW ME!
WAHOO.
ALL J.W.'S HAVE TO GET A MINISTRY-APPROVED 4 DOOR VEHICLE.
WOW, YOU SNAZZIED THIS PLACE UP.
ROSES FROM SOMEONE?
YOU'RE IN COLLEGE! WHY?
WOW, YOU ARE DIFFERENT?
I HAVE BEEN SEEING SOMEONE, TOO. HE'S NOT A J.W. I WANTED TO TELL YOU BEFORE DAD.
YOU'RE IN DEEP! DON'T WORRY. TIMMY WILL WITNESS TO HIM.
I AM NOT WORRIED. I'M FINE. AND HAPPY.
DON'T WORRY SIS. I SURVIVED A LOT ALREADY. LET'S JUST HAVE A NICE VISIT. LET'S PACK UP THE BOYS AND GO HAVE SOME FUN!
J.W.'S ARE TAUGHT THAT EVERYONE WHO FADES OR LEAVES IS UNHAPPY. IT'S VERY IMPORTANT TO ALWAYS SHOW YOUR COURAGE AND STRENGTH!

MOM

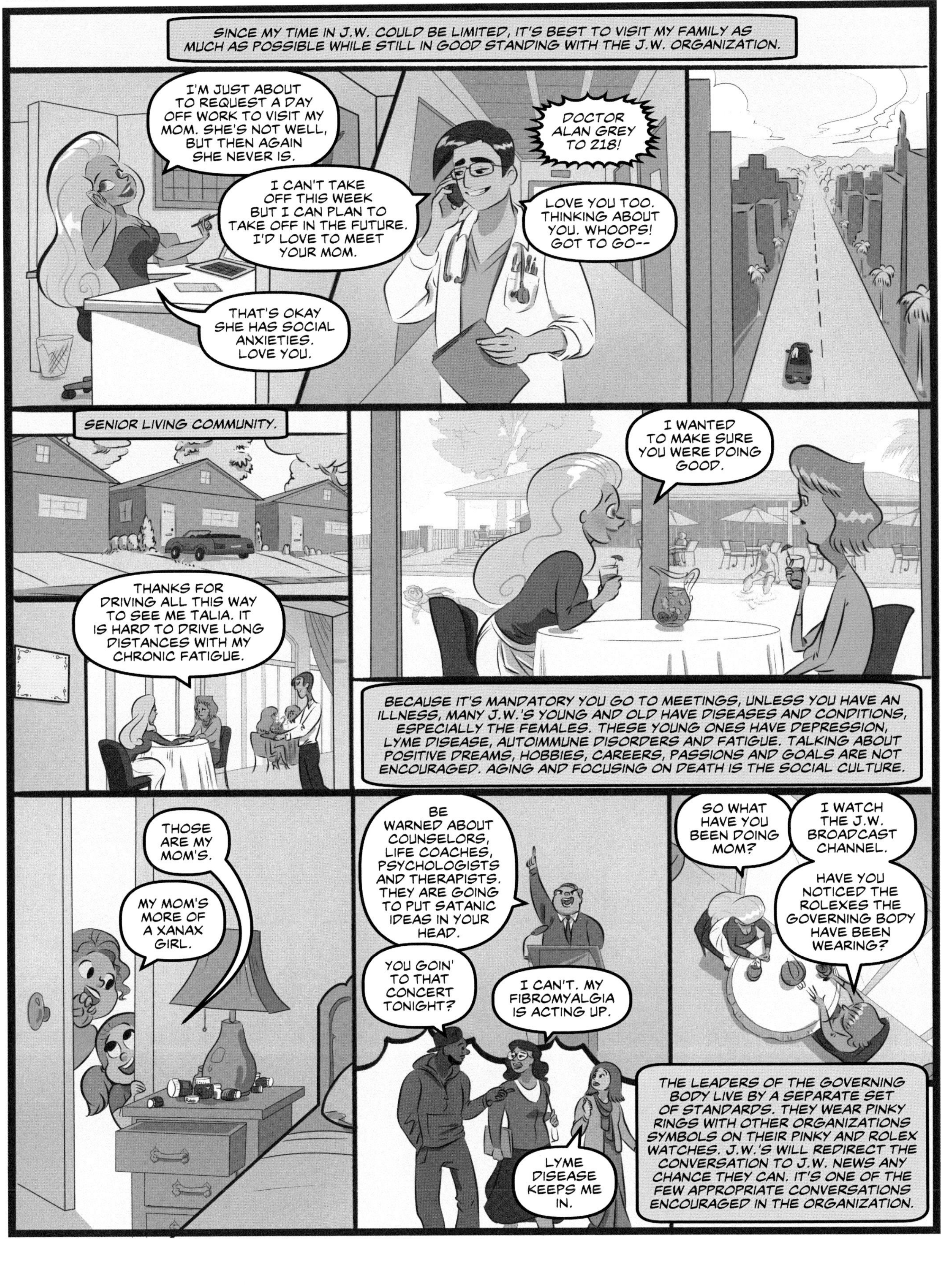

SINCE MY TIME IN J.W. COULD BE LIMITED, IT'S BEST TO VISIT MY FAMILY AS MUCH AS POSSIBLE WHILE STILL IN GOOD STANDING WITH THE J.W. ORGANIZATION.
I'M JUST ABOUT TO REQUEST A DAY OFF WORK TO VISIT MY MOM. SHE'S NOT WELL, BUT THEN AGAIN SHE NEVER IS.
I CAN'T TAKE OFF THIS WEEK BUT I CAN PLAN TO TAKE OFF IN THE FUTURE. I'D LOVE TO MEET YOUR MOM.
THAT'S OKAY SHE HAS SOCIAL ANXIETIES. LOVE YOU.
DOCTOR ALAN GREY TO 218!
LOVE YOU TOO. THINKING ABOUT YOU. WHOOPS! GOT TO GO--
SENIOR LIVING COMMUNITY.
THANKS FOR DRIVING ALL THIS WAY TO SEE ME TALIA. IT IS HARD TO DRIVE LONG DISTANCES WITH MY CHRONIC FATIGUE.
I WANTED TO MAKE SURE YOU WERE DOING GOOD.
BECAUSE IT'S MANDATORY YOU GO TO MEETINGS, UNLESS YOU HAVE AN ILLNESS, MANY J.W.'S YOUNG AND OLD HAVE DISEASES AND CONDITIONS, ESPECIALLY THE FEMALES. THESE YOUNG ONES HAVE DEPRESSION, LYME DISEASE, AUTOIMMUNE DISORDERS AND FATIGUE. TALKING ABOUT POSITIVE DREAMS, HOBBIES, CAREERS, PASSIONS AND GOALS ARE NOT ENCOURAGED. AGING AND FOCUSING ON DEATH IS THE SOCIAL CULTURE.
THOSE ARE MY MOM'S.
MY MOM'S MORE OF A XANAX GIRL.
BE WARNED ABOUT COUNSELORS, LIFE COACHES, PSYCHOLOGISTS AND THERAPISTS. THEY ARE GOING TO PUT SATANIC IDEAS IN YOUR HEAD.
YOU GOIN' TO THAT CONCERT TONIGHT?
I CAN'T. MY FIBROMYALGIA IS ACTING UP.
LYME DISEASE KEEPS ME IN.
SO WHAT HAVE YOU BEEN DOING MOM?
I WATCH THE J.W. BROADCAST CHANNEL.
HAVE YOU NOTICED THE ROLEXES THE GOVERNING BODY HAVE BEEN WEARING?
THE LEADERS OF THE GOVERNING BODY LIVE BY A SEPARATE SET OF STANDARDS. THEY WEAR PINKY RINGS WITH OTHER ORGANIZATIONS SYMBOLS ON THEIR PINKY AND ROLEX WATCHES. J.W.'S WILL REDIRECT THE CONVERSATION TO J.W. NEWS ANY CHANCE THEY CAN. IT'S ONE OF THE FEW APPROPRIATE CONVERSATIONS ENCOURAGED IN THE ORGANIZATION.

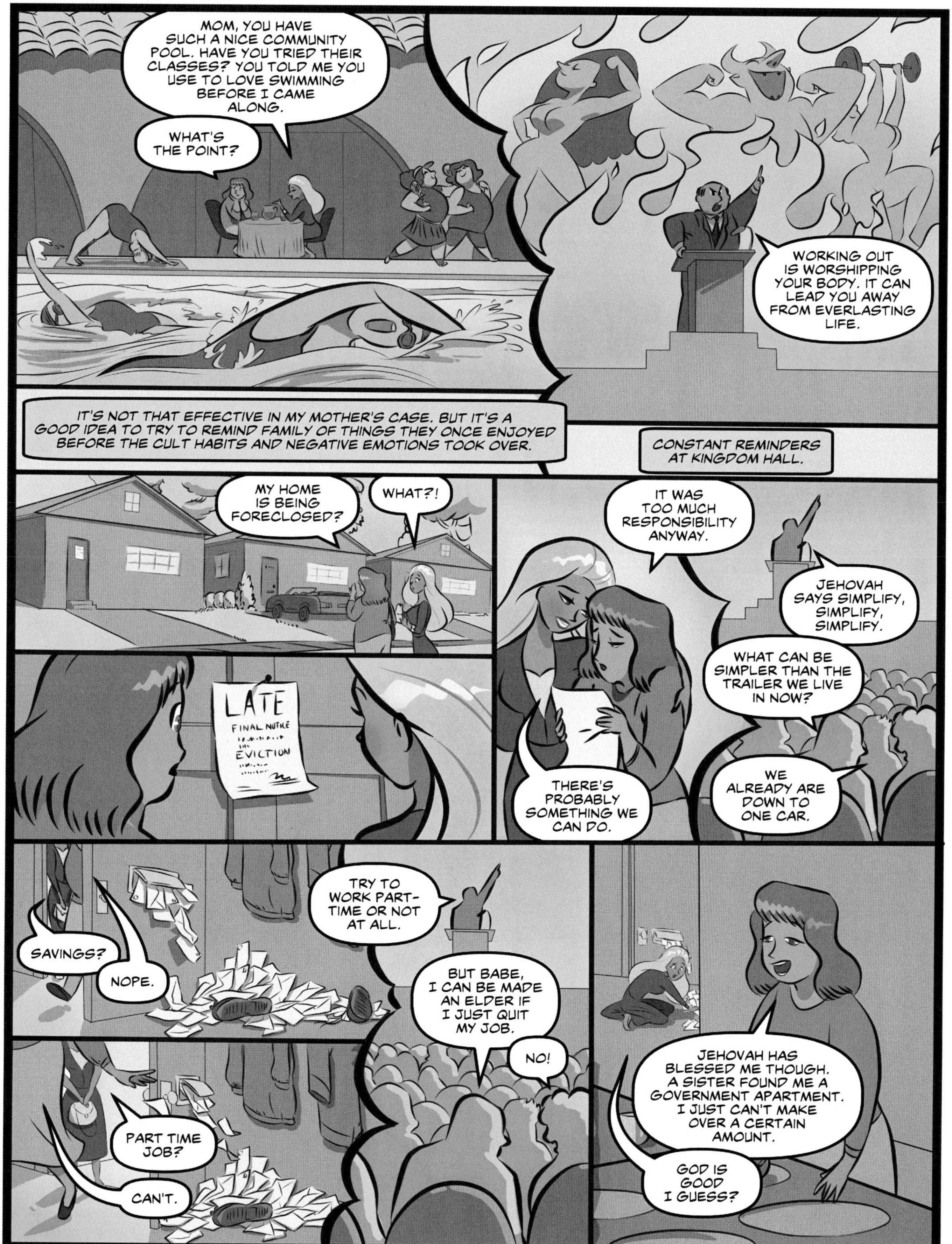
MOM, YOU HAVE SUCH A NICE COMMUNITY POOL. HAVE YOU TRIED THEIR CLASSES? YOU TOLD ME YOU USE TO LOVE SWIMMING BEFORE I CAME ALONG.
WHAT'S THE POINT?
WORKING OUT IS WORSHIPPING YOUR BODY. IT CAN LEAD YOU AWAY FROM EVERLASTING LIFE.
IT'S NOT THAT EFFECTIVE IN MY MOTHER'S CASE. BUT IT'S A GOOD IDEA TO TRY TO REMIND FAMILY OF THINGS THEY ONCE ENJOYED BEFORE THE CULT HABITS AND NEGATIVE EMOTIONS TOOK OVER.
CONSTANT REMINDERS AT KINGDOM HALL.
MY HOME IS BEING FORECLOSED?
WHAT?!
LATE
FINAL NOTICE
EVICTION
IT WAS TOO MUCH RESPONSIBILITY ANYWAY.
JEHOVAH SAYS SIMPLIFY, SIMPLIFY, SIMPLIFY.
WHAT CAN BE SIMPLER THAN THE TRAILER WE LIVE IN NOW?
THERE'S PROBABLY SOMETHING WE CAN DO.
WE ALREADY ARE DOWN TO ONE CAR.
SAVINGS?
NOPE.
TRY TO WORK PART-TIME OR NOT AT ALL.
BUT BABE, I CAN BE MADE AN ELDER IF I JUST QUIT MY JOB.
NO!
PART TIME JOB?
CAN'T.
JEHOVAH HAS BLESSED ME THOUGH. A SISTER FOUND ME A GOVERNMENT APARTMENT. I JUST CAN'T MAKE OVER A CERTAIN AMOUNT.
GOD IS GOOD I GUESS?

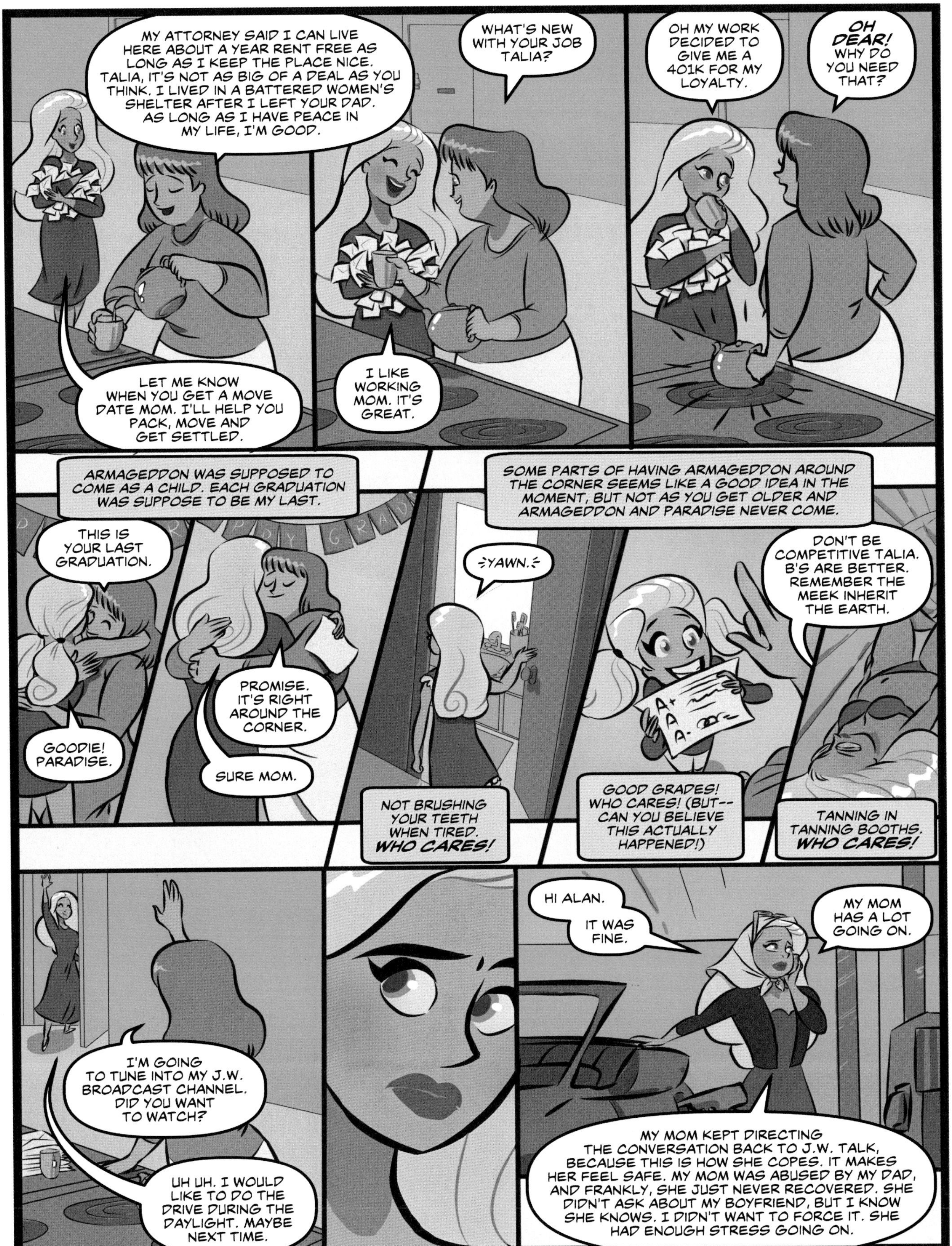
MY ATTORNEY SAID I CAN LIVE HERE ABOUT A YEAR RENT FREE AS LONG AS I KEEP THE PLACE NICE. TALIA, IT'S NOT AS BIG OF A DEAL AS YOU THINK. I LIVED IN A BATTERED WOMEN'S SHELTER AFTER I LEFT YOUR DAD. AS LONG AS I HAVE PEACE IN MY LIFE, I'M GOOD.
LET ME KNOW WHEN YOU GET A MOVE DATE MOM. I'LL HELP YOU PACK, MOVE AND GET SETTLED.
WHAT'S NEW WITH YOUR JOB TALIA?
I LIKE WORKING MOM. IT'S GREAT.
OH MY WORK DECIDED TO GIVE ME A 401K FOR MY LOYALTY.
OH DEAR! WHY DO YOU NEED THAT?
ARMAGEDDON WAS SUPPOSED TO COME AS A CHILD. EACH GRADUATION WAS SUPPOSE TO BE MY LAST.
THIS IS YOUR LAST GRADUATION.
GOODIE! PARADISE.
PROMISE. IT'S RIGHT AROUND THE CORNER.
SURE MOM.
SOME PARTS OF HAVING ARMAGEDDON AROUND THE CORNER SEEMS LIKE A GOOD IDEA IN THE MOMENT, BUT NOT AS YOU GET OLDER AND ARMAGEDDON AND PARADISE NEVER COME.
YAWN.
NOT BRUSHING YOUR TEETH WHEN TIRED. WHO CARES!
DON'T BE COMPETITIVE TALIA. B'S ARE BETTER. REMEMBER THE MEEK INHERIT THE EARTH.
GOOD GRADES! WHO CARES! (BUT--CAN YOU BELIEVE THIS ACTUALLY HAPPENED!)
TANNING IN TANNING BOOTHS. WHO CARES!
I'M GOING TO TUNE INTO MY J.W. BROADCAST CHANNEL. DID YOU WANT TO WATCH?
UH UH. I WOULD LIKE TO DO THE DRIVE DURING THE DAYLIGHT. MAYBE NEXT TIME.
HI ALAN.
IT WAS FINE.
MY MOM HAS A LOT GOING ON.
MY MOM KEPT DIRECTING THE CONVERSATION BACK TO J.W. TALK, BECAUSE THIS IS HOW SHE COPES. IT MAKES HER FEEL SAFE. MY MOM WAS ABUSED BY MY DAD, AND FRANKLY, SHE JUST NEVER RECOVERED. SHE DIDN'T ASK ABOUT MY BOYFRIEND, BUT I KNOW SHE KNOWS. I DIDN'T WANT TO FORCE IT. SHE HAD ENOUGH STRESS GOING ON.

EASTER

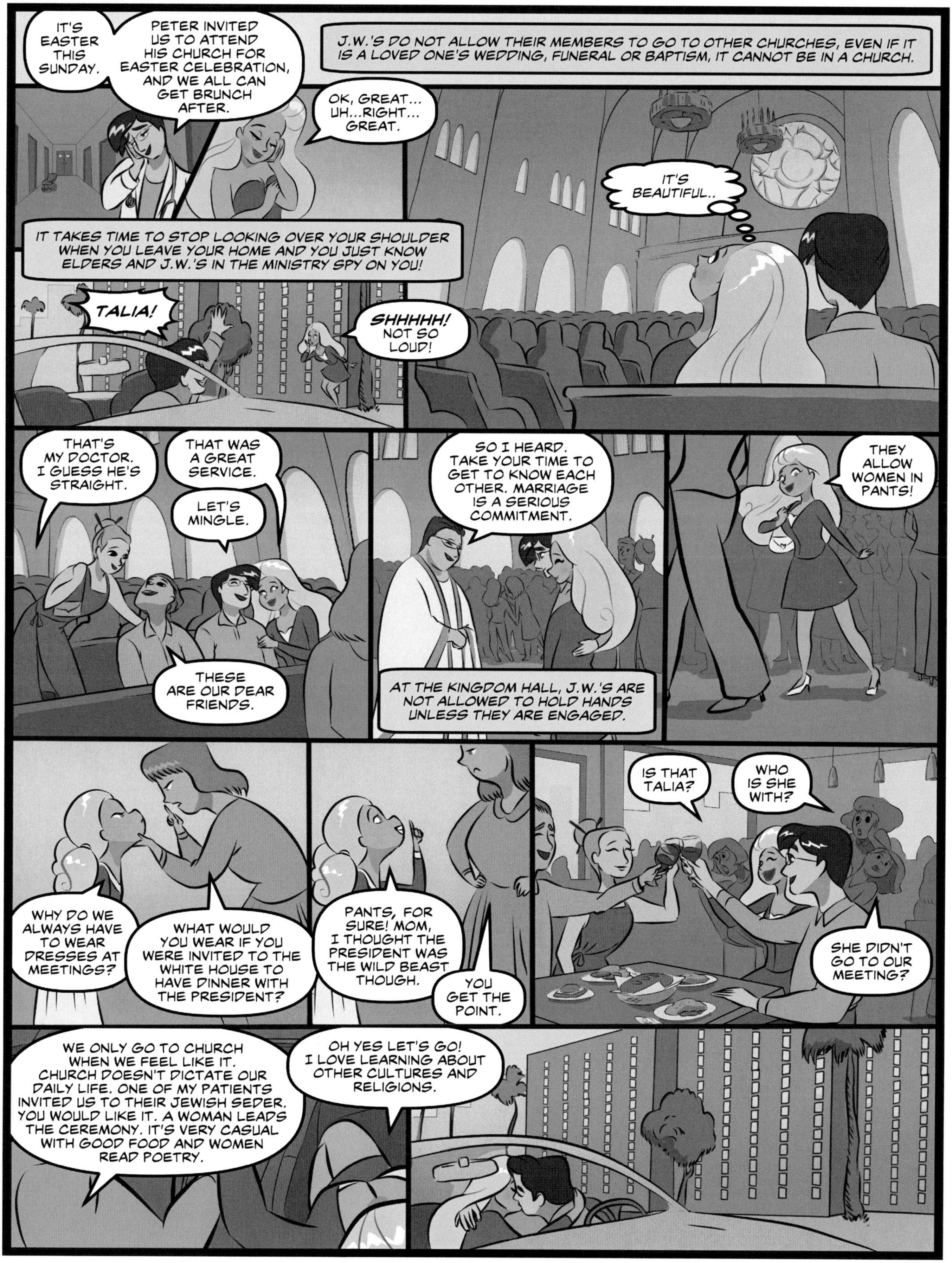

IT'S EASTER THIS SUNDAY.
PETER INVITED US TO ATTEND HIS CHURCH FOR EASTER CELEBRATION, AND WE ALL CAN GET BRUNCH AFTER.
J.W.'S DO NOT ALLOW THEIR MEMBERS TO GO TO OTHER CHURCHES, EVEN IF IT IS A LOVED ONE'S WEDDING, FUNERAL OR BAPTISM, IT CANNOT BE IN A CHURCH.
OK, GREAT... UH...RIGHT... GREAT.
IT TAKES TIME TO STOP LOOKING OVER YOUR SHOULDER WHEN YOU LEAVE YOUR HOME AND YOU JUST KNOW ELDERS AND J.W.'S IN THE MINISTRY SPY ON YOU!
TALIA!
SHHHHH! NOT SO LOUD!
IT'S BEAUTIFUL..
THAT'S MY DOCTOR. I GUESS HE'S STRAIGHT.
THAT WAS A GREAT SERVICE.
LET'S MINGLE.
THESE ARE OUR DEAR FRIENDS.
SO I HEARD. TAKE YOUR TIME TO GET TO KNOW EACH OTHER. MARRIAGE IS A SERIOUS COMMITMENT.
AT THE KINGDOM HALL, J.W.'S ARE NOT ALLOWED TO HOLD HANDS UNLESS THEY ARE ENGAGED.
THEY ALLOW WOMEN IN PANTS!
WHY DO WE ALWAYS HAVE TO WEAR DRESSES AT MEETINGS?
WHAT WOULD YOU WEAR IF YOU WERE INVITED TO THE WHITE HOUSE TO HAVE DINNER WITH THE PRESIDENT?
PANTS, FOR SURE! MOM, I THOUGHT THE PRESIDENT WAS THE WILD BEAST THOUGH.
YOU GET THE POINT.
IS THAT TALIA?
WHO IS SHE WITH?
SHE DIDN'T GO TO OUR MEETING?
WE ONLY GO TO CHURCH WHEN WE FEEL LIKE IT. CHURCH DOESN'T DICTATE OUR DAILY LIFE. ONE OF MY PATIENTS INVITED US TO THEIR JEWISH SEDER. YOU WOULD LIKE IT. A WOMAN LEADS THE CEREMONY. IT'S VERY CASUAL WITH GOOD FOOD AND WOMEN READ POETRY.
OH YES LET'S GO! I LOVE LEARNING ABOUT OTHER CULTURES AND RELIGIONS.

DAD

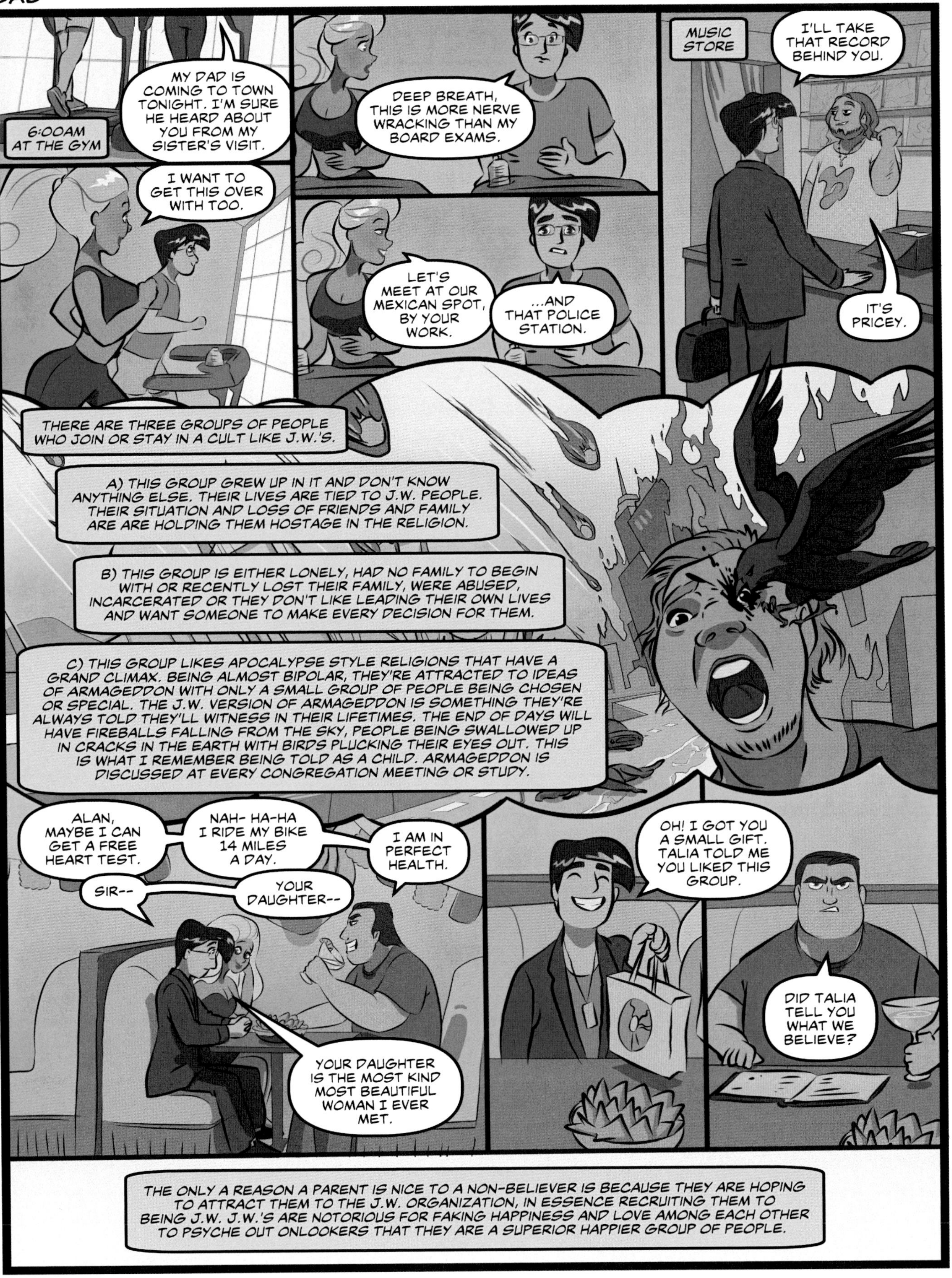
6:00AM AT THE GYM
MY DAD IS COMING TO TOWN TONIGHT. I'M SURE HE HEARD ABOUT YOU FROM MY SISTER'S VISIT.
DEEP BREATH, THIS IS MORE NERVE WRACKING THAN MY BOARD EXAMS.
I WANT TO GET THIS OVER WITH TOO.
LET'S MEET AT OUR MEXICAN SPOT, BY YOUR WORK.
...AND THAT POLICE STATION.
MUSIC STORE
I'LL TAKE THAT RECORD BEHIND YOU.
IT'S PRICEY.
THERE ARE THREE GROUPS OF PEOPLE WHO JOIN OR STAY IN A CULT LIKE J.W.'S.
A) THIS GROUP GREW UP IN IT AND DON'T KNOW ANYTHING ELSE. THEIR LIVES ARE TIED TO J.W. PEOPLE. THEIR SITUATION AND LOSS OF FRIENDS AND FAMILY ARE ARE HOLDING THEM HOSTAGE IN THE RELIGION.
B) THIS GROUP IS EITHER LONELY, HAD NO FAMILY TO BEGIN WITH OR RECENTLY LOST THEIR FAMILY, WERE ABUSED, INCARCERATED OR THEY DON'T LIKE LEADING THEIR OWN LIVES AND WANT SOMEONE TO MAKE EVERY DECISION FOR THEM.
C) THIS GROUP LIKES APOCALYPSE STYLE RELIGIONS THAT HAVE A GRAND CLIMAX. BEING ALMOST BIPOLAR, THEY'RE ATTRACTED TO IDEAS OF ARMAGEDDON WITH ONLY A SMALL GROUP OF PEOPLE BEING CHOSEN OR SPECIAL. THE J.W. VERSION OF ARMAGEDDON IS SOMETHING THEY'RE ALWAYS TOLD THEY'LL WITNESS IN THEIR LIFETIMES. THE END OF DAYS WILL HAVE FIREBALLS FALLING FROM THE SKY, PEOPLE BEING SWALLOWED UP IN CRACKS IN THE EARTH WITH BIRDS PLUCKING THEIR EYES OUT. THIS IS WHAT I REMEMBER BEING TOLD AS A CHILD. ARMAGEDDON IS DISCUSSED AT EVERY CONGREGATION MEETING OR STUDY.
ALAN, MAYBE I CAN GET A FREE HEART TEST.
NAH- HA-HA I RIDE MY BIKE 14 MILES A DAY.
I AM IN PERFECT HEALTH.
SIR--
YOUR DAUGHTER--
YOUR DAUGHTER IS THE MOST KIND MOST BEAUTIFUL WOMAN I EVER MET.
OH! I GOT YOU A SMALL GIFT. TALIA TOLD ME YOU LIKED THIS GROUP.
DID TALIA TELL YOU WHAT WE BELIEVE?
THE ONLY A REASON A PARENT IS NICE TO A NON-BELIEVER IS BECAUSE THEY ARE HOPING TO ATTRACT THEM TO THE J.W. ORGANIZATION, IN ESSENCE RECRUITING THEM TO BEING J.W. J.W.'S ARE NOTORIOUS FOR FAKING HAPPINESS AND LOVE AMONG EACH OTHER TO PSYCHE OUT ONLOOKERS THAT THEY ARE A SUPERIOR HAPPIER GROUP OF PEOPLE.

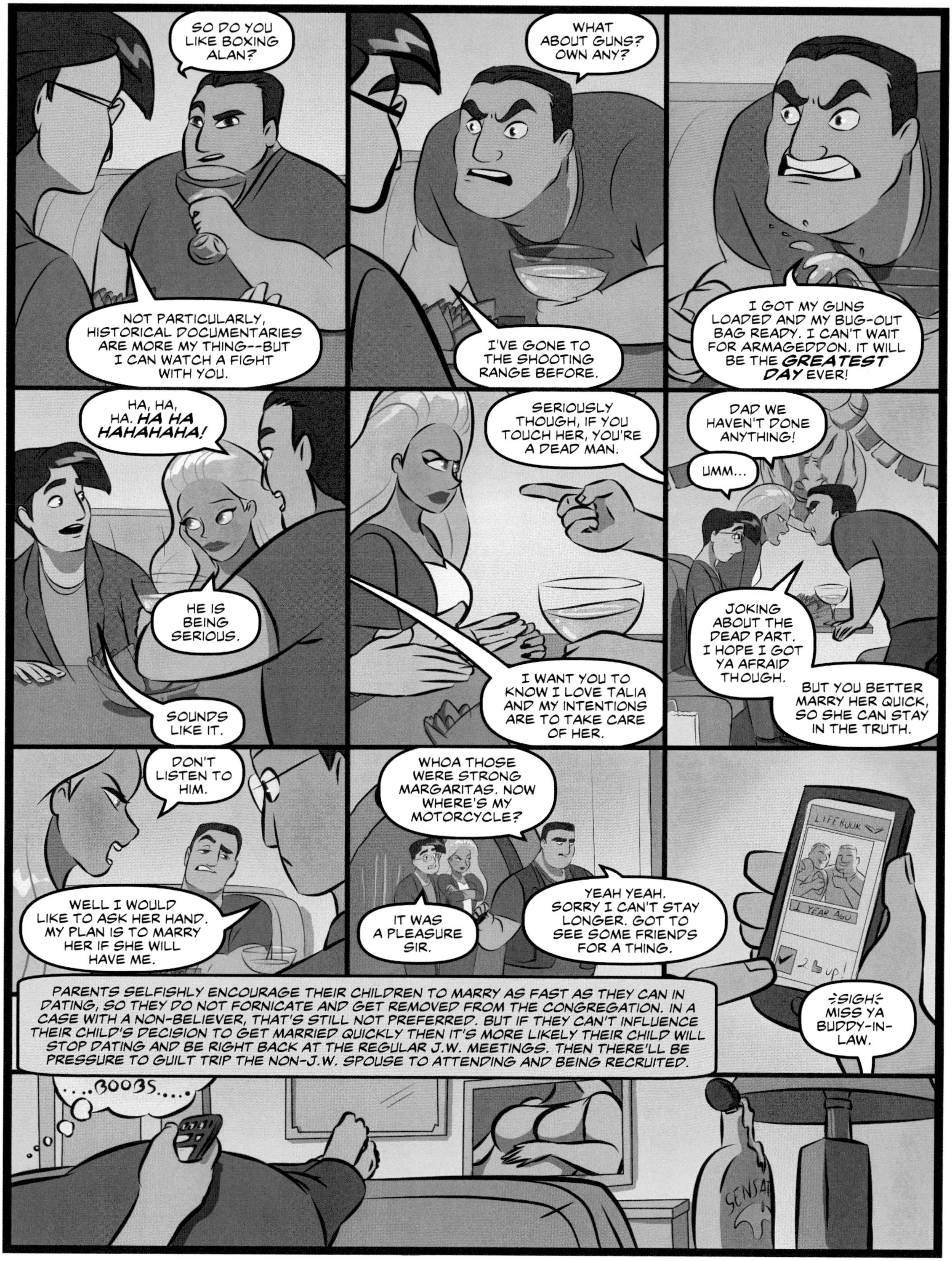
SO DO YOU LIKE BOXING ALAN?
NOT PARTICULARLY, HISTORICAL DOCUMENTARIES ARE MORE MY THING--BUT I CAN WATCH A FIGHT WITH YOU.
WHAT ABOUT GUNS? OWN ANY?
I'VE GONE TO THE SHOOTING RANGE BEFORE.
I GOT MY GUNS LOADED AND MY BUG-OUT BAG READY. I CAN'T WAIT FOR ARMAGEDDON. IT WILL BE THE ***GREATEST DAY*** EVER!
HA, HA, HA. ***HA HA HAHAHAHA!***
HE IS BEING SERIOUS.
SOUNDS LIKE IT.
SERIOUSLY THOUGH, IF YOU TOUCH HER, YOU'RE A DEAD MAN.
I WANT YOU TO KNOW I LOVE TALIA AND MY INTENTIONS ARE TO TAKE CARE OF HER.
DAD WE HAVEN'T DONE ANYTHING!
UMM...
JOKING ABOUT THE DEAD PART. I HOPE I GOT YA AFRAID THOUGH.
BUT YOU BETTER MARRY HER QUICK, SO SHE CAN STAY IN THE TRUTH.
DON'T LISTEN TO HIM.
WELL I WOULD LIKE TO ASK HER HAND. MY PLAN IS TO MARRY HER IF SHE WILL HAVE ME.
WHOA THOSE WERE STRONG MARGARITAS. NOW WHERE'S MY MOTORCYCLE?
IT WAS A PLEASURE SIR.
YEAH YEAH. SORRY I CAN'T STAY LONGER. GOT TO SEE SOME FRIENDS FOR A THING.
LIFEBOOK
1 YEAR AGO
2 up!
SIGH MISS YA BUDDY-IN-LAW.
PARENTS SELFISHLY ENCOURAGE THEIR CHILDREN TO MARRY AS FAST AS THEY CAN IN DATING, SO THEY DO NOT FORNICATE AND GET REMOVED FROM THE CONGREGATION. IN A CASE WITH A NON-BELIEVER, THAT'S STILL NOT PREFERRED. BUT IF THEY CAN'T INFLUENCE THEIR CHILD'S DECISION TO GET MARRIED QUICKLY THEN IT'S MORE LIKELY THEIR CHILD WILL STOP DATING AND BE RIGHT BACK AT THE REGULAR J.W. MEETINGS. THEN THERE'LL BE PRESSURE TO GUILT TRIP THE NON-J.W. SPOUSE TO ATTENDING AND BEING RECRUITED.
...BOOBS.....
SENSAT

DOCTOR'S OFFICE

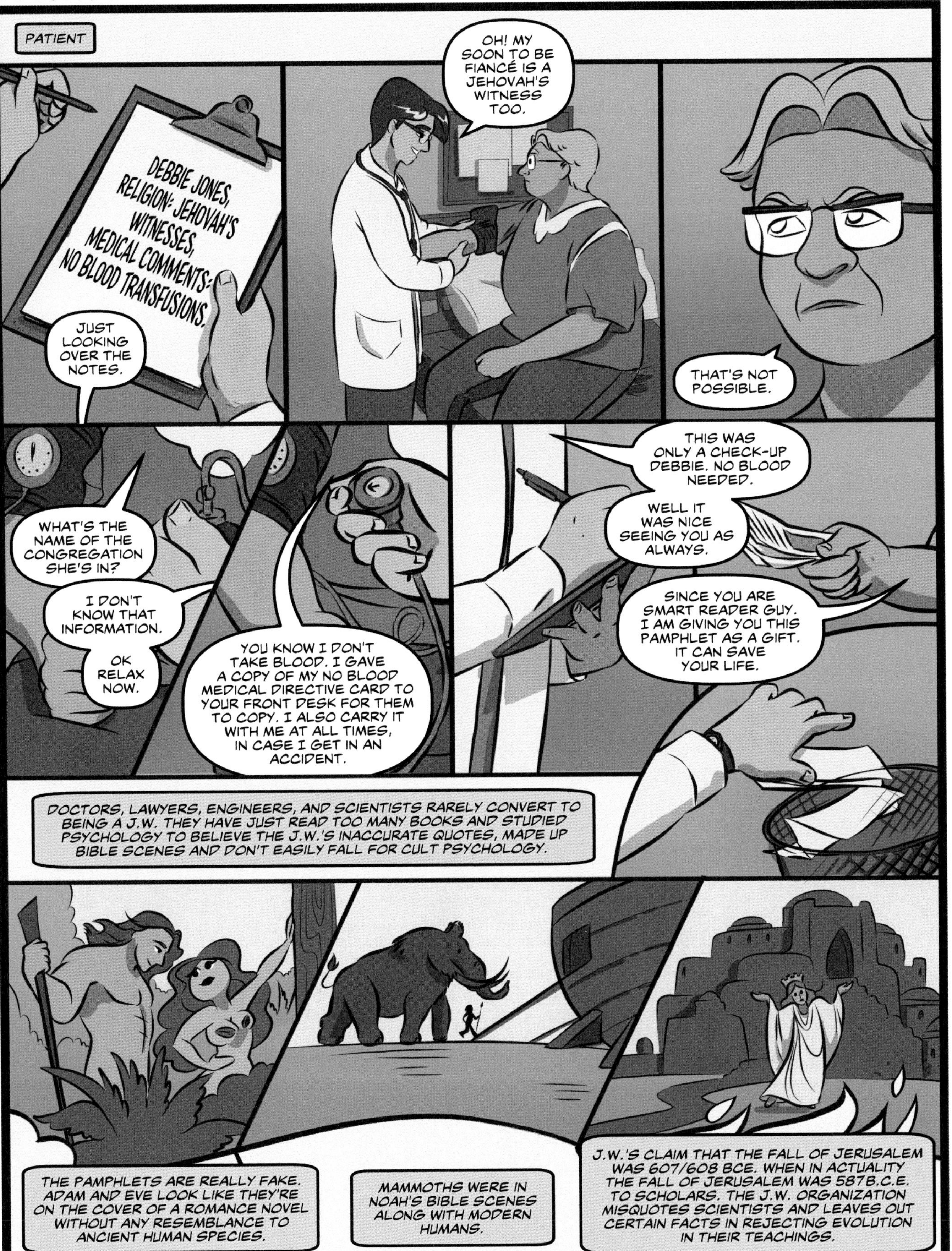
PATIENT
DEBBIE JONES, RELIGION: JEHOVAH'S WITNESSES, MEDICAL COMMENTS: NO BLOOD TRANSFUSIONS.
JUST LOOKING OVER THE NOTES.
OH! MY SOON TO BE FIANCÉ IS A JEHOVAH'S WITNESS TOO.
THAT'S NOT POSSIBLE.
WHAT'S THE NAME OF THE CONGREGATION SHE'S IN?
I DON'T KNOW THAT INFORMATION.
OK RELAX NOW.
YOU KNOW I DON'T TAKE BLOOD. I GAVE A COPY OF MY NO BLOOD MEDICAL DIRECTIVE CARD TO YOUR FRONT DESK FOR THEM TO COPY. I ALSO CARRY IT WITH ME AT ALL TIMES, IN CASE I GET IN AN ACCIDENT.
THIS WAS ONLY A CHECK-UP DEBBIE. NO BLOOD NEEDED.
WELL IT WAS NICE SEEING YOU AS ALWAYS.
SINCE YOU ARE SMART READER GUY. I AM GIVING YOU THIS PAMPHLET AS A GIFT. IT CAN SAVE YOUR LIFE.
DOCTORS, LAWYERS, ENGINEERS, AND SCIENTISTS RARELY CONVERT TO BEING A J.W. THEY HAVE JUST READ TOO MANY BOOKS AND STUDIED PSYCHOLOGY TO BELIEVE THE J.W.'S INACCURATE QUOTES, MADE UP BIBLE SCENES AND DON'T EASILY FALL FOR CULT PSYCHOLOGY.
THE PAMPHLETS ARE REALLY FAKE. ADAM AND EVE LOOK LIKE THEY'RE ON THE COVER OF A ROMANCE NOVEL WITHOUT ANY RESEMBLANCE TO ANCIENT HUMAN SPECIES.
MAMMOTHS WERE IN NOAH'S BIBLE SCENES ALONG WITH MODERN HUMANS.
J.W.'S CLAIM THAT THE FALL OF JERUSALEM WAS 607/608 BCE. WHEN IN ACTUALITY THE FALL OF JERUSALEM WAS 587B.C.E. TO SCHOLARS. THE J.W. ORGANIZATION MISQUOTES SCIENTISTS AND LEAVES OUT CERTAIN FACTS IN REJECTING EVOLUTION IN THEIR TEACHINGS.

AS A J.W. YOU ARE NOT TAUGHT TO CARE FOR THE EARTH, BECAUSE IT'S ALL GOING TO BE DESTROYED IN ARMAGEDDON. YOU ARE ALSO NOT ALLOWED TO VOLUNTEER FOR OTHER CAUSES BECAUSE IT TAKES AWAY FROM J.W RECRUITING TIME AND YOU CANNOT SIGN PETITIONS, BECAUSE THAT IS GETTING INVOLVED IN SATAN'S POLITICAL SYSTEM. EVEN IF THE PETITIONS INVOLVE CHILDREN, ANIMALS OR THE ENVIRONMENT.

PLEASE SIGN TO HELP FREE CAGED ANIMALS.

AGAINST MY RELIGION!

MOMMY, CAN I TAKE THESE BOTTLES TO THE SCHOOL DRIVE INSTEAD?

NO, JEHOVAH IS GOING TO SOLVE EARTH'S PROBLEMS.

CAN YOU BELIEVE IT? SATAN IS FULL OF TRICKS.

SAVE THE ANIMALS

HELP the HOMELESS

J.W.'S DON'T HELP THE POOR, HUNGRY OR HOMELESS BECAUSE PARADISE IS GOING TO SOLVE EARTH'S PROBLEMS, AND THEY NEED TO WORK ON THEIR AFTER LIFE, NOT THE CURRENT LIFE. THE REAL REASON THE J.W. ORGANIZATION DOESN'T WANT YOU DOING WORK FOR OTHER CAUSES IS THAT IT TAKES AWAY TIME AND MONEY THAT COULD HAVE BEEN USED FOR THE J.W. ORGANIZATION'S EFFORTS.

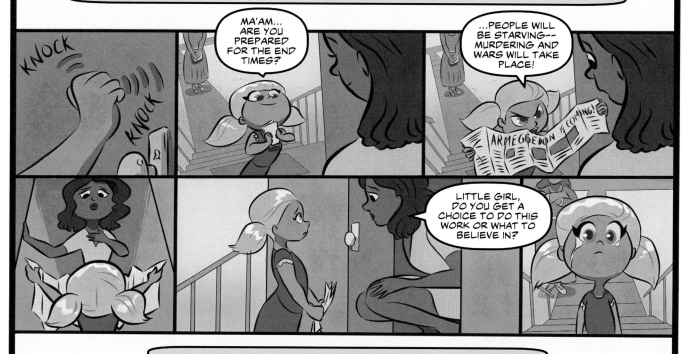

KNOCK

KNOCK

MA'AM... ARE YOU PREPARED FOR THE END TIMES?

...PEOPLE WILL BE STARVING-- MURDERING AND WARS WILL TAKE PLACE!

ARMEGGEDON IS COMING!

LITTLE GIRL, DO YOU GET A CHOICE TO DO THIS WORK OR WHAT TO BELIEVE IN?

WHEN I WAS A LITTLE GIRL THE PRESENTATIONS WERE TO SCARE THE PEOPLE WHO ANSWERED THE DOOR. ALSO CHILDREN WERE USED AND ARE STILL USED TO GET LITERATURE IN THE HOMEOWNER'S HANDS. CHILDREN HAVE TO MEMORIZE LINES, PRESENTATIONS AND SCRIPTURES.

SISTER VISIT WITH TIMMY

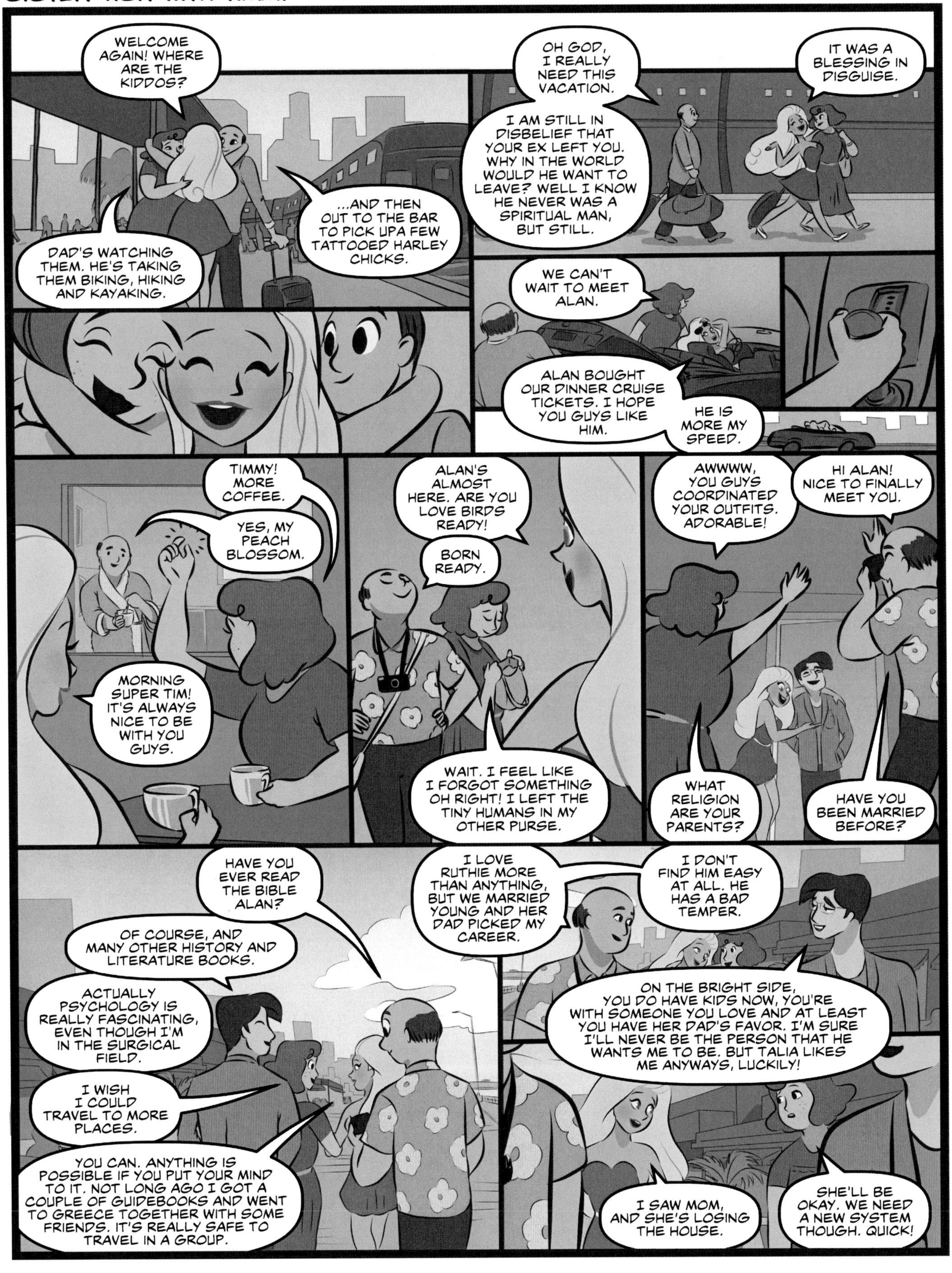

WELCOME AGAIN! WHERE ARE THE KIDDOS?
DAD'S WATCHING THEM. HE'S TAKING THEM BIKING, HIKING AND KAYAKING.
...AND THEN OUT TO THE BAR TO PICK UPA FEW TATTOOED HARLEY CHICKS.
OH GOD, I REALLY NEED THIS VACATION.
I AM STILL IN DISBELIEF THAT YOUR EX LEFT YOU. WHY IN THE WORLD WOULD HE WANT TO LEAVE? WELL I KNOW HE NEVER WAS A SPIRITUAL MAN, BUT STILL.
IT WAS A BLESSING IN DISGUISE.
WE CAN'T WAIT TO MEET ALAN.
ALAN BOUGHT OUR DINNER CRUISE TICKETS. I HOPE YOU GUYS LIKE HIM.
HE IS MORE MY SPEED.
TIMMY! MORE COFFEE.
YES, MY PEACH BLOSSOM.
MORNING SUPER TIM! IT'S ALWAYS NICE TO BE WITH YOU GUYS.
ALAN'S ALMOST HERE. ARE YOU LOVE BIRDS READY!
BORN READY.
WAIT. I FEEL LIKE I FORGOT SOMETHING OH RIGHT! I LEFT THE TINY HUMANS IN MY OTHER PURSE.
AWWWW, YOU GUYS COORDINATED YOUR OUTFITS. ADORABLE!
HI ALAN! NICE TO FINALLY MEET YOU.
WHAT RELIGION ARE YOUR PARENTS?
HAVE YOU BEEN MARRIED BEFORE?
HAVE YOU EVER READ THE BIBLE ALAN?
OF COURSE, AND MANY OTHER HISTORY AND LITERATURE BOOKS.
ACTUALLY PSYCHOLOGY IS REALLY FASCINATING, EVEN THOUGH I'M IN THE SURGICAL FIELD.
I WISH I COULD TRAVEL TO MORE PLACES.
YOU CAN. ANYTHING IS POSSIBLE IF YOU PUT YOUR MIND TO IT. NOT LONG AGO I GOT A COUPLE OF GUIDEBOOKS AND WENT TO GREECE TOGETHER WITH SOME FRIENDS. IT'S REALLY SAFE TO TRAVEL IN A GROUP.
I LOVE RUTHIE MORE THAN ANYTHING, BUT WE MARRIED YOUNG AND HER DAD PICKED MY CAREER.
I DON'T FIND HIM EASY AT ALL. HE HAS A BAD TEMPER.
ON THE BRIGHT SIDE, YOU DO HAVE KIDS NOW, YOU'RE WITH SOMEONE YOU LOVE AND AT LEAST YOU HAVE HER DAD'S FAVOR. I'M SURE I'LL NEVER BE THE PERSON THAT HE WANTS ME TO BE. BUT TALIA LIKES ME ANYWAYS, LUCKILY!
I SAW MOM, AND SHE'S LOSING THE HOUSE.
SHE'LL BE OKAY. WE NEED A NEW SYSTEM THOUGH. QUICK!

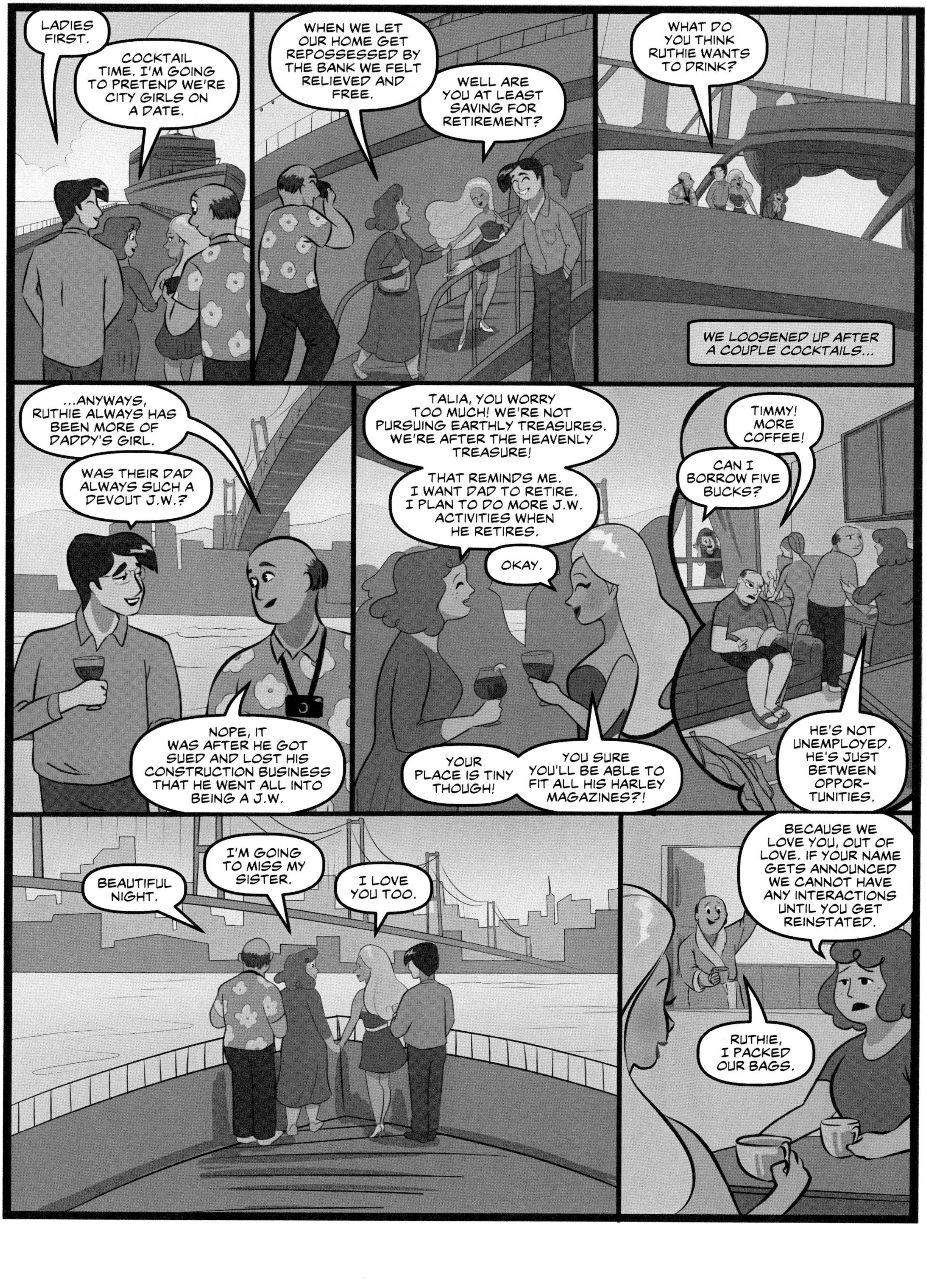
LADIES FIRST.
COCKTAIL TIME. I'M GOING TO PRETEND WE'RE CITY GIRLS ON A DATE.
WHEN WE LET OUR HOME GET REPOSSESSED BY THE BANK WE FELT RELIEVED AND FREE.
WELL ARE YOU AT LEAST SAVING FOR RETIREMENT?
WHAT DO YOU THINK RUTHIE WANTS TO DRINK?
WE LOOSENED UP AFTER A COUPLE COCKTAILS...
...ANYWAYS, RUTHIE ALWAYS HAS BEEN MORE OF DADDY'S GIRL.
WAS THEIR DAD ALWAYS SUCH A DEVOUT J.W.?
NOPE, IT WAS AFTER HE GOT SUED AND LOST HIS CONSTRUCTION BUSINESS THAT HE WENT ALL INTO BEING A J.W.
TALIA, YOU WORRY TOO MUCH! WE'RE NOT PURSUING EARTHLY TREASURES. WE'RE AFTER THE HEAVENLY TREASURE!
THAT REMINDS ME. I WANT DAD TO RETIRE. I PLAN TO DO MORE J.W. ACTIVITIES WHEN HE RETIRES.
OKAY.
YOUR PLACE IS TINY THOUGH!
YOU SURE YOU'LL BE ABLE TO FIT ALL HIS HARLEY MAGAZINES?!
TIMMY! MORE COFFEE!
CAN I BORROW FIVE BUCKS?
HE'S NOT UNEMPLOYED. HE'S JUST BETWEEN OPPOR-TUNITIES.
BEAUTIFUL NIGHT.
I'M GOING TO MISS MY SISTER.
I LOVE YOU TOO.
BECAUSE WE LOVE YOU, OUT OF LOVE. IF YOUR NAME GETS ANNOUNCED WE CANNOT HAVE ANY INTERACTIONS UNTIL YOU GET REINSTATED.
RUTHIE, I PACKED OUR BAGS.

THE HUNT – J.W. HARASSMENT

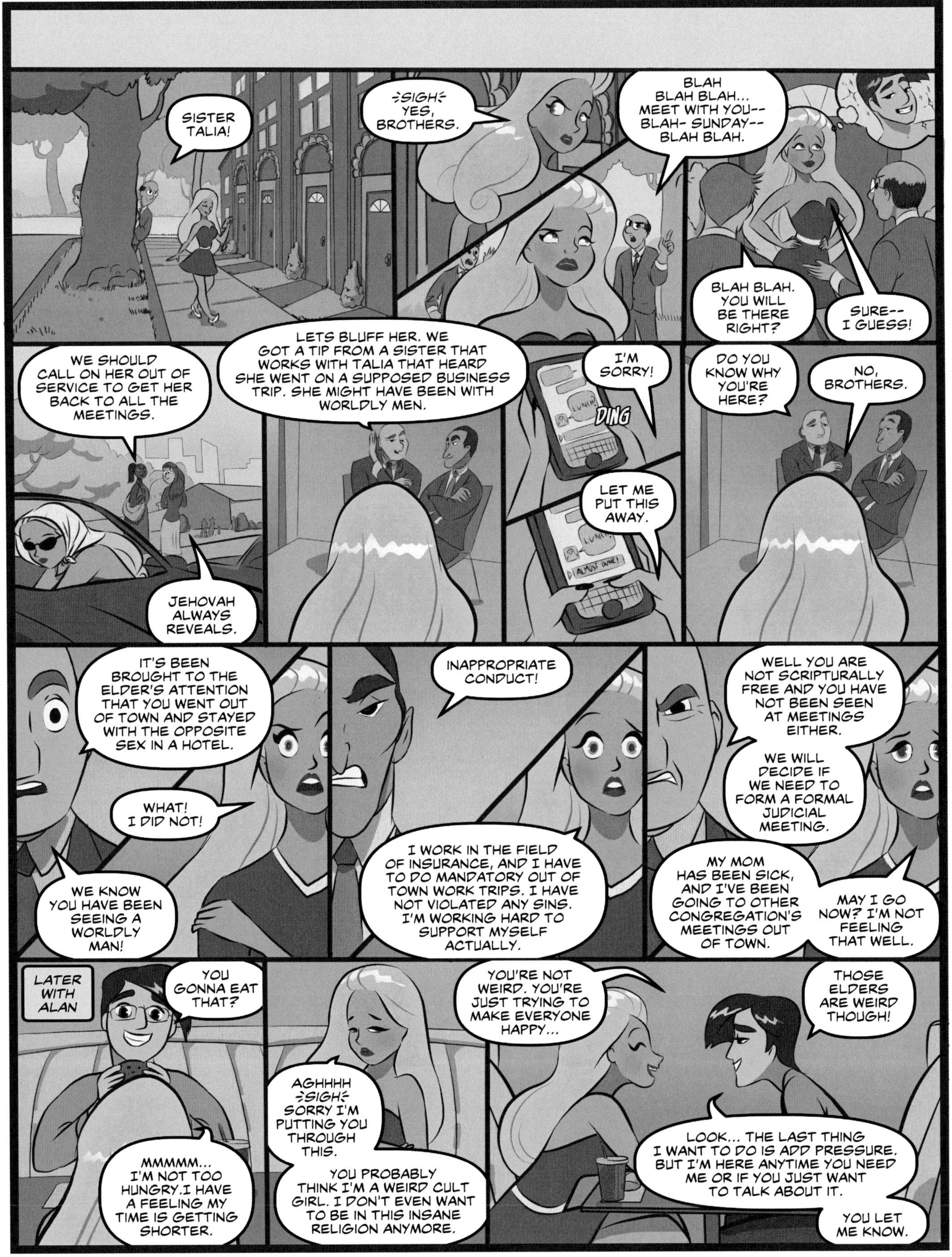
SISTER TALIA!
⫶SIGH⫶ YES, BROTHERS.
BLAH BLAH BLAH... MEET WITH YOU-- BLAH- SUNDAY-- BLAH BLAH.
BLAH BLAH. YOU WILL BE THERE RIGHT?
SURE-- I GUESS!
WE SHOULD CALL ON HER OUT OF SERVICE TO GET HER BACK TO ALL THE MEETINGS.
JEHOVAH ALWAYS REVEALS.
LETS BLUFF HER. WE GOT A TIP FROM A SISTER THAT WORKS WITH TALIA THAT HEARD SHE WENT ON A SUPPOSED BUSINESS TRIP. SHE MIGHT HAVE BEEN WITH WORLDLY MEN.
I'M SORRY!
LUNCH?
DING
LET ME PUT THIS AWAY.
ALMOST DONE!
DO YOU KNOW WHY YOU'RE HERE?
NO, BROTHERS.
IT'S BEEN BROUGHT TO THE ELDER'S ATTENTION THAT YOU WENT OUT OF TOWN AND STAYED WITH THE OPPOSITE SEX IN A HOTEL.
WHAT! I DID NOT!
WE KNOW YOU HAVE BEEN SEEING A WORLDLY MAN!
INAPPROPRIATE CONDUCT!
I WORK IN THE FIELD OF INSURANCE, AND I HAVE TO DO MANDATORY OUT OF TOWN WORK TRIPS. I HAVE NOT VIOLATED ANY SINS. I'M WORKING HARD TO SUPPORT MYSELF ACTUALLY.
WELL YOU ARE NOT SCRIPTURALLY FREE AND YOU HAVE NOT BEEN SEEN AT MEETINGS EITHER.
WE WILL DECIDE IF WE NEED TO FORM A FORMAL JUDICIAL MEETING.
MY MOM HAS BEEN SICK, AND I'VE BEEN GOING TO OTHER CONGREGATION'S MEETINGS OUT OF TOWN.
MAY I GO NOW? I'M NOT FEELING THAT WELL.
LATER WITH ALAN
YOU GONNA EAT THAT?
MMMMM... I'M NOT TOO HUNGRY. I HAVE A FEELING MY TIME IS GETTING SHORTER.
AGHHHH ⫶SIGH⫶ SORRY I'M PUTTING YOU THROUGH THIS.
YOU PROBABLY THINK I'M A WEIRD CULT GIRL. I DON'T EVEN WANT TO BE IN THIS INSANE RELIGION ANYMORE.
YOU'RE NOT WEIRD. YOU'RE JUST TRYING TO MAKE EVERYONE HAPPY...
THOSE ELDERS ARE WEIRD THOUGH!
LOOK... THE LAST THING I WANT TO DO IS ADD PRESSURE. BUT I'M HERE ANYTIME YOU NEED ME OR IF YOU JUST WANT TO TALK ABOUT IT.
YOU LET ME KNOW.

DOMINO EFFECT

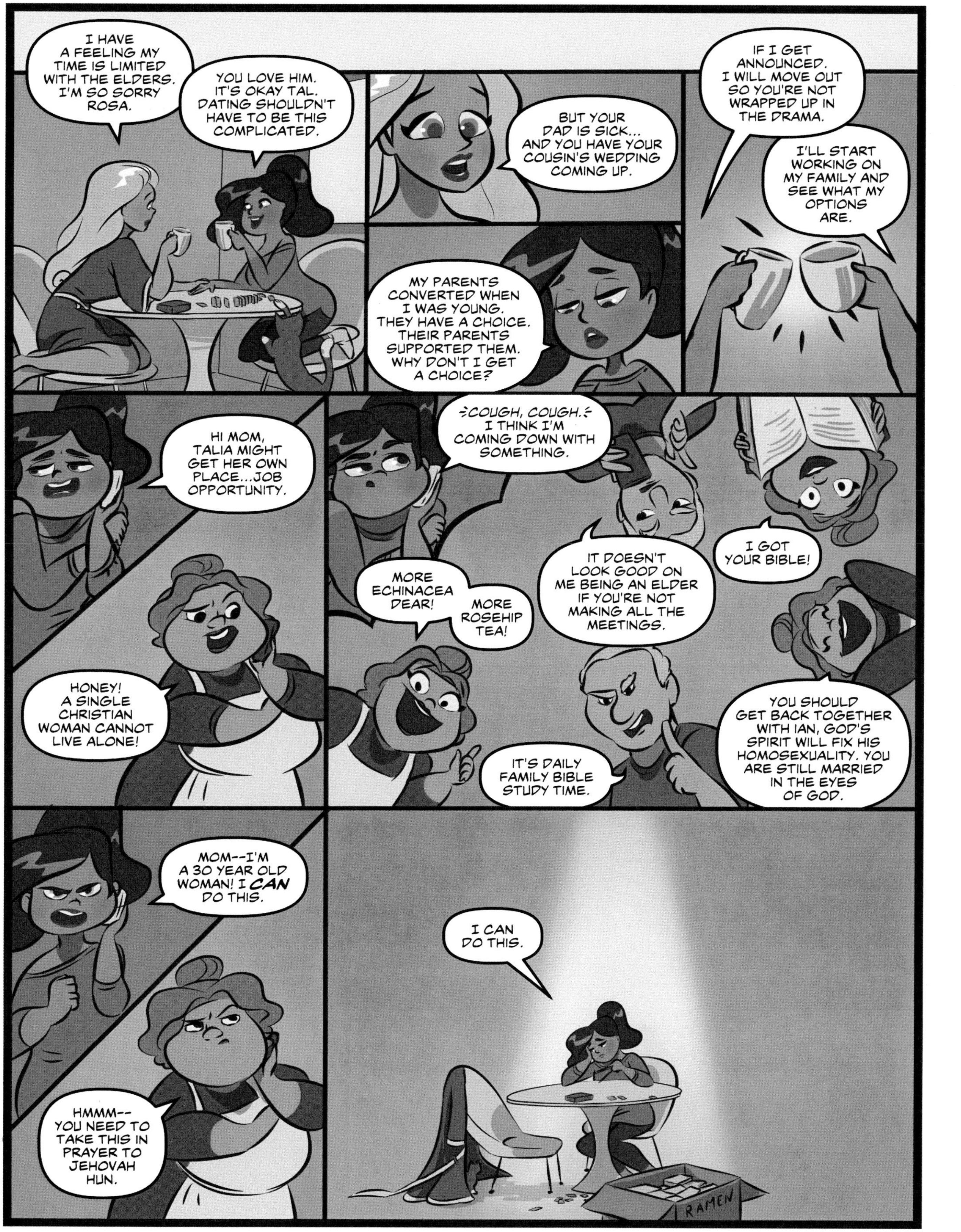

I HAVE A FEELING MY TIME IS LIMITED WITH THE ELDERS. I'M SO SORRY ROSA.
YOU LOVE HIM. IT'S OKAY TAL. DATING SHOULDN'T HAVE TO BE THIS COMPLICATED.
BUT YOUR DAD IS SICK... AND YOU HAVE YOUR COUSIN'S WEDDING COMING UP.
MY PARENTS CONVERTED WHEN I WAS YOUNG. THEY HAVE A CHOICE. THEIR PARENTS SUPPORTED THEM. WHY DON'T I GET A CHOICE?
IF I GET ANNOUNCED. I WILL MOVE OUT SO YOU'RE NOT WRAPPED UP IN THE DRAMA.
I'LL START WORKING ON MY FAMILY AND SEE WHAT MY OPTIONS ARE.
HI MOM, TALIA MIGHT GET HER OWN PLACE...JOB OPPORTUNITY.
HONEY! A SINGLE CHRISTIAN WOMAN CANNOT LIVE ALONE!
COUGH, COUGH. I THINK I'M COMING DOWN WITH SOMETHING.
IT DOESN'T LOOK GOOD ON ME BEING AN ELDER IF YOU'RE NOT MAKING ALL THE MEETINGS.
I GOT YOUR BIBLE!
MORE ECHINACEA DEAR!
MORE ROSEHIP TEA!
IT'S DAILY FAMILY BIBLE STUDY TIME.
YOU SHOULD GET BACK TOGETHER WITH IAN, GOD'S SPIRIT WILL FIX HIS HOMOSEXUALITY. YOU ARE STILL MARRIED IN THE EYES OF GOD.
MOM--I'M A 30 YEAR OLD WOMAN! I CAN DO THIS.
HMMM--YOU NEED TO TAKE THIS IN PRAYER TO JEHOVAH HUN.
I CAN DO THIS.
RAMEN

FURNITURE SHOPPING

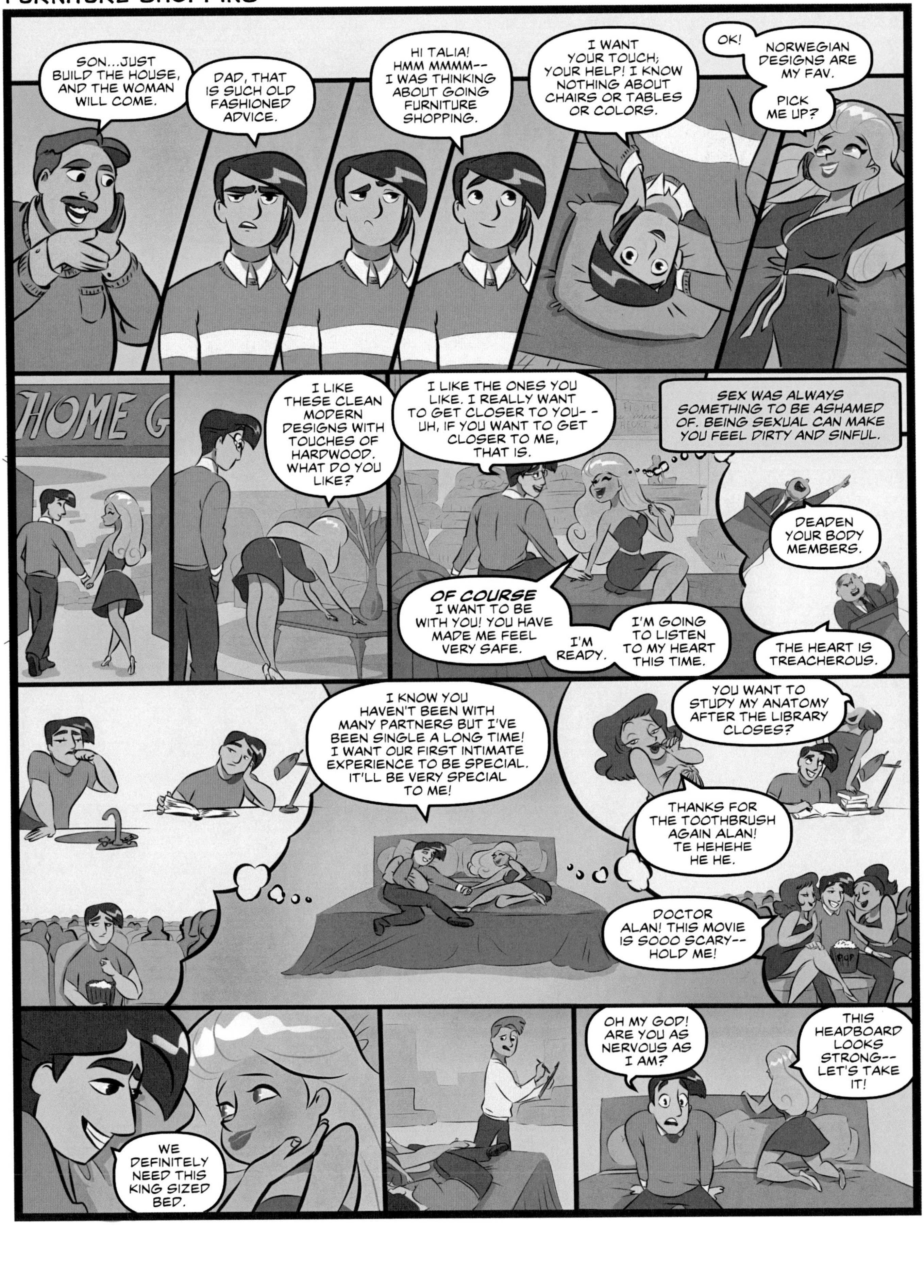

SON...JUST BUILD THE HOUSE, AND THE WOMAN WILL COME.
DAD, THAT IS SUCH OLD FASHIONED ADVICE.
HI TALIA! HMM MMMM-- I WAS THINKING ABOUT GOING FURNITURE SHOPPING.
I WANT YOUR TOUCH; YOUR HELP! I KNOW NOTHING ABOUT CHAIRS OR TABLES OR COLORS.
OK!
NORWEGIAN DESIGNS ARE MY FAV.
PICK ME UP?
HOME G
I LIKE THESE CLEAN MODERN DESIGNS WITH TOUCHES OF HARDWOOD. WHAT DO YOU LIKE?
I LIKE THE ONES YOU LIKE. I REALLY WANT TO GET CLOSER TO YOU-- UH, IF YOU WANT TO GET CLOSER TO ME, THAT IS.
SEX WAS ALWAYS SOMETHING TO BE ASHAMED OF. BEING SEXUAL CAN MAKE YOU FEEL DIRTY AND SINFUL.
DEADEN YOUR BODY MEMBERS.
OF COURSE I WANT TO BE WITH YOU! YOU HAVE MADE ME FEEL VERY SAFE.
I'M READY.
I'M GOING TO LISTEN TO MY HEART THIS TIME.
THE HEART IS TREACHEROUS.
I KNOW YOU HAVEN'T BEEN WITH MANY PARTNERS BUT I'VE BEEN SINGLE A LONG TIME! I WANT OUR FIRST INTIMATE EXPERIENCE TO BE SPECIAL. IT'LL BE VERY SPECIAL TO ME!
YOU WANT TO STUDY MY ANATOMY AFTER THE LIBRARY CLOSES?
THANKS FOR THE TOOTHBRUSH AGAIN ALAN! TE HEHEHE HE HE.
DOCTOR ALAN! THIS MOVIE IS SOOO SCARY-- HOLD ME!
POP
WE DEFINITELY NEED THIS KING SIZED BED.
OH MY GOD! ARE YOU AS NERVOUS AS I AM?
THIS HEADBOARD LOOKS STRONG-- LET'S TAKE IT!

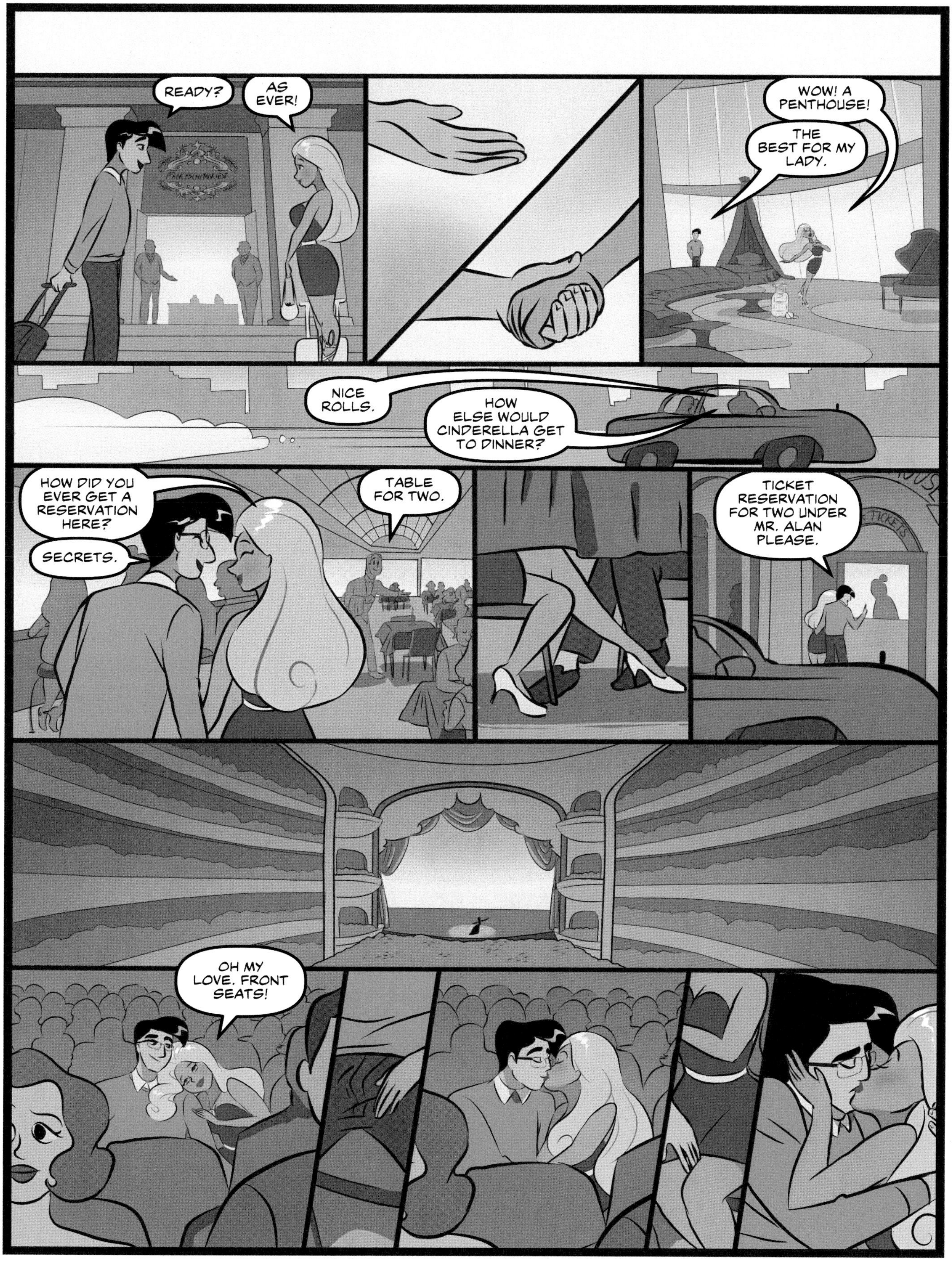
READY?
AS EVER!
FANCYSCHMANCY
WOW! A PENTHOUSE!
THE BEST FOR MY LADY.
NICE ROLLS.
HOW ELSE WOULD CINDERELLA GET TO DINNER?
HOW DID YOU EVER GET A RESERVATION HERE?
SECRETS.
TABLE FOR TWO.
TICKET RESERVATION FOR TWO UNDER MR. ALAN PLEASE.
TICKETS
OH MY LOVE. FRONT SEATS!

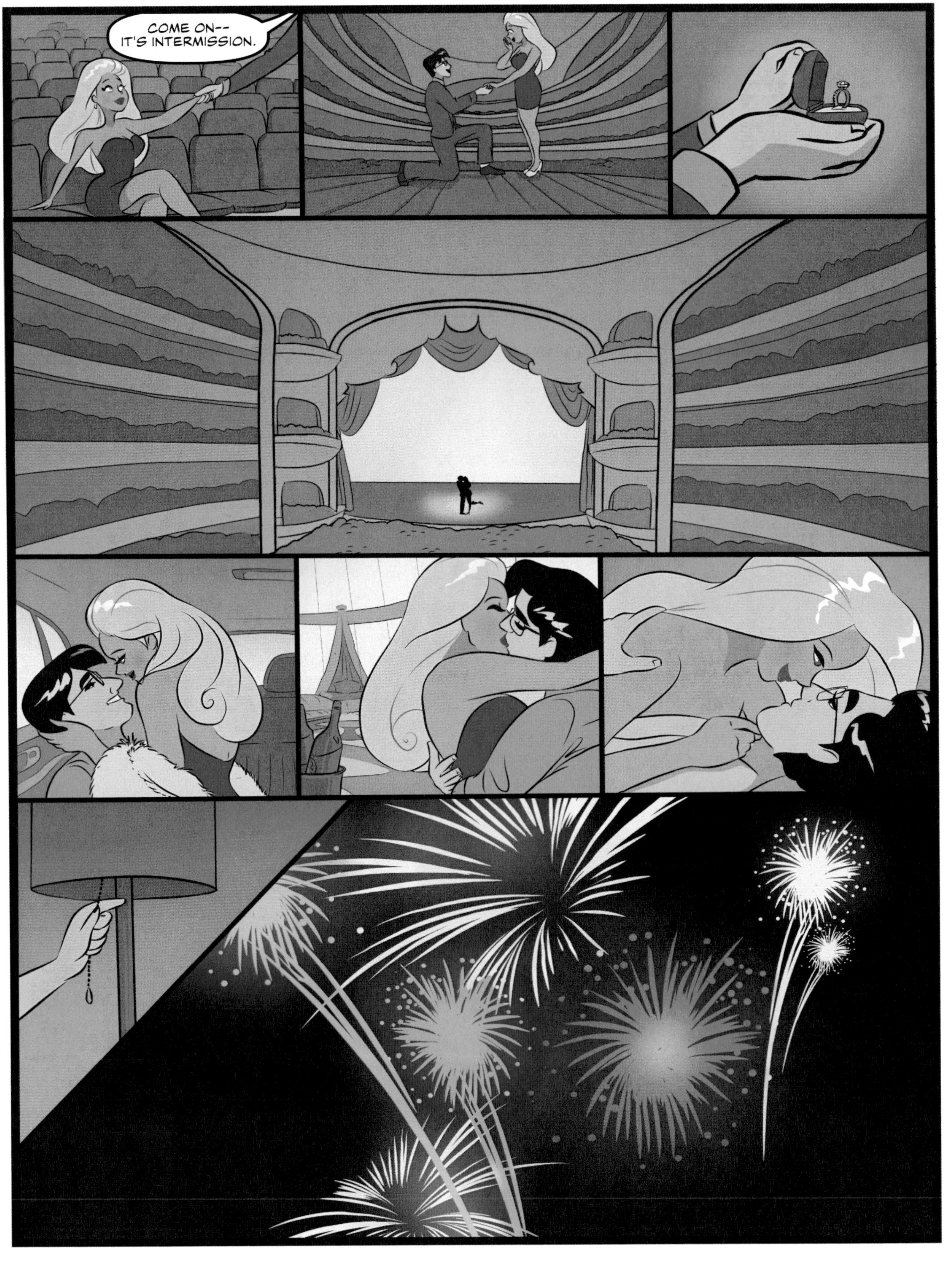
COME ON--
IT'S INTERMISSION.

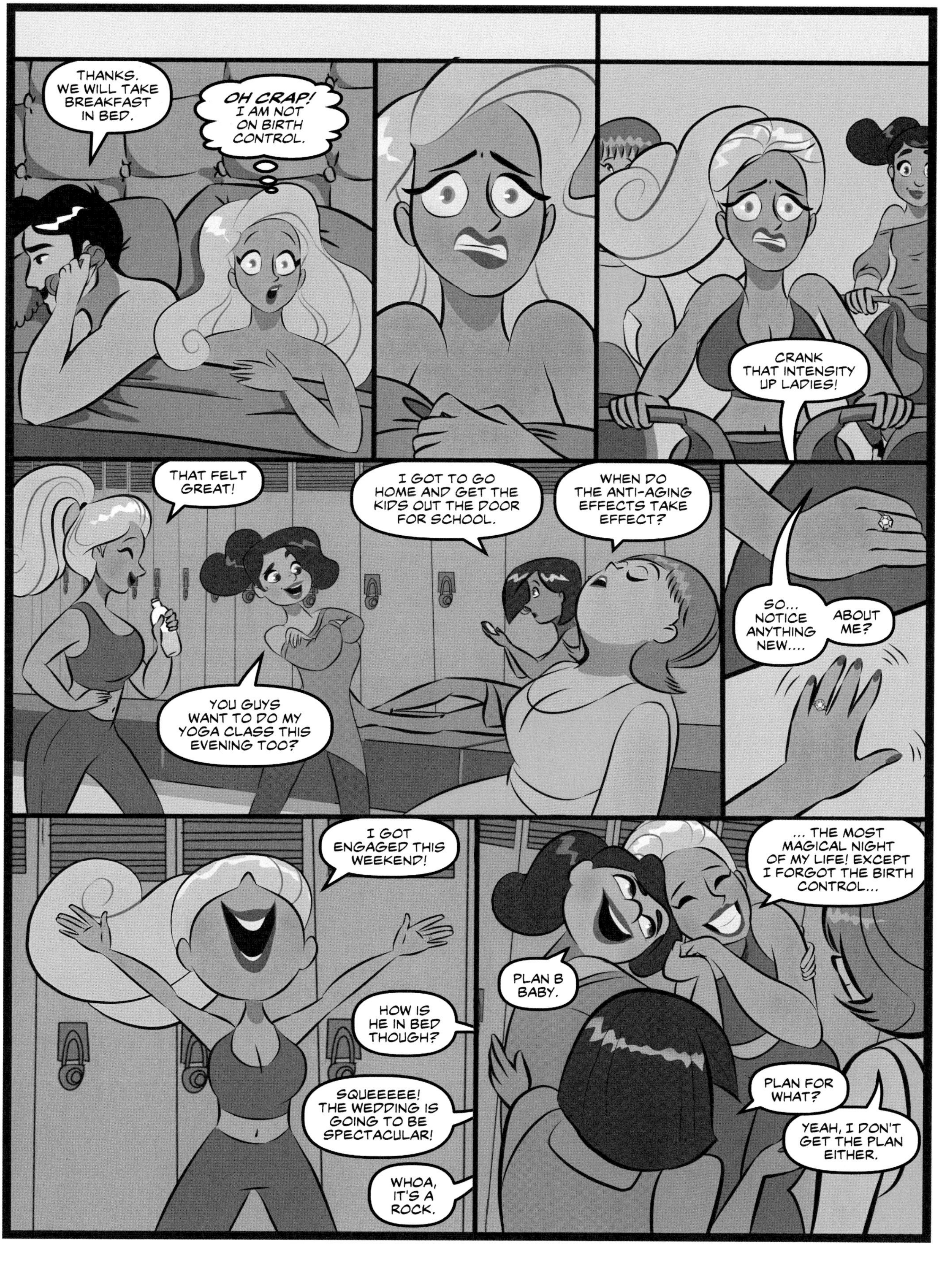
THANKS. WE WILL TAKE BREAKFAST IN BED.
OH CRAP! I AM NOT ON BIRTH CONTROL.
CRANK THAT INTENSITY UP LADIES!
THAT FELT GREAT!
I GOT TO GO HOME AND GET THE KIDS OUT THE DOOR FOR SCHOOL.
WHEN DO THE ANTI-AGING EFFECTS TAKE EFFECT?
YOU GUYS WANT TO DO MY YOGA CLASS THIS EVENING TOO?
SO... NOTICE ANYTHING NEW....
ABOUT ME?
I GOT ENGAGED THIS WEEKEND!
HOW IS HE IN BED THOUGH?
SQUEEEEE! THE WEDDING IS GOING TO BE SPECTACULAR!
WHOA, IT'S A ROCK.
... THE MOST MAGICAL NIGHT OF MY LIFE! EXCEPT I FORGOT THE BIRTH CONTROL...
PLAN B BABY.
PLAN FOR WHAT?
YEAH, I DON'T GET THE PLAN EITHER.

PLAN B

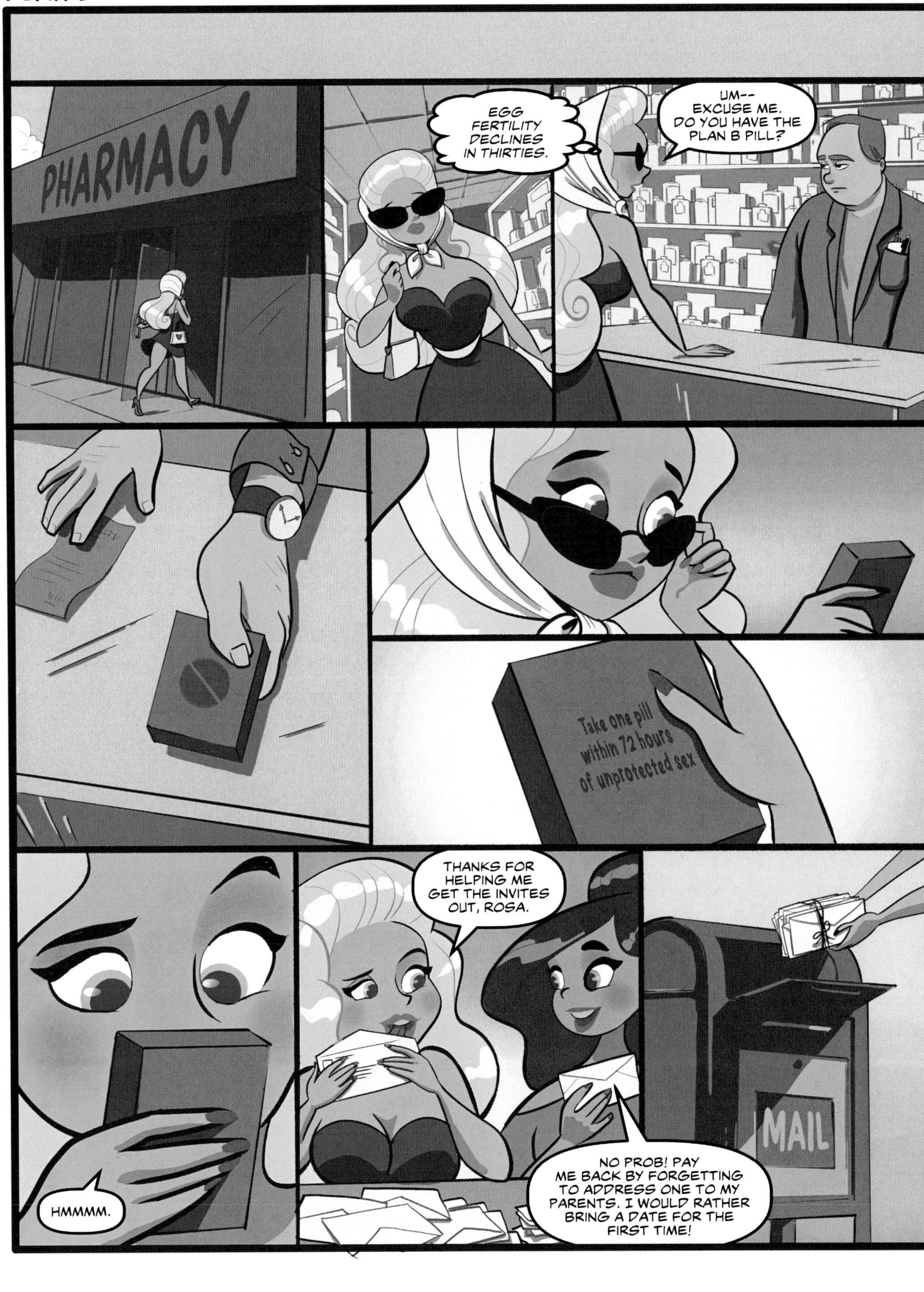
PHARMACY
EGG FERTILITY DECLINES IN THIRTIES.
UM-- EXCUSE ME. DO YOU HAVE THE PLAN B PILL?
Take one pill within 72 hours of unprotected sex
HMMMM.
THANKS FOR HELPING ME GET THE INVITES OUT, ROSA.
NO PROB! PAY ME BACK BY FORGETTING TO ADDRESS ONE TO MY PARENTS. I WOULD RATHER BRING A DATE FOR THE FIRST TIME!
MAIL

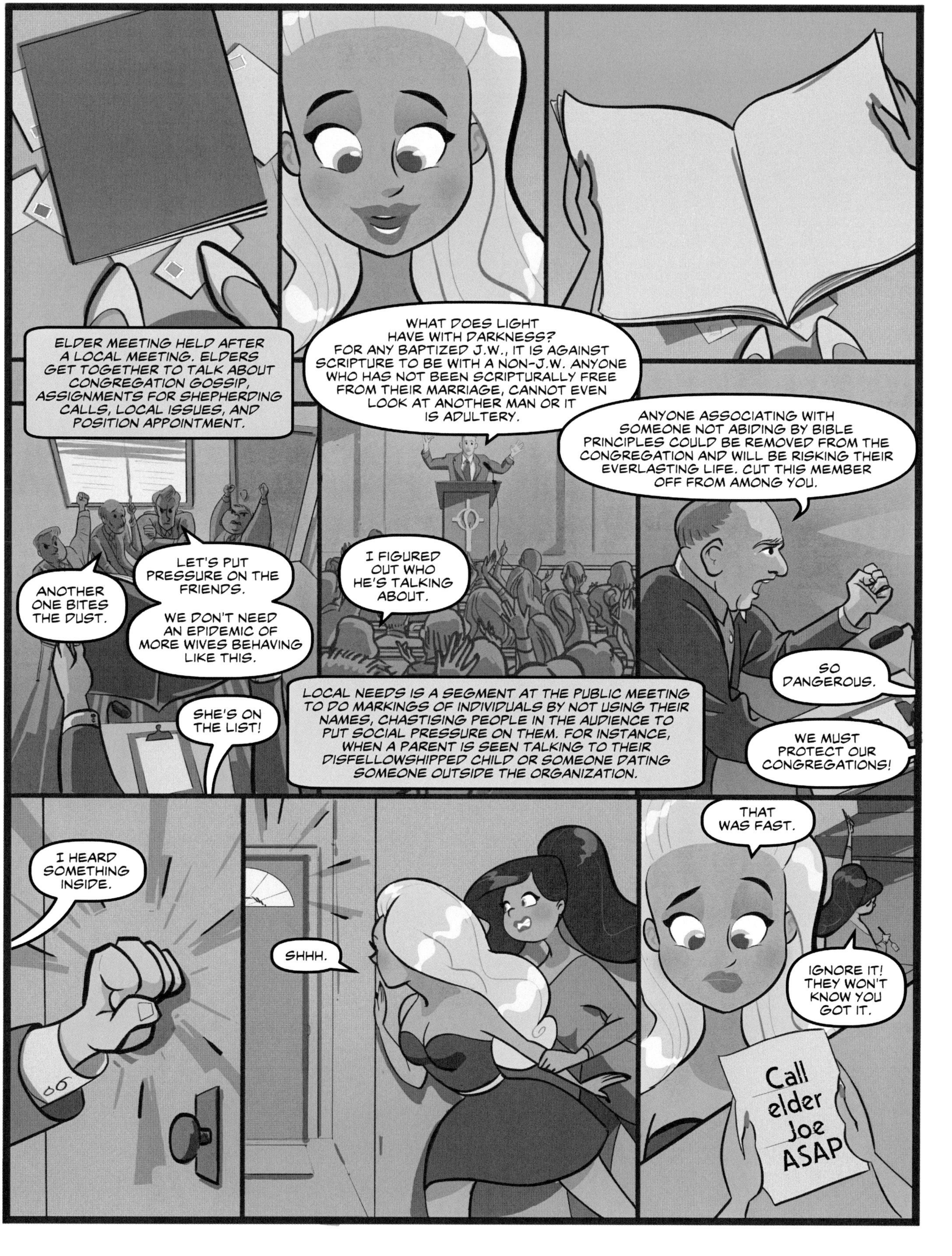
ELDER MEETING HELD AFTER A LOCAL MEETING. ELDERS GET TOGETHER TO TALK ABOUT CONGREGATION GOSSIP, ASSIGNMENTS FOR SHEPHERDING CALLS, LOCAL ISSUES, AND POSITION APPOINTMENT.
WHAT DOES LIGHT HAVE WITH DARKNESS? FOR ANY BAPTIZED J.W., IT IS AGAINST SCRIPTURE TO BE WITH A NON-J.W. ANYONE WHO HAS NOT BEEN SCRIPTURALLY FREE FROM THEIR MARRIAGE, CANNOT EVEN LOOK AT ANOTHER MAN OR IT IS ADULTERY.
ANYONE ASSOCIATING WITH SOMEONE NOT ABIDING BY BIBLE PRINCIPLES COULD BE REMOVED FROM THE CONGREGATION AND WILL BE RISKING THEIR EVERLASTING LIFE. CUT THIS MEMBER OFF FROM AMONG YOU.
ANOTHER ONE BITES THE DUST.
LET'S PUT PRESSURE ON THE FRIENDS.
WE DON'T NEED AN EPIDEMIC OF MORE WIVES BEHAVING LIKE THIS.
I FIGURED OUT WHO HE'S TALKING ABOUT.
SHE'S ON THE LIST!
LOCAL NEEDS IS A SEGMENT AT THE PUBLIC MEETING TO DO MARKINGS OF INDIVIDUALS BY NOT USING THEIR NAMES, CHASTISING PEOPLE IN THE AUDIENCE TO PUT SOCIAL PRESSURE ON THEM. FOR INSTANCE, WHEN A PARENT IS SEEN TALKING TO THEIR DISFELLOWSHIPPED CHILD OR SOMEONE DATING SOMEONE OUTSIDE THE ORGANIZATION.
SO DANGEROUS.
WE MUST PROTECT OUR CONGREGATIONS!
I HEARD SOMETHING INSIDE.
SHHH.
THAT WAS FAST.
IGNORE IT! THEY WON'T KNOW YOU GOT IT.
Call elder Joe ASAP

HEAD OF THE HOUSE

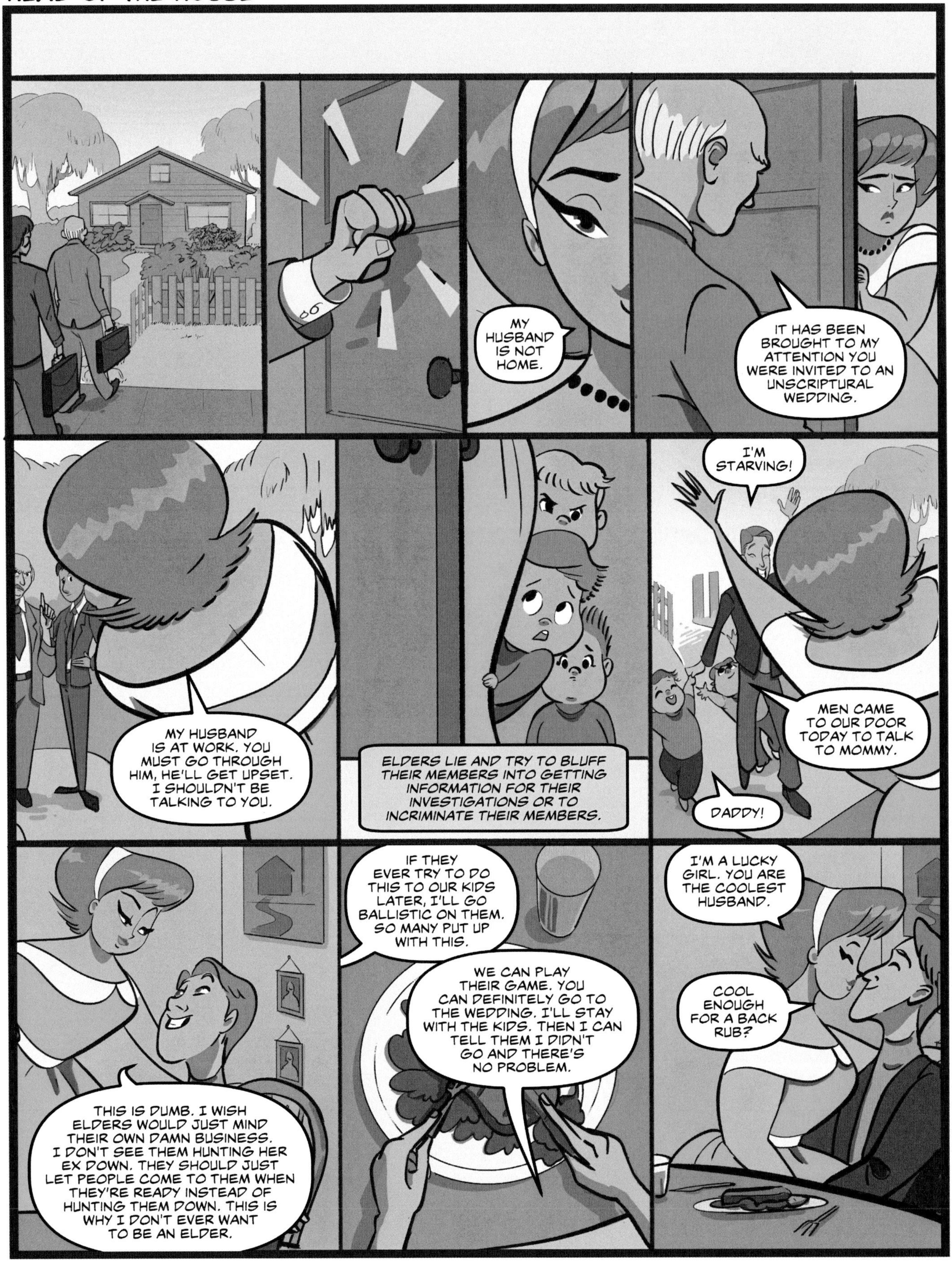

MY HUSBAND IS NOT HOME.
IT HAS BEEN BROUGHT TO MY ATTENTION YOU WERE INVITED TO AN UNSCRIPTURAL WEDDING.
MY HUSBAND IS AT WORK. YOU MUST GO THROUGH HIM, HE'LL GET UPSET. I SHOULDN'T BE TALKING TO YOU.
ELDERS LIE AND TRY TO BLUFF THEIR MEMBERS INTO GETTING INFORMATION FOR THEIR INVESTIGATIONS OR TO INCRIMINATE THEIR MEMBERS.
I'M STARVING!
MEN CAME TO OUR DOOR TODAY TO TALK TO MOMMY.
DADDY!
THIS IS DUMB. I WISH ELDERS WOULD JUST MIND THEIR OWN DAMN BUSINESS. I DON'T SEE THEM HUNTING HER EX DOWN. THEY SHOULD JUST LET PEOPLE COME TO THEM WHEN THEY'RE READY INSTEAD OF HUNTING THEM DOWN. THIS IS WHY I DON'T EVER WANT TO BE AN ELDER.
IF THEY EVER TRY TO DO THIS TO OUR KIDS LATER, I'LL GO BALLISTIC ON THEM. SO MANY PUT UP WITH THIS.
WE CAN PLAY THEIR GAME. YOU CAN DEFINITELY GO TO THE WEDDING. I'LL STAY WITH THE KIDS. THEN I CAN TELL THEM I DIDN'T GO AND THERE'S NO PROBLEM.
I'M A LUCKY GIRL. YOU ARE THE COOLEST HUSBAND.
COOL ENOUGH FOR A BACK RUB?

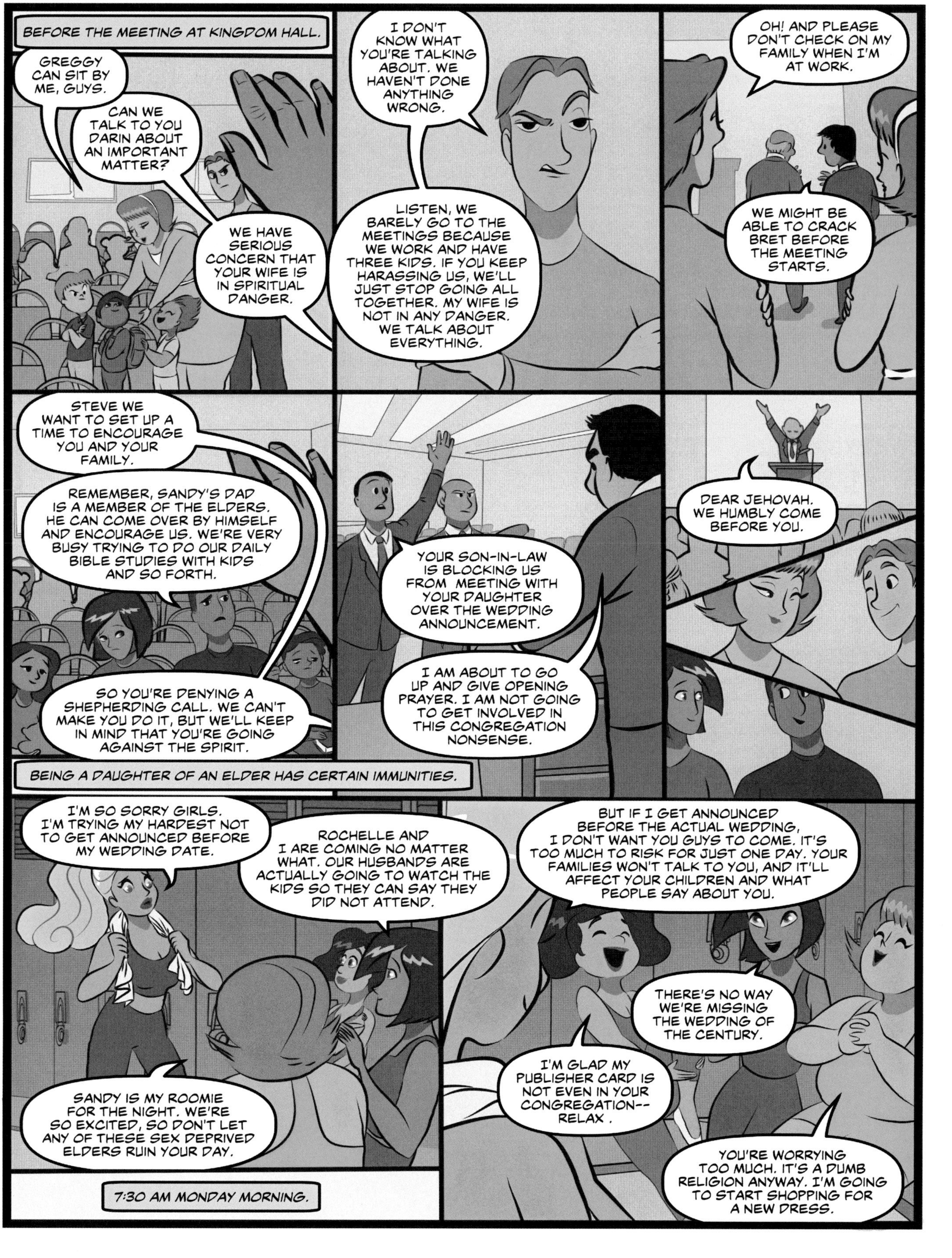
BEFORE THE MEETING AT KINGDOM HALL.
GREGGY CAN SIT BY ME, GUYS.
CAN WE TALK TO YOU DARIN ABOUT AN IMPORTANT MATTER?
WE HAVE SERIOUS CONCERN THAT YOUR WIFE IS IN SPIRITUAL DANGER.
I DON'T KNOW WHAT YOU'RE TALKING ABOUT. WE HAVEN'T DONE ANYTHING WRONG.
LISTEN, WE BARELY GO TO THE MEETINGS BECAUSE WE WORK AND HAVE THREE KIDS. IF YOU KEEP HARASSING US, WE'LL JUST STOP GOING ALL TOGETHER. MY WIFE IS NOT IN ANY DANGER. WE TALK ABOUT EVERYTHING.
OH! AND PLEASE DON'T CHECK ON MY FAMILY WHEN I'M AT WORK.
WE MIGHT BE ABLE TO CRACK BRET BEFORE THE MEETING STARTS.
STEVE WE WANT TO SET UP A TIME TO ENCOURAGE YOU AND YOUR FAMILY.
REMEMBER, SANDY'S DAD IS A MEMBER OF THE ELDERS. HE CAN COME OVER BY HIMSELF AND ENCOURAGE US. WE'RE VERY BUSY TRYING TO DO OUR DAILY BIBLE STUDIES WITH KIDS AND SO FORTH.
SO YOU'RE DENYING A SHEPHERDING CALL. WE CAN'T MAKE YOU DO IT, BUT WE'LL KEEP IN MIND THAT YOU'RE GOING AGAINST THE SPIRIT.
YOUR SON-IN-LAW IS BLOCKING US FROM MEETING WITH YOUR DAUGHTER OVER THE WEDDING ANNOUNCEMENT.
I AM ABOUT TO GO UP AND GIVE OPENING PRAYER. I AM NOT GOING TO GET INVOLVED IN THIS CONGREGATION NONSENSE.
DEAR JEHOVAH. WE HUMBLY COME BEFORE YOU.
BEING A DAUGHTER OF AN ELDER HAS CERTAIN IMMUNITIES.
I'M SO SORRY GIRLS. I'M TRYING MY HARDEST NOT TO GET ANNOUNCED BEFORE MY WEDDING DATE.
ROCHELLE AND I ARE COMING NO MATTER WHAT. OUR HUSBANDS ARE ACTUALLY GOING TO WATCH THE KIDS SO THEY CAN SAY THEY DID NOT ATTEND.
SANDY IS MY ROOMIE FOR THE NIGHT. WE'RE SO EXCITED, SO DON'T LET ANY OF THESE SEX DEPRIVED ELDERS RUIN YOUR DAY.
BUT IF I GET ANNOUNCED BEFORE THE ACTUAL WEDDING, I DON'T WANT YOU GUYS TO COME. IT'S TOO MUCH TO RISK FOR JUST ONE DAY. YOUR FAMILIES WON'T TALK TO YOU, AND IT'LL AFFECT YOUR CHILDREN AND WHAT PEOPLE SAY ABOUT YOU.
THERE'S NO WAY WE'RE MISSING THE WEDDING OF THE CENTURY.
I'M GLAD MY PUBLISHER CARD IS NOT EVEN IN YOUR CONGREGATION-- RELAX .
YOU'RE WORRYING TOO MUCH. IT'S A DUMB RELIGION ANYWAY. I'M GOING TO START SHOPPING FOR A NEW DRESS.
7:30 AM MONDAY MORNING.

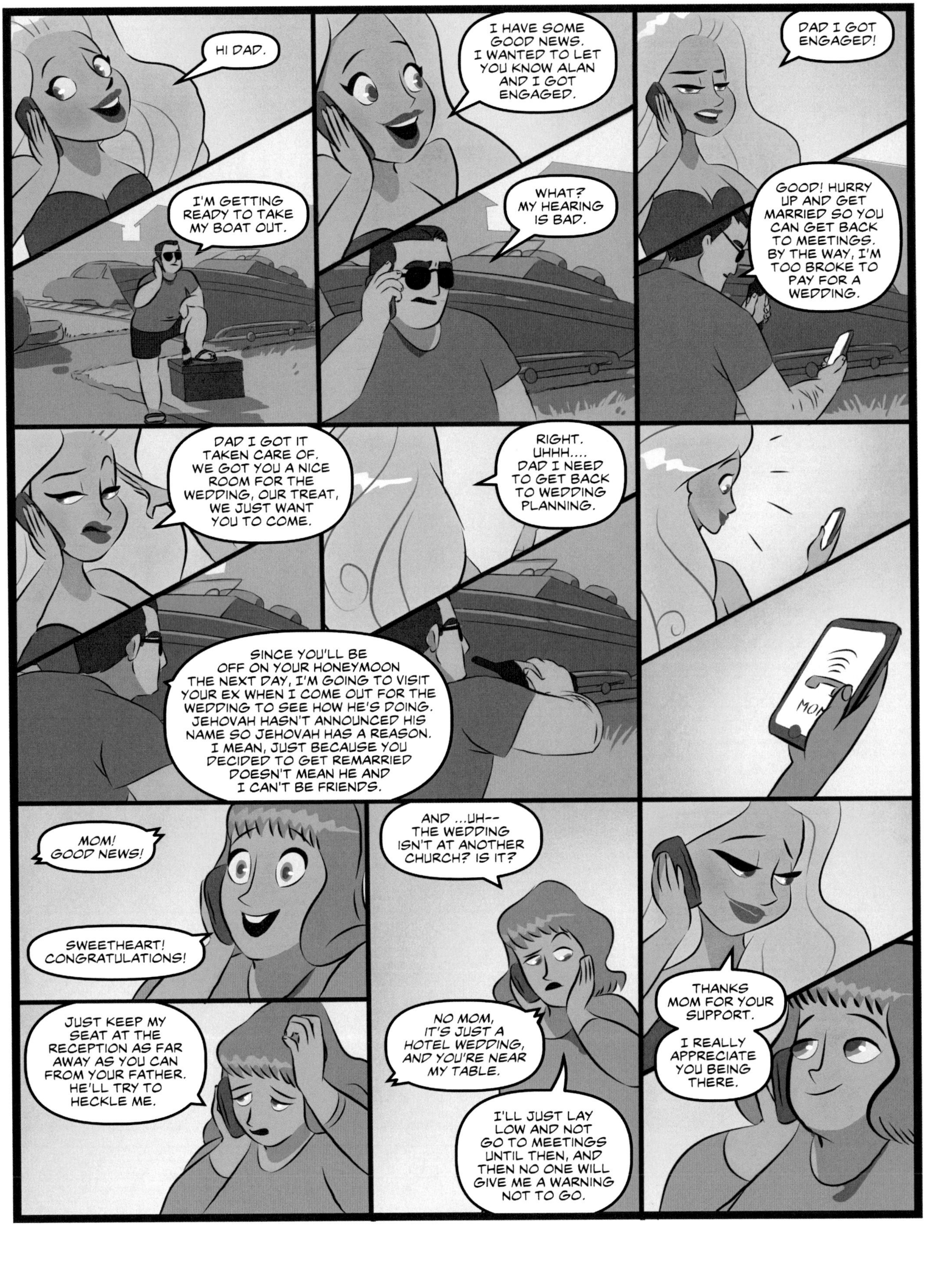
HI DAD.
I HAVE SOME GOOD NEWS. I WANTED TO LET YOU KNOW ALAN AND I GOT ENGAGED.
DAD I GOT ENGAGED!
I'M GETTING READY TO TAKE MY BOAT OUT.
WHAT? MY HEARING IS BAD.
GOOD! HURRY UP AND GET MARRIED SO YOU CAN GET BACK TO MEETINGS. BY THE WAY, I'M TOO BROKE TO PAY FOR A WEDDING.
DAD I GOT IT TAKEN CARE OF. WE GOT YOU A NICE ROOM FOR THE WEDDING, OUR TREAT, WE JUST WANT YOU TO COME.
RIGHT. UHHH.... DAD I NEED TO GET BACK TO WEDDING PLANNING.
SINCE YOU'LL BE OFF ON YOUR HONEYMOON THE NEXT DAY, I'M GOING TO VISIT YOUR EX WHEN I COME OUT FOR THE WEDDING TO SEE HOW HE'S DOING. JEHOVAH HASN'T ANNOUNCED HIS NAME SO JEHOVAH HAS A REASON. I MEAN, JUST BECAUSE YOU DECIDED TO GET REMARRIED DOESN'T MEAN HE AND I CAN'T BE FRIENDS.
MOM! GOOD NEWS!
SWEETHEART! CONGRATULATIONS!
JUST KEEP MY SEAT AT THE RECEPTION AS FAR AWAY AS YOU CAN FROM YOUR FATHER. HE'LL TRY TO HECKLE ME.
AND ...UH-- THE WEDDING ISN'T AT ANOTHER CHURCH? IS IT?
NO MOM, IT'S JUST A HOTEL WEDDING, AND YOU'RE NEAR MY TABLE.
I'LL JUST LAY LOW AND NOT GO TO MEETINGS UNTIL THEN, AND THEN NO ONE WILL GIVE ME A WARNING NOT TO GO.
THANKS MOM FOR YOUR SUPPORT.
I REALLY APPRECIATE YOU BEING THERE.

CERTIFIED LETTER

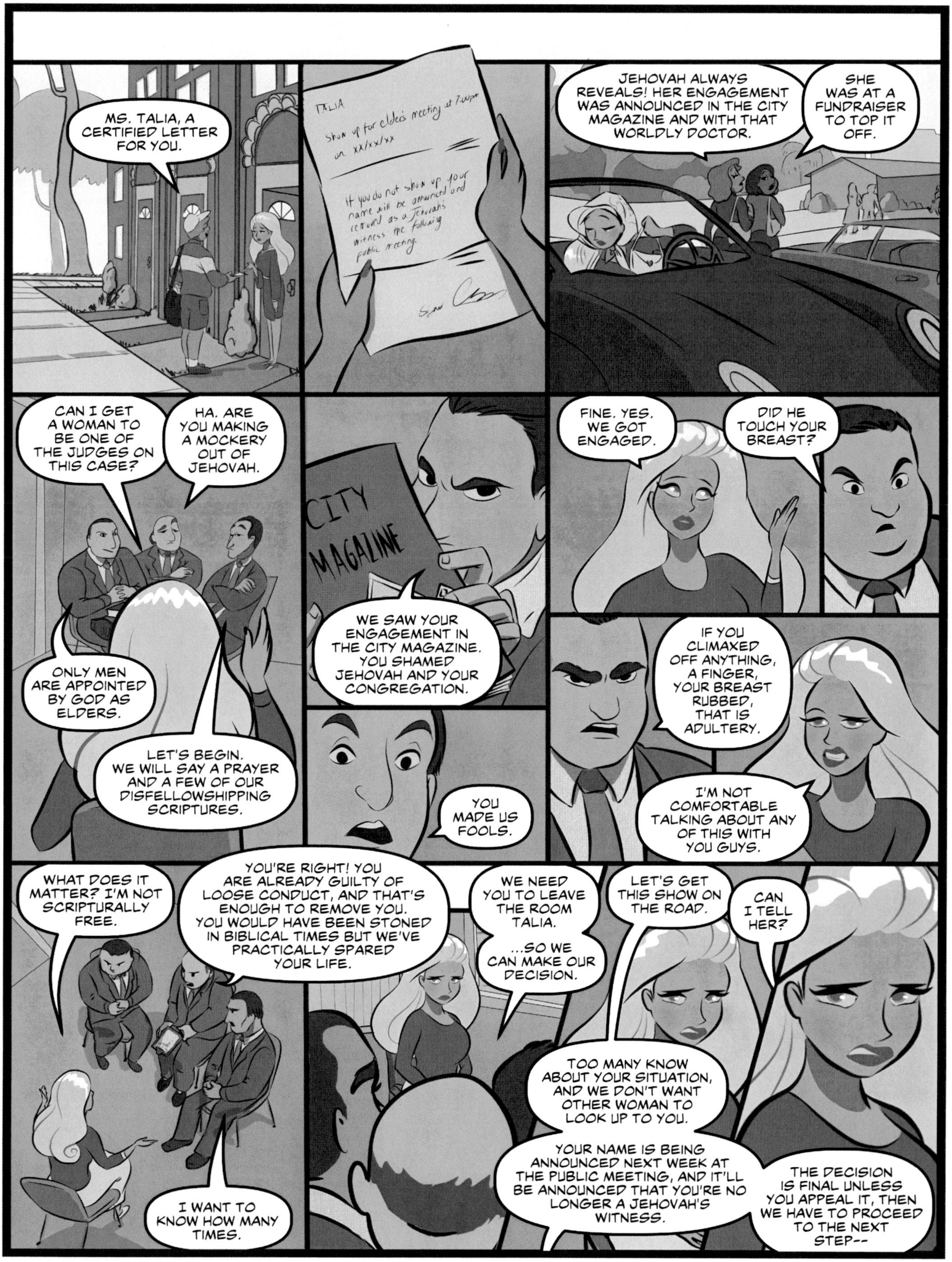

MS. TALIA, A CERTIFIED LETTER FOR YOU.
TALIA
Show up for elder's meeting at 7:00pm on XX/XX/XX
If you do not show up your name will be announced and removed as a Jehovah's witness the following public meeting.
JEHOVAH ALWAYS REVEALS! HER ENGAGEMENT WAS ANNOUNCED IN THE CITY MAGAZINE AND WITH THAT WORLDLY DOCTOR.
SHE WAS AT A FUNDRAISER TO TOP IT OFF.
CAN I GET A WOMAN TO BE ONE OF THE JUDGES ON THIS CASE?
HA. ARE YOU MAKING A MOCKERY OUT OF JEHOVAH.
ONLY MEN ARE APPOINTED BY GOD AS ELDERS.
LET'S BEGIN. WE WILL SAY A PRAYER AND A FEW OF OUR DISFELLOWSHIPPING SCRIPTURES.
CITY MAGAZINE
WE SAW YOUR ENGAGEMENT IN THE CITY MAGAZINE. YOU SHAMED JEHOVAH AND YOUR CONGREGATION.
YOU MADE US FOOLS.
FINE. YES. WE GOT ENGAGED.
DID HE TOUCH YOUR BREAST?
IF YOU CLIMAXED OFF ANYTHING, A FINGER, YOUR BREAST RUBBED, THAT IS ADULTERY.
I'M NOT COMFORTABLE TALKING ABOUT ANY OF THIS WITH YOU GUYS.
WHAT DOES IT MATTER? I'M NOT SCRIPTURALLY FREE.
YOU'RE RIGHT! YOU ARE ALREADY GUILTY OF LOOSE CONDUCT, AND THAT'S ENOUGH TO REMOVE YOU. YOU WOULD HAVE BEEN STONED IN BIBLICAL TIMES BUT WE'VE PRACTICALLY SPARED YOUR LIFE.
I WANT TO KNOW HOW MANY TIMES.
WE NEED YOU TO LEAVE THE ROOM TALIA.
...SO WE CAN MAKE OUR DECISION.
LET'S GET THIS SHOW ON THE ROAD.
CAN I TELL HER?
TOO MANY KNOW ABOUT YOUR SITUATION, AND WE DON'T WANT OTHER WOMAN TO LOOK UP TO YOU.
YOUR NAME IS BEING ANNOUNCED NEXT WEEK AT THE PUBLIC MEETING, AND IT'LL BE ANNOUNCED THAT YOU'RE NO LONGER A JEHOVAH'S WITNESS.
THE DECISION IS FINAL UNLESS YOU APPEAL IT, THEN WE HAVE TO PROCEED TO THE NEXT STEP--

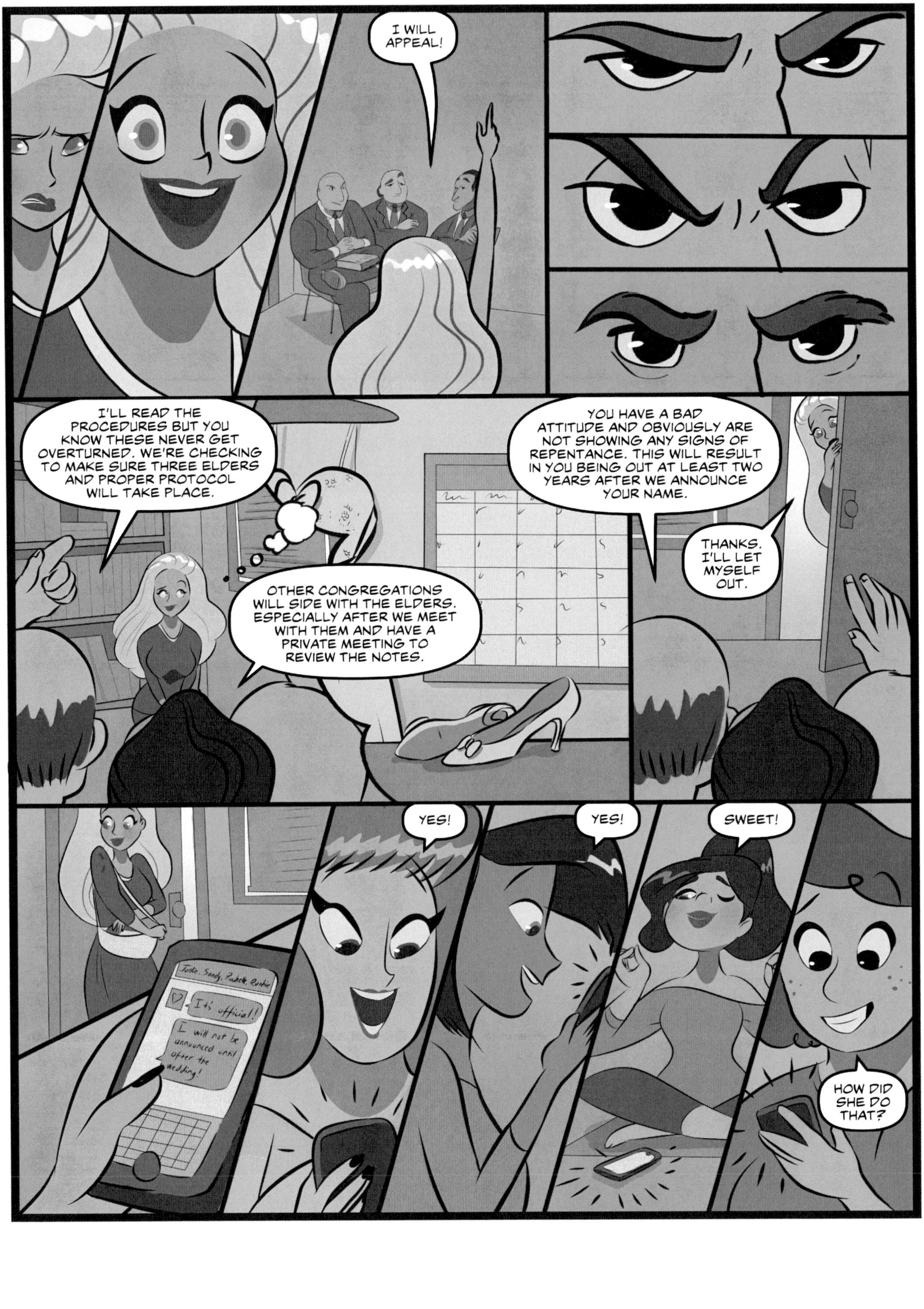
I WILL APPEAL!
I'LL READ THE PROCEDURES BUT YOU KNOW THESE NEVER GET OVERTURNED. WE'RE CHECKING TO MAKE SURE THREE ELDERS AND PROPER PROTOCOL WILL TAKE PLACE.
OTHER CONGREGATIONS WILL SIDE WITH THE ELDERS. ESPECIALLY AFTER WE MEET WITH THEM AND HAVE A PRIVATE MEETING TO REVIEW THE NOTES.
YOU HAVE A BAD ATTITUDE AND OBVIOUSLY ARE NOT SHOWING ANY SIGNS OF REPENTANCE. THIS WILL RESULT IN YOU BEING OUT AT LEAST TWO YEARS AFTER WE ANNOUNCE YOUR NAME.
THANKS. I'LL LET MYSELF OUT.
Jodie, Sandy, Rachelle, Rosalie
It's official!
I will not be announced until after the wedding!
YES!
YES!
SWEET!
HOW DID SHE DO THAT?

WEDDING DAY

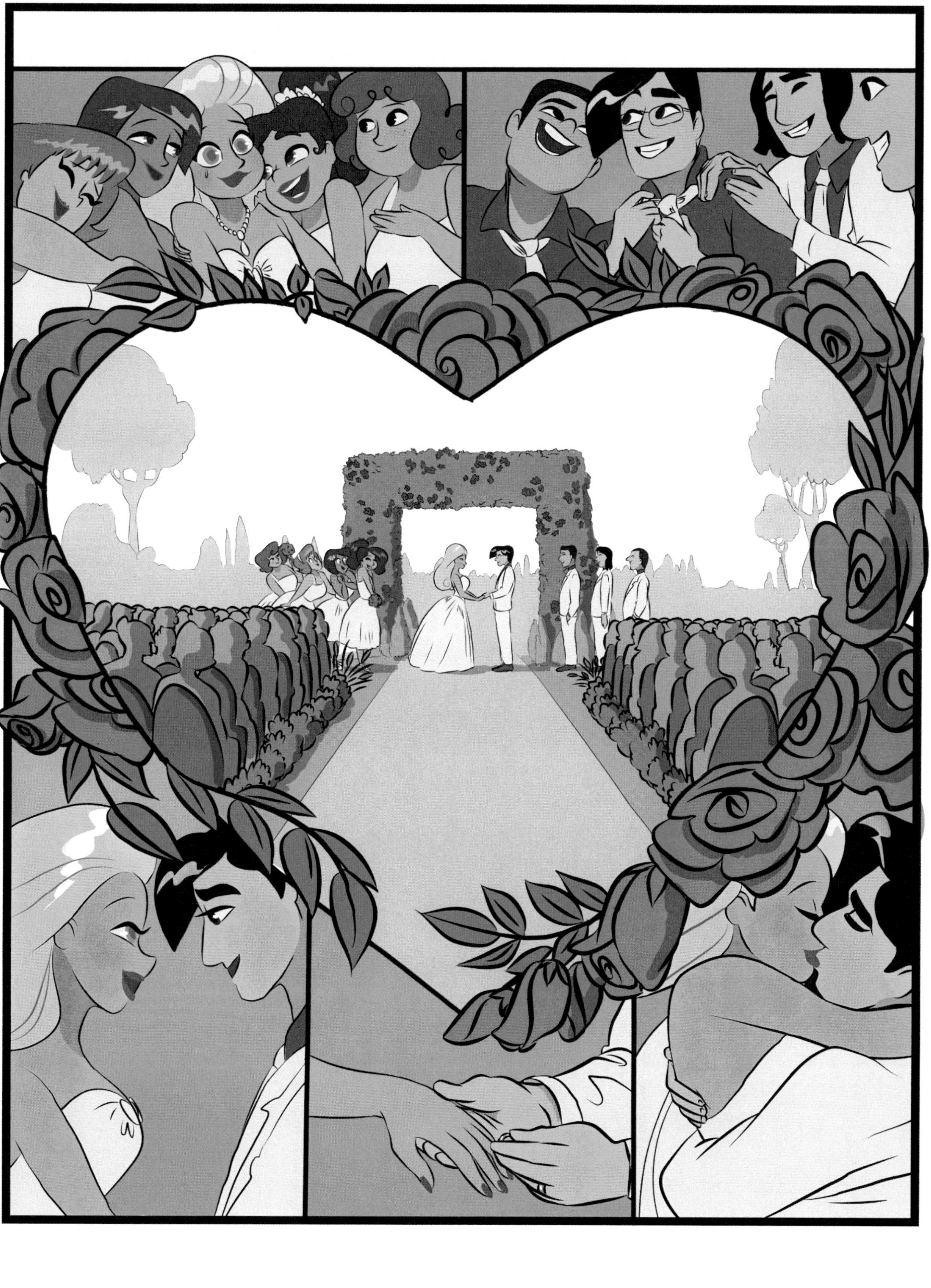

WEDDING RECEPTION

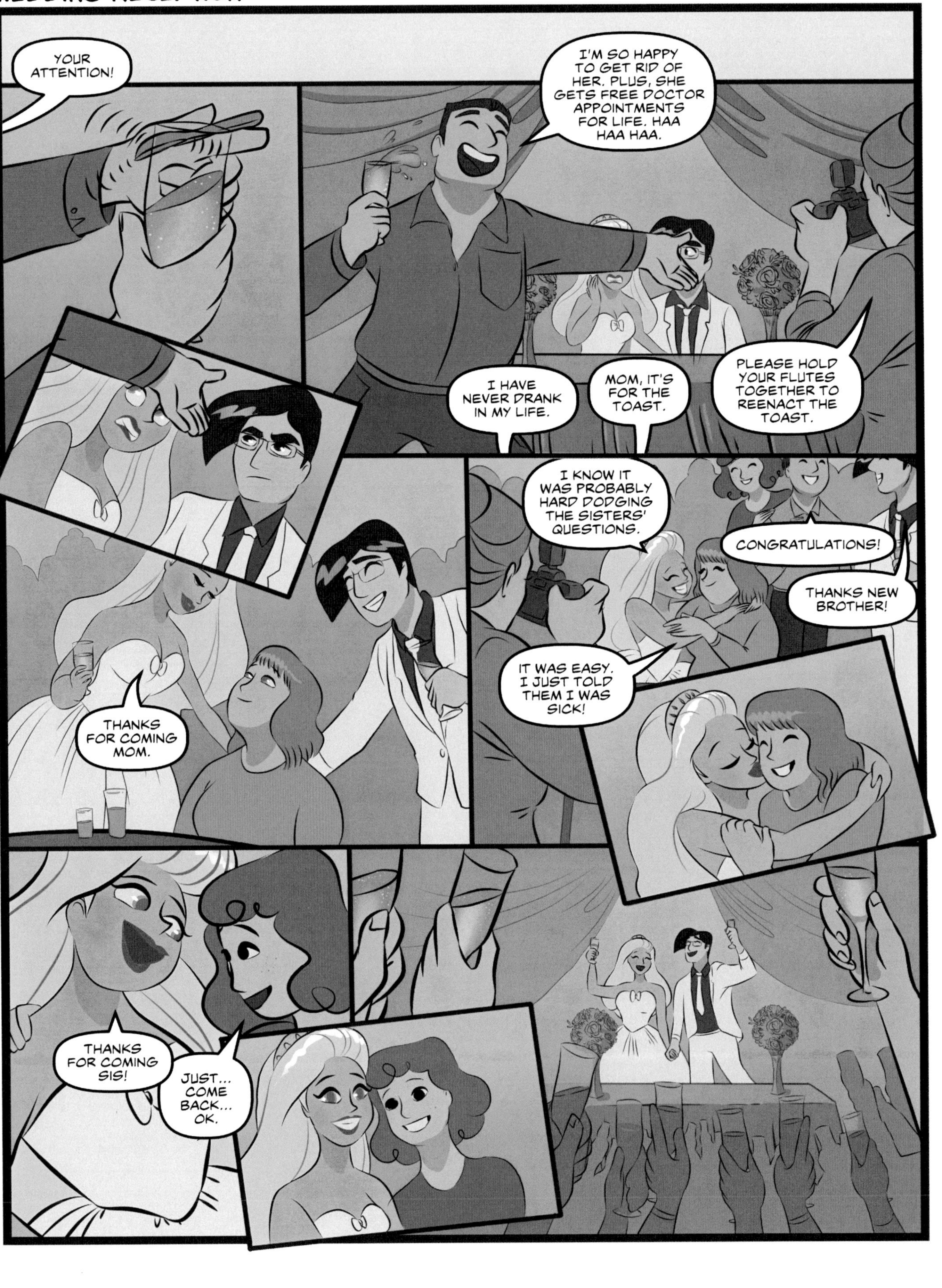
YOUR ATTENTION!
I'M SO HAPPY TO GET RID OF HER. PLUS, SHE GETS FREE DOCTOR APPOINTMENTS FOR LIFE. HAA HAA HAA.
I HAVE NEVER DRANK IN MY LIFE.
MOM, IT'S FOR THE TOAST.
PLEASE HOLD YOUR FLUTES TOGETHER TO REENACT THE TOAST.
THANKS FOR COMING MOM.
I KNOW IT WAS PROBABLY HARD DODGING THE SISTERS' QUESTIONS.
CONGRATULATIONS!
THANKS NEW BROTHER!
IT WAS EASY. I JUST TOLD THEM I WAS SICK!
THANKS FOR COMING SIS!
JUST... COME BACK... OK.

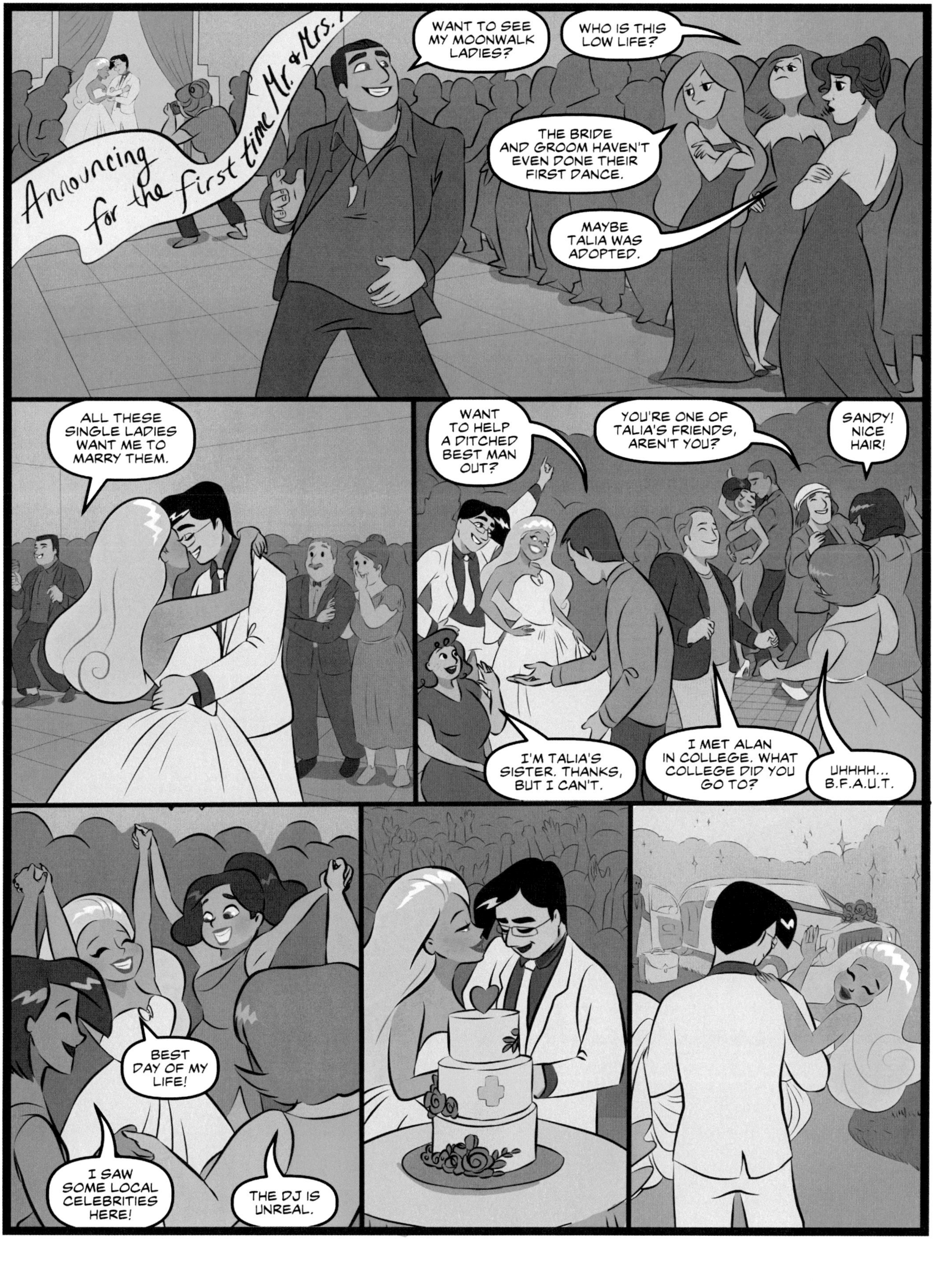
Announcing for the first time Mr. & Mrs. !
WANT TO SEE MY MOONWALK LADIES?
WHO IS THIS LOW LIFE?
THE BRIDE AND GROOM HAVEN'T EVEN DONE THEIR FIRST DANCE.
MAYBE TALIA WAS ADOPTED.
ALL THESE SINGLE LADIES WANT ME TO MARRY THEM.
WANT TO HELP A DITCHED BEST MAN OUT?
I'M TALIA'S SISTER. THANKS, BUT I CAN'T.
YOU'RE ONE OF TALIA'S FRIENDS, AREN'T YOU?
I MET ALAN IN COLLEGE. WHAT COLLEGE DID YOU GO TO?
SANDY! NICE HAIR!
UHHHH... B.F.A.U.T.
BEST DAY OF MY LIFE!
I SAW SOME LOCAL CELEBRITIES HERE!
THE DJ IS UNREAL.

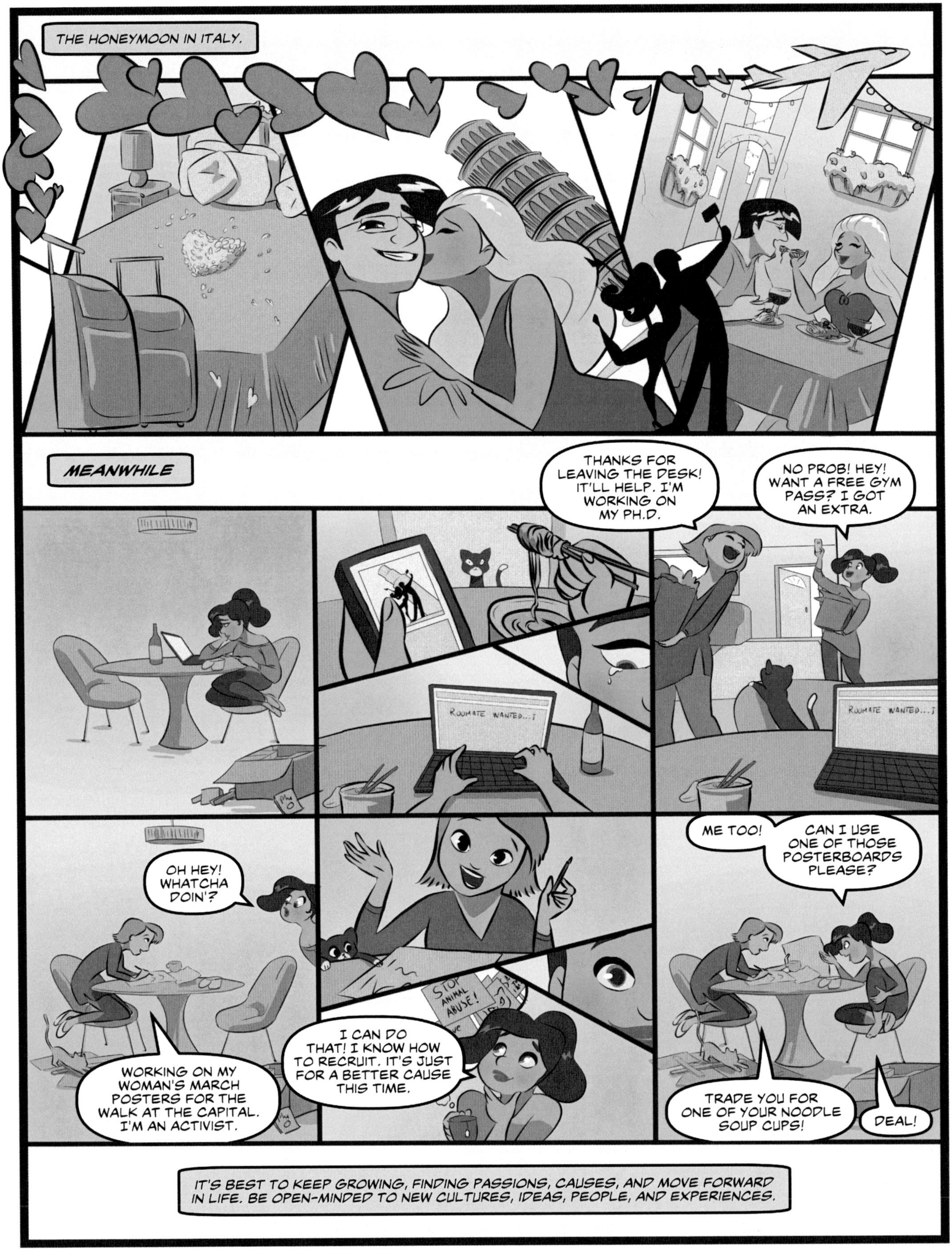

THE HONEYMOON IN ITALY.
MEANWHILE
ROOMATE WANTED...!
THANKS FOR LEAVING THE DESK! IT'LL HELP. I'M WORKING ON MY PH.D.
NO PROB! HEY! WANT A FREE GYM PASS? I GOT AN EXTRA.
ROOMATE WANTED...!
OH HEY! WHATCHA DOIN'?
WORKING ON MY WOMAN'S MARCH POSTERS FOR THE WALK AT THE CAPITAL. I'M AN ACTIVIST.
STOP ANIMAL ABUSE!
I CAN DO THAT! I KNOW HOW TO RECRUIT. IT'S JUST FOR A BETTER CAUSE THIS TIME.
ME TOO!
CAN I USE ONE OF THOSE POSTERBOARDS PLEASE?
TRADE YOU FOR ONE OF YOUR NOODLE SOUP CUPS!
DEAL!
IT'S BEST TO KEEP GROWING, FINDING PASSIONS, CAUSES, AND MOVE FORWARD IN LIFE. BE OPEN-MINDED TO NEW CULTURES, IDEAS, PEOPLE, AND EXPERIENCES.

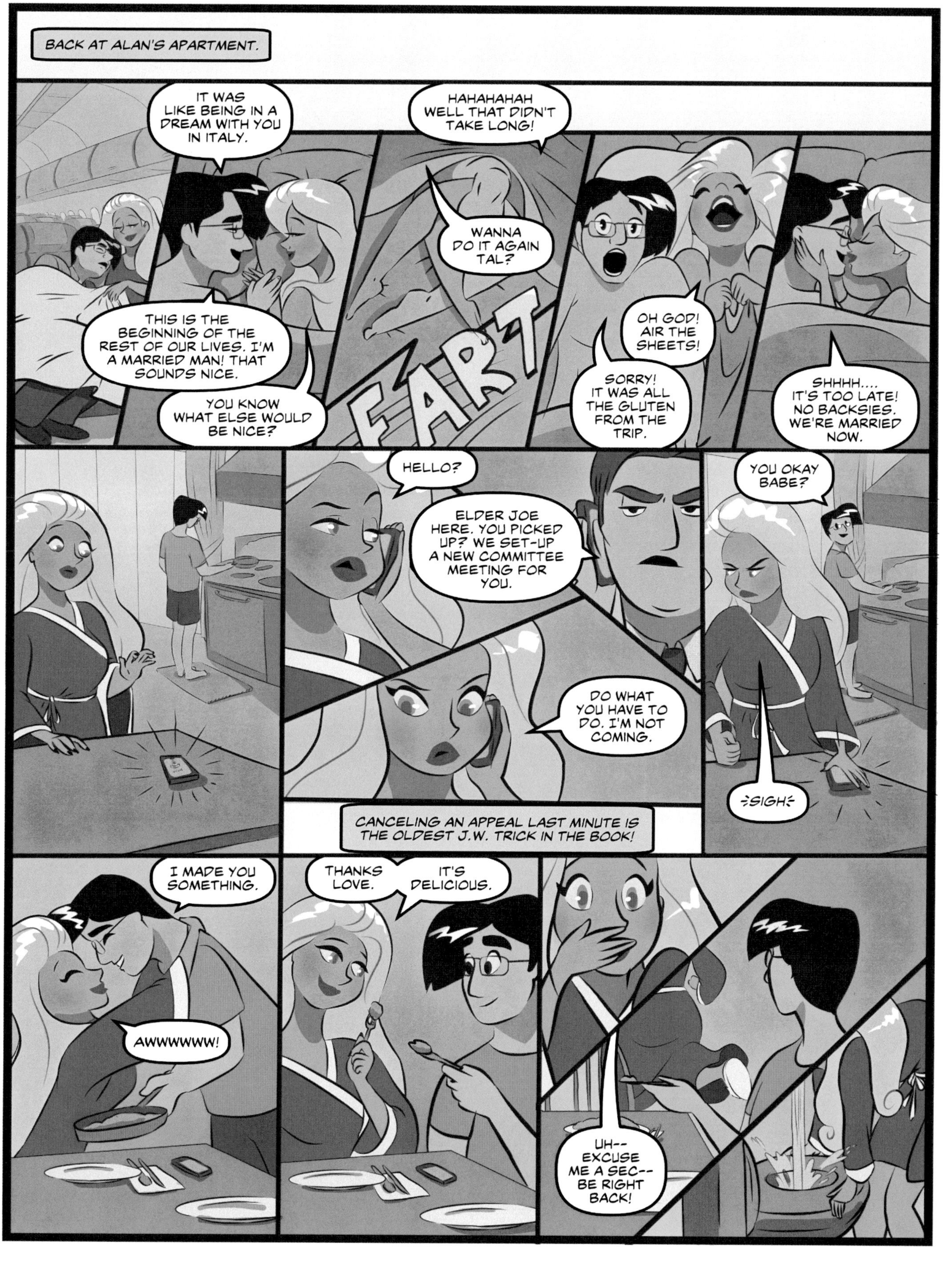
BACK AT ALAN'S APARTMENT.
IT WAS LIKE BEING IN A DREAM WITH YOU IN ITALY.
THIS IS THE BEGINNING OF THE REST OF OUR LIVES. I'M A MARRIED MAN! THAT SOUNDS NICE.
YOU KNOW WHAT ELSE WOULD BE NICE?
HAHAHAHAH WELL THAT DIDN'T TAKE LONG!
WANNA DO IT AGAIN TAL?
FART
OH GOD! AIR THE SHEETS!
SORRY! IT WAS ALL THE GLUTEN FROM THE TRIP.
SHHHH.... IT'S TOO LATE! NO BACKSIES. WE'RE MARRIED NOW.
HELLO?
ELDER JOE HERE. YOU PICKED UP? WE SET-UP A NEW COMMITTEE MEETING FOR YOU.
DO WHAT YOU HAVE TO DO. I'M NOT COMING.
CANCELING AN APPEAL LAST MINUTE IS THE OLDEST J.W. TRICK IN THE BOOK!
YOU OKAY BABE?
SIGH
I MADE YOU SOMETHING.
AWWWWWW!
THANKS LOVE.
IT'S DELICIOUS.
UH-- EXCUSE ME A SEC-- BE RIGHT BACK!

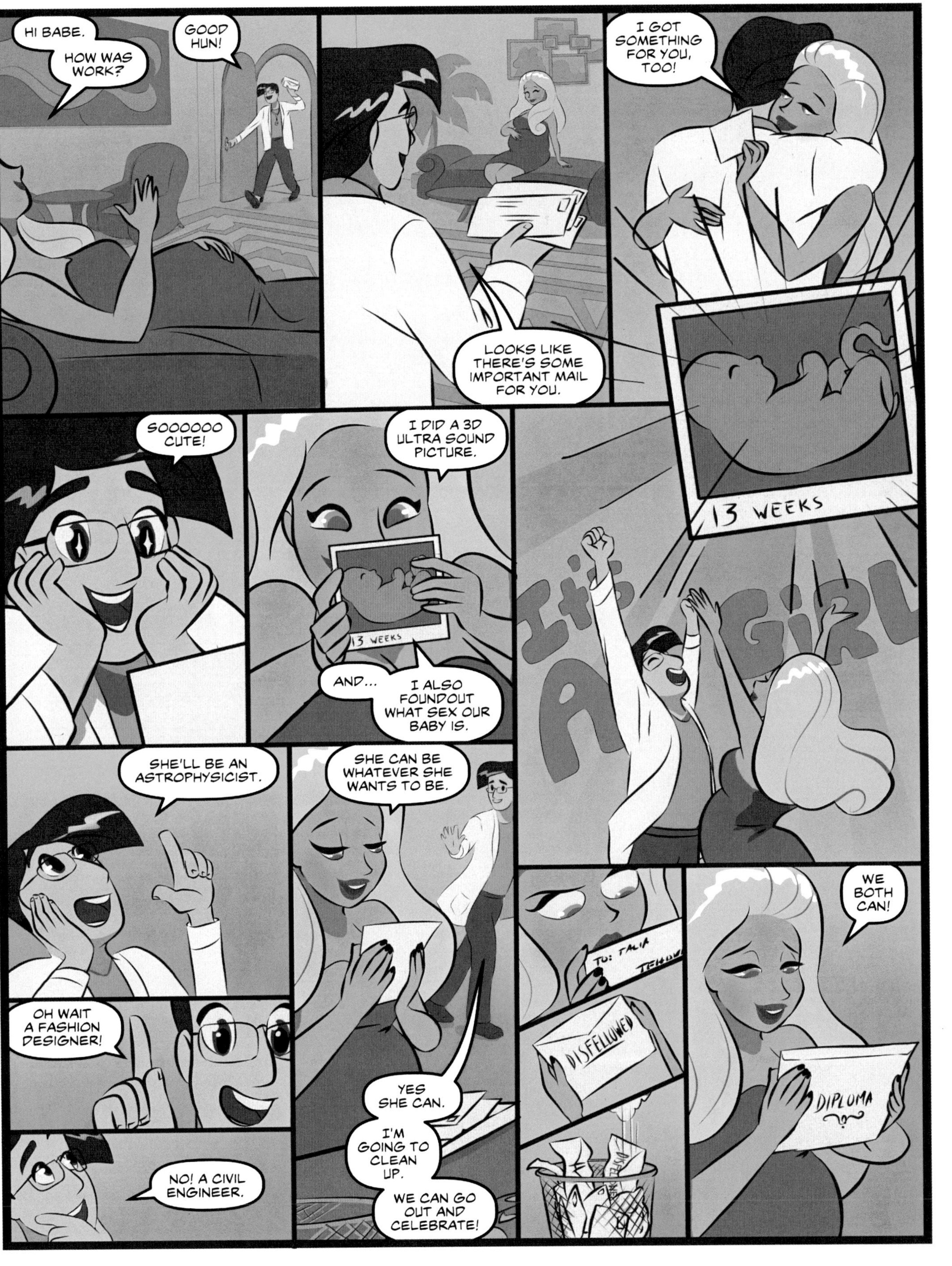

HI BABE.
HOW WAS WORK?
GOOD HUN!
LOOKS LIKE THERE'S SOME IMPORTANT MAIL FOR YOU.
I GOT SOMETHING FOR YOU, TOO!
13 WEEKS
SOOOOOO CUTE!
I DID A 3D ULTRA SOUND PICTURE.
13 WEEKS
AND...
I ALSO FOUNDOUT WHAT SEX OUR BABY IS.
It's A GiRL
SHE'LL BE AN ASTROPHYSICIST.
OH WAIT A FASHION DESIGNER!
NO! A CIVIL ENGINEER.
SHE CAN BE WHATEVER SHE WANTS TO BE.
YES SHE CAN.
I'M GOING TO CLEAN UP.
WE CAN GO OUT AND CELEBRATE!
TO: TALIA
DISFELLOWED
WE BOTH CAN!
DIPLOMA

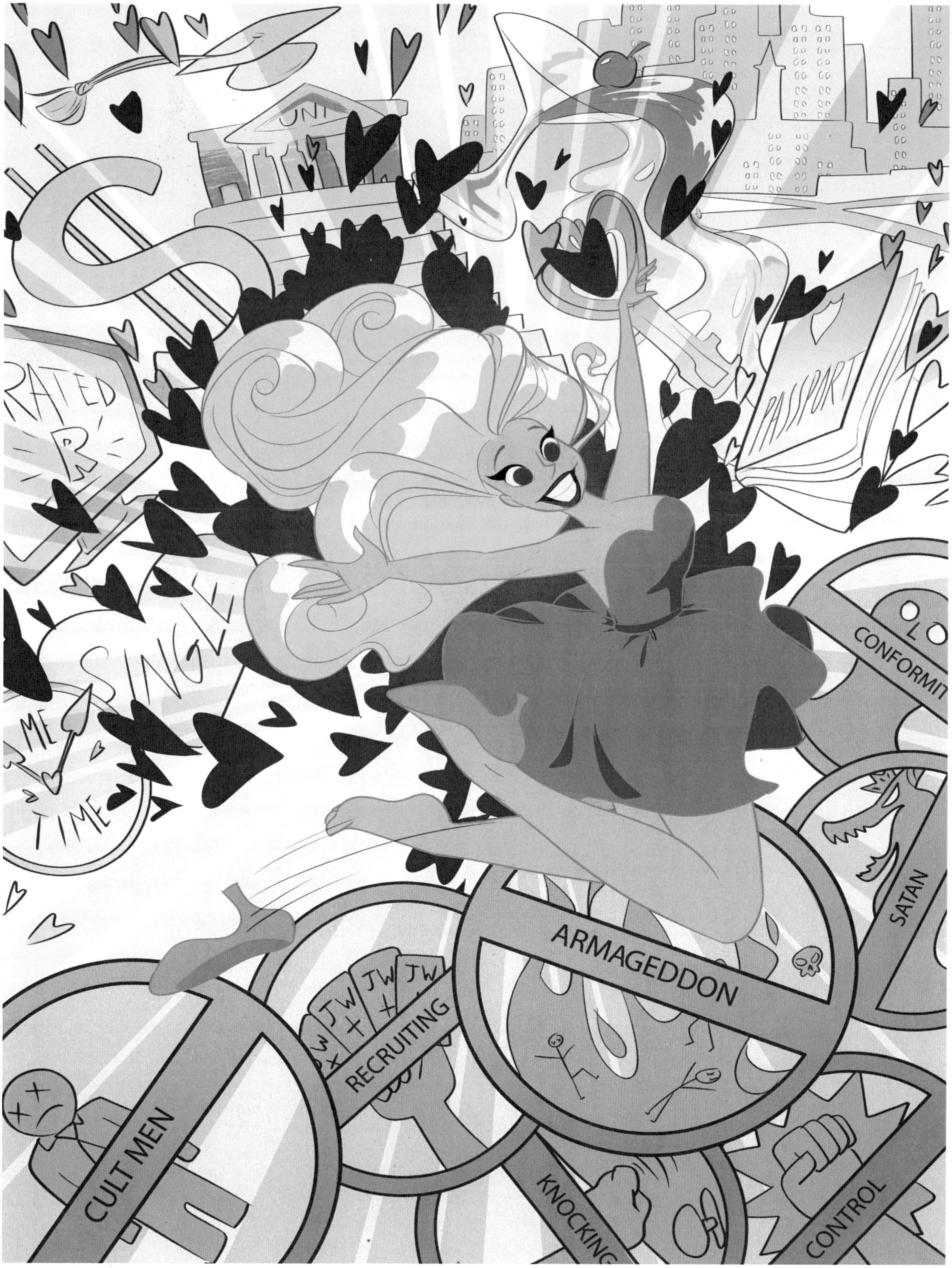
RATED R
SINGLE
ME TIME
PASSPORT
SATAN
ARMAGEDDON
JW
RECRUITING
CULT MEN
CONTROL

THE CHARACTERS: Where Are They Now?

GIRL TALK
ConGrats!

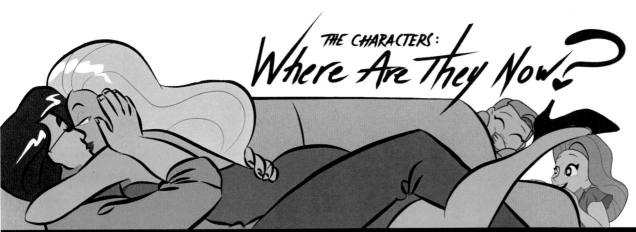

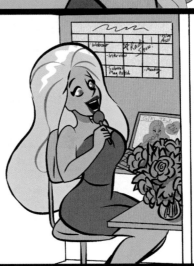

TALIA GREY is a happily remarried mother of two and a college graduate. Since freeing herself from the cult, she has become a successful business woman in real estate and insurance. She passionately advocates for legal reforms to protect children from pedophiles in religious organizations. She engages in charity work for women escaping abusive relationships and religions. She has been on various forms of media advocating awareness of cults and suppressive religions to encourage woman to become the best version of themselves.

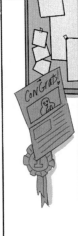

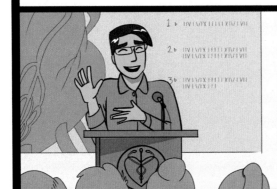

ALAN travels with his wife and beautiful children, giving cutting edge medical lectures. He volunteers a lot of time to children with heart conditions. He is a hands-on dad and loves being a father. Alan and Talia spend a lot of time with his enormous family. Their children are showered with love by wonderful grandparents who assist in raising them.

HOLY BIBLE

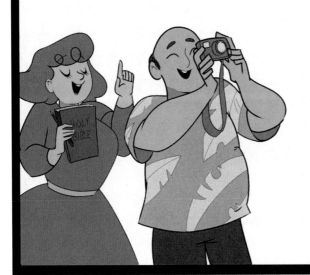

RUTHIE AND TIMMY moved to the country and live mostly off the grid. They built a little guest house for Ruthie's dad to later retire. Their eldest son lives in that home and works in the family business, breeding horses. The twins learned Spanish and moved to South America serving as ministers and conducting bible studies for the J.W.s. They rely on donations and small jobs in their local town. Ruthie is a pioneer and spends most of her time writing letters and mailing pamphlets to neighbors. She hasn't spoken to Talia since the day her name was removed as a Jehovah Witness.

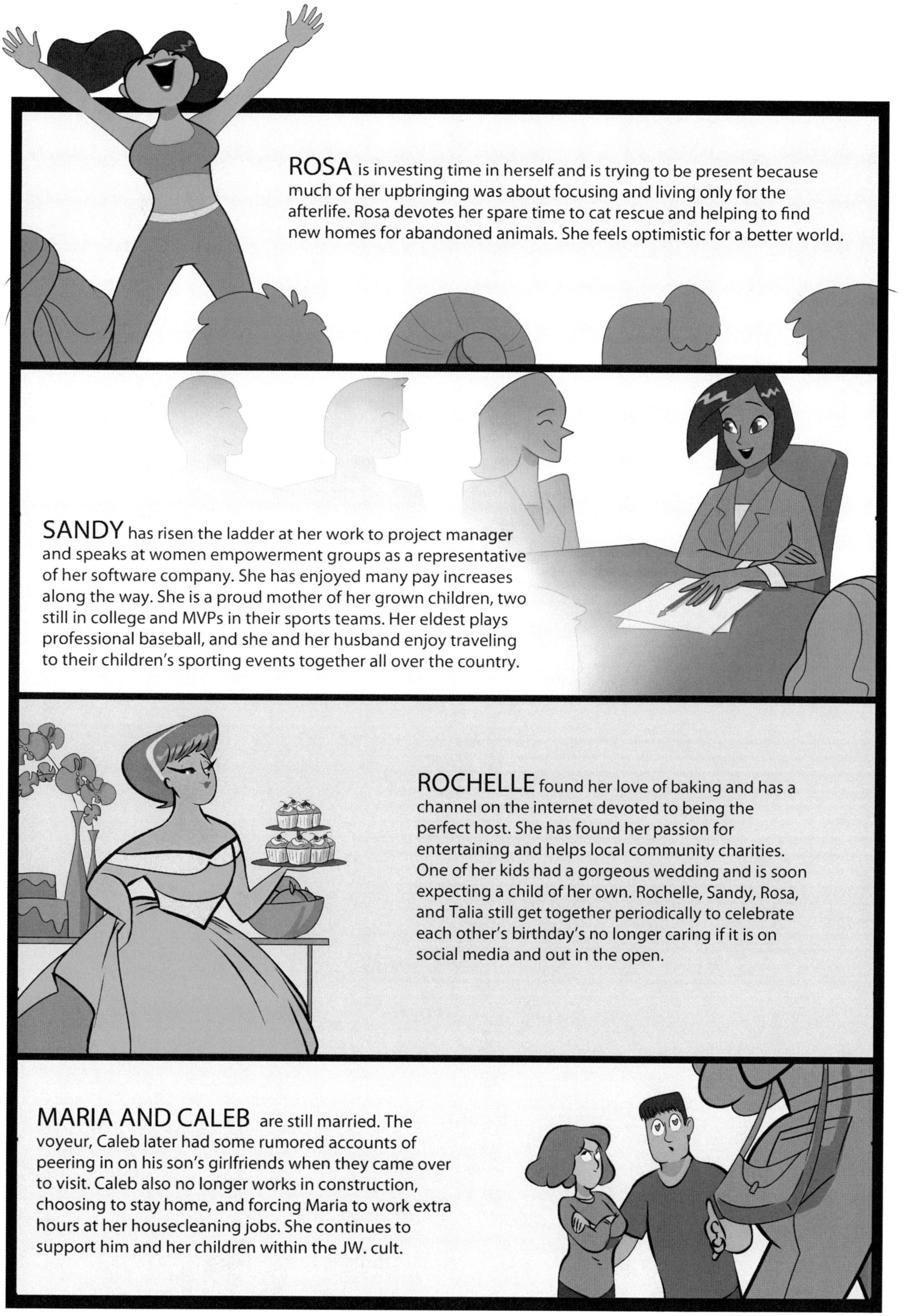
ROSA is investing time in herself and is trying to be present because much of her upbringing was about focusing and living only for the afterlife. Rosa devotes her spare time to cat rescue and helping to find new homes for abandoned animals. She feels optimistic for a better world.
SANDY has risen the ladder at her work to project manager and speaks at women empowerment groups as a representative of her software company. She has enjoyed many pay increases along the way. She is a proud mother of her grown children, two still in college and MVPs in their sports teams. Her eldest plays professional baseball, and she and her husband enjoy traveling to their children's sporting events together all over the country.
ROCHELLE found her love of baking and has a channel on the internet devoted to being the perfect host. She has found her passion for entertaining and helps local community charities. One of her kids had a gorgeous wedding and is soon expecting a child of her own. Rochelle, Sandy, Rosa, and Talia still get together periodically to celebrate each other's birthday's no longer caring if it is on social media and out in the open.
MARIA AND CALEB are still married. The voyeur, Caleb later had some rumored accounts of peering in on his son's girlfriends when they came over to visit. Caleb also no longer works in construction, choosing to stay home, and forcing Maria to work extra hours at her housecleaning jobs. She continues to support him and her children within the JW. cult.

Made in United States
Orlando, FL
19 December 2022